TEACHINGS OF PRESIDENTS OF THE CHURCH

GORDON B. HINCKLEY

D1206438

Published by
The Church of Jesus Christ of Latter-day Saints
Salt Lake City, Utah

To obtain copies of these books, go to a Church distribution center or visit store.lds.org. The books are also available in digital formats at LDS.org and on the Gospel Library mobile application.

Your comments and suggestions about this book would be appreciated. Please submit them to:

Curriculum Development
50 East North Temple Street
Salt Lake City, UT 84150-0024 USA
Email: pth-development@ldschurch.org

Please give your name, address, ward, and stake. Be sure to include the title of the book. Then offer your comments and suggestions about the book's strengths and areas of potential improvement.

Contents

Introduction

The First Presidency and the Quorum of the Twelve Apostles have established the *Teachings of Presidents of the Church* series to help you draw closer to your Heavenly Father and deepen your understanding of the restored gospel of Jesus Christ. As the Church adds volumes to this series, you will build a collection of gospel reference books for your home. These books are designed to be used for personal study and as resources for teaching. They can also help you prepare family home evening lessons, prepare other lessons or talks, and answer questions about Church doctrine.

This book features the teachings of President Gordon B. Hinckley, who served as President of The Church of Jesus Christ of Latter-day Saints from March 12, 1995, to January 27, 2008.

Personal Study

As you study the teachings of President Gordon B. Hinckley, prayerfully seek the inspiration of the Holy Ghost. The questions at the end of each chapter will help you ponder, understand, and apply President Hinckley's teachings. The following ideas may also be helpful:

- Write thoughts and feelings that come to you from the Holy Ghost as you study.

- Underline passages you want to remember. Consider memorizing these passages or noting them in your scriptures next to related verses.

- Read a chapter or passage more than once so you can understand it more deeply.

- Ask yourself questions such as "How do President Hinckley's teachings increase my understanding of gospel principles?" or

"What does the Lord want me to learn from these teachings? What does He want me to do?"

- Ask yourself how the teachings in this book can help you with personal challenges and concerns.

- Share what you learn with family members and friends.

Teaching from This Book

The following guidelines will help you teach from this book, whether at home or at church.

Prepare to Teach

Seek the guidance of the Holy Ghost as you prepare to teach. Study the chapter to become confident in your understanding of President Hinckley's teachings, and prayerfully select the teachings that you feel will be most helpful.

You may want to encourage those you teach to study the chapter themselves and to give special attention to the "Suggestions for Study and Teaching" section at the end of the chapter.

Encourage Discussion about President Hinckley's Teachings

As you teach from this book, invite others to share their thoughts, ask questions, testify, and teach one another. When they actively participate, they will be more prepared to learn and to receive personal revelation.

Allow good discussions to continue rather than trying to cover all the teachings. Guide the discussions to help participants read President Hinckley's teachings and discover ways to apply those teachings in their lives.

The questions at the end of each chapter are a valuable resource for encouraging discussion. You may also develop your own questions specifically for those you are teaching. Some other ideas for encouraging discussion are provided below:

- Ask participants to share what they have learned from their personal study of the chapter.

- Assign selected questions at the end of the chapter to individuals or small groups. Ask participants to look for teachings in the chapter that relate to the questions. Then invite them to share their thoughts and insights.

- Read together some of President Hinckley's teachings in the chapter. Ask participants to share examples from the scriptures and from their own experiences that relate to those teachings.

- Ask participants to choose one section and read it silently. Invite them to gather in groups of two or three people who chose the same section and discuss what they learned.

Encourage Application and Sharing

President Hinckley's teachings will be most meaningful when individuals apply them in their lives and share them with others. You may want to use one or more of the following ideas:

- Ask participants how they can apply President Hinckley's teachings in their responsibilities at home, in the Church, and in other settings.

- Invite participants to share experiences they have had as they have followed President Hinckley's counsel.

- Encourage participants to share some of President Hinckley's teachings with family members and friends.

Conclude the Discussion

Briefly summarize the lesson or ask one or two others to do so. Testify of the teachings you have discussed, and encourage participants to apply what they have learned. You may also want to invite others to share their testimonies.

Information about Source Materials

The teachings in this book are direct quotations from President Gordon B. Hinckley's sermons, writings, and interviews. Quotations from published sources have retained the punctuation, spelling, capitalization, and paragraphing of the original sources unless editorial or typographic changes have been necessary to improve readability. Because the quotations maintain fidelity to published sources, you may notice minor stylistic inconsistencies in the text. For example, pronouns referring to Deity are lowercased in some quotations and capitalized in others.

President Hinckley often used the terms *men, man,* and *mankind* to refer to all people, both male and female. He also frequently used the pronouns *he, his,* and *him* to refer to both genders. These language conventions were common in his era.

Historical Summary

The following chronology provides a brief overview of major events in the life of President Gordon B. Hinckley.

June 23, 1910	Born to Bryant S. Hinckley and Ada Bitner Hinckley in Salt Lake City, Utah.
1922	Attends a stake priesthood meeting with his father and gains a testimony of the prophetic calling of Joseph Smith.
1932	Graduates from the University of Utah, having studied English, journalism, and ancient languages.
1933 to 1935	Serves as a full-time missionary in the European Mission, spending the entire time in England.
1935 to 1943	Works as executive secretary of the Church's Radio, Publicity, and Mission Literature Committee.
1937	Called to the Sunday School general board.
April 29, 1937	Marries Marjorie Pay in the Salt Lake Temple.
1943 to 1945	Works as an assistant superintendent for the Denver and Rio Grande Railroad in Salt Lake City, Utah, and Denver, Colorado.
1945 to 1958	Returns to Church employment; in 1951 begins overseeing the day-to-day operations of the newly formed Missionary Department.

1953 to 1955	Under the direction of President David O. McKay, recommends and oversees the production of the temple endowment on film to accommodate multiple languages.
October 28, 1956	Called to serve as president of the East Mill Creek Stake.
April 6, 1958	Sustained as an Assistant to the Twelve.
October 5, 1961	Ordained an Apostle and set apart as a member of the Quorum of the Twelve by President David O. McKay.
July 23, 1981	Called to serve as a counselor in the First Presidency, to assist President Spencer W. Kimball and Presidents Marion G. Romney and N. Eldon Tanner.
December 2, 1982	Called to serve as the Second Counselor to President Kimball.
November 10, 1985	Called to serve as the First Counselor to President Ezra Taft Benson.
June 5, 1994	Called to serve as the First Counselor to President Howard W. Hunter.
March 3, 1995	Becomes the senior Apostle at the death of President Hunter.
March 12, 1995	Set apart as President of The Church of Jesus Christ of Latter-day Saints.
September 23, 1995	Issues "The Family: A Proclamation to the World" during the general Relief Society meeting.
February 1996	The number of Church members outside the United States exceeds the number of Church members inside the United States.
April 7, 1996	Appears on the United States television program *60 Minutes*.

May 26, 1996	Dedicates the Hong Kong China Temple, the first of 77 temples that were dedicated during his presidency, 63 of which he dedicated himself.
April 5, 1997	Organizes three new Quorums of Seventy.
October 4, 1997	Announces a plan for smaller temples to be built throughout the world.
January 1, 2000	With his fellow Apostles in the First Presidency and Quorum of the Twelve, publishes "The Living Christ: The Testimony of the Apostles."
October 1, 2000	Dedicates the Boston Massachusetts Temple, the 100th temple in operation.
October 8, 2000	Dedicates the Conference Center.
March 31, 2001	Announces the creation of the Perpetual Education Fund.
February 8, 2002	Welcomes visitors from around the world to Salt Lake City for the Winter Olympics.
June 27, 2002	Dedicates the Nauvoo Illinois Temple on the 158th anniversary of the martyrdom of Joseph and Hyrum Smith.
January 11, 2003	Presides over the first worldwide leadership training broadcast.
February 8, 2003	Speaks to one million Primary children via satellite broadcast to celebrate the Primary's 125th anniversary.
April 6, 2004	Mourns the death of his wife, Marjorie.
June 23, 2004	Is awarded the Presidential Medal of Freedom, the highest civilian award given in the United States.
June 26, 2007	Announces that Church membership has surpassed 13 million and that the one-millionth missionary has served since the Church was organized.
January 27, 2008	Dies at his home in Salt Lake City, Utah.

The Life and Ministry of Gordon B. Hinckley

On February 16, 1998, about 6,700 Latter-day Saints gathered at Independence Square in Accra, Ghana. They came to welcome their prophet, President Gordon B. Hinckley.[1] He stood before them, with a smile on his face, and announced the long-awaited news that a temple would be built in their homeland. Elder Jeffrey R. Holland of the Quorum of the Twelve Apostles said that when President Hinckley made this announcement, the people "stood and cheered, wept and danced, held each other, and cried."[2] Years later, after the temple had been built and dedicated, a woman who was present that day recalled the feelings of joy and expressed how the temple had blessed her:

"I still have a vivid picture in my mind of the Prophet Gordon B. Hinckley's visit to Ghana and his announcement of a temple in our Motherland. The excitement on everyone's face, the happiness, the shouts of joy are all still clear in my mind. . . .

"Today, because of a temple in our land, I am married and sealed to my husband for time and all eternity. The blessing of living with my family beyond this mortality gives me great hope as I strive to do all that I can to be with my family forever."[3]

Throughout the world, President Hinckley helped people find this "great hope" in striving to live the gospel of Jesus Christ. As illustrated by the event in Ghana, he often ministered to thousands at the same time. He also reached out to people one by one. Elder Adney Y. Komatsu of the Seventy told of his feelings as a mission president when President Hinckley visited his mission:

"Never once in my three years did he criticize me, despite all my weaknesses. . . . And that spurred me on. . . . Every time he came off the plane he would grab my hand like he was pumping water out of a well with great enthusiasm. 'Well, President Komatsu, how are you getting along? . . . You're doing great work.' He encouraged me like that . . . and when he left I felt I should give 105 percent, not just 100 percent."[4]

People felt encouragement from President Hinckley not just because of his inspiring words but because of the way he lived. President Russell M. Nelson of the Quorum of the Twelve recounted:

"While [President and Sister Hinckley were] going from a chapel to an airport in Central America, their vehicle was involved in an accident. Sister Nelson and I were traveling behind them and saw it occur. A truck [that was] loaded on top with unsecured metal rods approached them at an intersection. To avoid a collision, its driver suddenly stopped the truck, launching those iron rods like javelins to pierce the Hinckleys' car. Windows were smashed; fenders and doors were dented. The accident could have been very serious. While shattered glass was being removed from their clothing and skin, President Hinckley said: 'Thank the Lord for His blessing; now let's continue on in another car.' "[5]

This statement, spoken spontaneously in a moment of crisis, is representative of President Hinckley's life and ministry as a disciple of Jesus Christ. He was, as Elder Holland observed, "always filled with faith in God and in the future."[6]

Family Heritage—A Foundation of Faith and Perseverance

When Gordon Bitner Hinckley was born on June 23, 1910, he was his mother's first child, but eight older siblings welcomed him into the family. Gordon's father, Bryant Stringham Hinckley, had married Ada Bitner after the death of his first wife, Christine. Ada and Bryant had four more children after Gordon, and they raised their large family with love—and without distinctions such as half brothers and half sisters. From his earliest days, Gordon learned to treasure his family.

Gordon's last name and middle name were reminders of his noble heritage. His Hinckley ancestors included early pilgrims in the land that would become the United States of America. Some had been banished to that land in the 1600s because of their Christian beliefs. Others had been passengers in 1620 on the *Mayflower,* one of the first ships to transport emigrants from Europe to North America. More than two centuries later, Gordon's paternal grandfather, Ira Nathaniel Hinckley, was one of the early Latter-day Saint pioneers. In 1843, as a recently orphaned 14-year-old, Ira joined the Church in Nauvoo, Illinois, after hearing Joseph and Hyrum Smith preach. Gordon's great-grandmother Anna Barr Musser Bitner Starr was also a pioneer. Her son Breneman Barr Bitner, Gordon's maternal grandfather, later recalled their journey to the Salt Lake Valley in 1849: "I [age 11] drove two yoke of oxen and a heavily laden wagon through heat and cold across the deserts and rivers and mountains to this valley."[7]

Bryant Hinckley often reminded his children and grandchildren of their rich heritage. Speaking of the *Mayflower* pilgrims' perilous journey and the long, bitter winter they faced when they reached their destination, he once said: "When the *Mayflower* was ready to return in the spring, only 49 [of the 102] people had survived. No one went back [to England]. This spirit is born in you fellows—the spirit of never turning back."[8] As Gordon stayed true to this principle, he received opportunities to learn and serve and testify that he never could have imagined.

Childhood—Learning to Be Optimistic, Diligent, and Faithful

As a young child, Gordon Hinckley was not the energetic, robust individual people came to know in his later years. He was "a spindly, frail boy," susceptible to illnesses.[9] When two-year-old Gordon "contracted a severe case of whooping cough, . . . a doctor told Ada the only remedy was clear, country air. Bryant responded by purchasing a five-acre farm . . . and building a small summer home."[10] The farm, located in an area of the Salt Lake Valley called East Mill Creek, was a blessing for the entire family, providing the children with a place to roam and play and to learn valuable lessons as they worked together.

Ada and Bryant Hinckley were optimistic, diligent parents who created opportunities for their children to grow and succeed. They held family home evenings as soon as the program was introduced in 1915. They shared bedtime stories, often from the scriptures. They set aside a room in their home as a library where the children could read good books. They inspired discipline in their children by encouraging them and expecting the best of them.

As Gordon grew up, his faith increased, nurtured by the constant influence of his parents' faith. Then one day he had an experience that helped form the foundation of his testimony of the Prophet Joseph Smith:

"When I was a boy, twelve years of age, my father took me to a meeting of the priesthood of the stake in which we lived. I sat on the back row while he, as president of the stake, sat on the stand. At the opening of that meeting, the first of its kind I had ever attended, three or four hundred men stood. They were men from varied backgrounds and many vocations, but each had in his heart the same conviction, out of which together they sang these great words:

Praise to the man who communed with Jehovah!
Jesus anointed that Prophet and Seer.
Blessed to open the last dispensation,
Kings shall extol him, and nations revere.

"Something happened within me as I heard those men of faith sing. There came into my boyish heart a knowledge, placed there by the Holy Spirit, that Joseph Smith was indeed a prophet of the Almighty." [11]

Continuing Education and Trying Times

In his early childhood, Gordon did not enjoy school, preferring the outdoors to the walls and desks of a classroom. As he matured, however, he learned to appreciate books, schools, and the library at home as much as the fields where he had run barefoot as a young boy. He graduated from high school in 1928 and began studies at the University of Utah that same year.

His four years at the university presented almost overwhelming challenges. In 1929 the United States stock market crashed, and the Great Depression rolled across the country and the world. Unemployment was about 35 percent in Salt Lake City, but Gordon

Gordon B. Hinckley as a young man

was fortunate to have a job as a maintenance worker to pay for his tuition and school supplies. Bryant, who worked as a manager at the Church's Deseret Gym, cut his own salary so other employees could keep their jobs.[12]

Eclipsing these financial pressures was the discovery that Gordon's mother had cancer. She died in 1930 at the age of 50, when Gordon was 20. The wounds that came with his mother's death "were deep and painful," Gordon said.[13] This personal trial, combined with the influence of worldly philosophies and the cynicism of the times, led him to ask difficult questions. "It was a time of terrible discouragement," Gordon recalled, "and it was felt strongly on campus. I felt some of it myself. I began to question some things, including perhaps in a slight measure the faith of my parents. That is not unusual for university students, but the atmosphere was particularly acute at that time."[14]

Gordon's emerging questions, while troubling, did not shake his faith. "There was for me an underlying foundation of love that came from great parents and a good family, a wonderful bishop, devoted and faithful teachers, and the scriptures to read and ponder," he recalled. Speaking of the challenges of those times for him and others his age, he said: "Although in our youth we had trouble understanding many things, there was in our hearts something of a love for God and his great work that carried us above any doubts and fears. We loved the Lord and we loved good and honorable friends. From such love we drew great strength."[15]

Missionary Service and Personal Conversion

Gordon graduated from the University of Utah in June 1932 with a major in English and a minor in ancient languages. A year later he found himself at a crossroads. He was looking forward to continuing his education so he could become a journalist. Even in the midst of the Depression, he had scraped together a modest savings account to support his education. He was also thinking about marriage. He and Marjorie Pay, a young woman who lived across the street, were becoming increasingly fond of one another.

Then, just before his 23rd birthday, Gordon met with his bishop, John C. Duncan, who asked whether he had thought about serving a mission. This was "a shocking suggestion" to Gordon,[16] since few young men were being called on missions during the Depression. Families simply did not have the resources to support them.

Gordon told Bishop Duncan that he would serve, but he worried about how his family would manage financially. His concerns increased when he learned that the bank that held his savings account had failed. "Nevertheless," he said, "I remember my father saying, 'We will do all we can to see that your needs are met,' and he and my brother committed to see me through my mission. It was at that time that we discovered a little savings account my mother had left—change saved from her grocery purchases and other shopping. With that little bit of help added, it appeared I could go on my mission." He considered his mother's coins to be sacred. "I guarded them with my honor," he said.[17] He was called to serve in the European Mission.

Sensing that his son was still feeling troubled, Bryant Hinckley prepared a simple reminder of the true source of strength. "When I left for a mission," Gordon later said, "my good father handed me a card on which were written five words . . . : 'Be not afraid, only believe' (Mark 5:36)."[18] Those words would inspire Elder Gordon B. Hinckley to serve a faithful, honorable mission, especially when they were combined with six more words from his father's pen several weeks later.

The additional six words came at a time of severe discouragement, which had begun on June 29, 1933, Elder Hinckley's first day in Preston, England. When he arrived at his apartment, his companion told him they would be speaking at the town square that evening. "You've got the wrong man to go with you," Elder Hinckley responded, only to find himself singing and speaking from a stand a few hours later, facing a crowd of unengaged spectators.[19]

Elder Hinckley discovered that many people were unwilling to listen to the message of the restored gospel. The poverty created by the worldwide financial depression seemed to penetrate the souls of the people who jostled him on the streetcars, and he found little to draw him to them. In addition, he felt wretched physically. He remembered, "In England the grass pollinates and turns to seed in late June and early July, which is exactly when I arrived."[20] This triggered his allergies, which made everything seem worse. He missed his family. He missed Marjorie. He missed the familiarity of his country. The work was frustrating. He and his fellow missionaries had very few opportunities to teach investigators, although they taught and spoke in the small branches every Sunday.

Feeling that he was wasting his time and his family's money, Elder Hinckley wrote a letter to his father explaining his unhappy situation. Bryant Hinckley replied with advice that his son would follow throughout his life. "Dear Gordon," he wrote, "I have your recent letter. I have only one suggestion." And then those six words

Elder Gordon B. Hinckley as a full-time missionary,
preaching in London's Hyde Park

that added weight to the five he had written earlier: "Forget yourself and go to work."[21] This counsel echoed a scripture passage Elder Hinckley had read with his companion earlier that day: "Whosoever will save his life shall lose it; but whosoever shall lose his life for my sake and the gospel's, the same shall save it" (Mark 8:35).

With his father's letter in his hand, the young Elder Hinckley got on his knees and made a pledge that he would give himself to the Lord. The effect was almost immediate. "The whole world changed," he said. "The fog lifted. The sun began to shine in my life. I had a new interest. I saw the beauty of this land. I saw the greatness of the people. I began to feel at home in this wonderful land."[22]

Remembering those days, Gordon explained that he also received help from his mother. He felt her comforting presence, especially during the dark and discouraging times. "I tried then, as I have tried since, to so conduct my life and perform my duty as to bring honor to her name," he said. "The thought of living beneath my mother's expectations has been painful, and has afforded a discipline that otherwise might have been lacking."[23]

He became a missionary with purpose and zeal. Records from the first eight months of his mission show that although he did not baptize anyone, he distributed 8,785 pamphlets, spent more than 440 hours with members, attended 191 meetings, had 220 gospel conversations, and confirmed one person.[24]

In March 1934, Elder Hinckley was transferred from Preston to London to work as an assistant to Elder Joseph F. Merrill of the Quorum of the Twelve Apostles, who presided over the British and European Missions.[25] He spent the rest of his mission there, working in the office by day and teaching the gospel in the evenings. Convert baptisms were few, but in the heart of Bryant and Ada Hinckley's son, the spark of conversion became an enduring flame.

A New Opportunity to Serve the Lord

When Gordon returned from his mission, he said, "I never want to travel again. I have traveled as far as I ever want to travel."[26] He and two missionary companions had toured Europe and the United States on their way home, a common practice in those days, and he was tired. When his family went on vacation soon after his return, he stayed behind. Despite his exhaustion, he enjoyed some satisfaction as he reflected on his travels: he felt that he had seen the fulfillment of part of his patriarchal blessing. Many years later he said:

"I received a patriarchal blessing when I was a boy. In that blessing it said that I would lift my voice in testimony of the truth in the nations of the earth. I had labored in London for a long time and given my testimony many times there. We [went to Amsterdam], and I had opportunity in a meeting to say a few words and offer my testimony. We then went to Berlin, where I had a similar opportunity.

We then went to Paris, where I had a similar opportunity. We then went to the United States, to Washington, D.C., and on a Sunday there I had a similar opportunity. When I arrived home, I was tired. . . . I said, '. . . I have completed [that] phase of my blessing. I have lifted my voice in the great capitals of the world. . . .' And I really felt that way."[27]

Before Gordon could consider his mission complete, he had to fulfill one more assignment. Elder Joseph F. Merrill had asked him to make an appointment with the First Presidency of the Church to report on needs in the British and European Missions. On the morning of August 20, 1935, less than a month after returning home, Gordon was ushered into the council room in the Church Administration Building. Shaking hands with each member of the First Presidency—Presidents Heber J. Grant, J. Reuben Clark Jr., and David O. McKay—he was suddenly overwhelmed with the task he had been given. President Grant said, "Brother Hinckley, we'll give you fifteen minutes to tell us what Elder Merrill wants us to hear."[28]

For the next 15 minutes, the recently returned missionary presented Elder Merrill's concern—that the missionaries needed better printed materials to help them in their work. In response, President Grant and his counselors asked question after question, and the meeting stretched an hour longer than had been planned.

On his way home from the meeting, Gordon could not have guessed how those 75 minutes would affect his life. Two days later he received a call from President McKay, who offered him a job as executive secretary of the newly formed Church Radio, Publicity, and Mission Literature Committee. This committee, made up of six members of the Quorum of the Twelve, would work to address the needs that Gordon had outlined in his meeting with the First Presidency.[29]

Once again, Gordon put off his plans for graduate school and a career as a journalist. He went to work developing scripts for radio programs and filmstrips, writing pamphlets for missionaries, developing professional relationships with media pioneers, and researching and writing about Church history. He contributed to messages designed to build the faith of Church members and connect with

*Gordon B. Hinckley as an employee of the Church Radio,
Publicity, and Mission Literature Committee*

people outside the Church. A friend once sent him a letter complimenting him on a radio script and asking how he had developed such a gift for writing and speaking. Gordon replied:

"If I have any talent for speaking or writing, I am extremely grateful to my Father in Heaven. I think very little of it is native ability; rather, any power that I might have has come through opportunities that have been opened to me."[30]

Gordon's work with the committee honed his skills as a writer. It also offered a valuable opportunity to learn from apostles and prophets. As Gordon saw the six members of the Twelve weigh decisions and teach one another, he better understood the holy calling of these diverse men and the revelatory process that occurred when they counseled together.

Elder Stephen L Richards, who later served as First Counselor in the First Presidency, was the chairman of the committee. Gordon described him as "thoughtful, deliberate, careful, and wise. He never rushed into action but looked cautiously before he proceeded.

I learned that you best proceed carefully in this work, because whatever decision you make has far-reaching ramifications and affects the lives of many people."[31]

The other five committee members were Elders Melvin J. Ballard, John A. Widtsoe, Charles A. Callis, Alonzo A. Hinckley (Gordon's uncle), and Albert E. Bowen. Concerning them, Gordon said:

"I got along wonderfully well with those great men, who were very kind to me. But I learned that they were human. They had weaknesses and problems, but that didn't bother me. In fact, it enhanced my estimation of them because I saw rising above their mortality an element of the divine, or at the very least an element of consecration to a tremendous cause that came first in their lives. I saw the inspiration that was at work in their lives. I had no doubt concerning their prophetic callings or of the fact that the Lord spoke and acted through them. I saw their human side, their foibles—and they all had a few. But I also saw the great overriding strength of their faith and love for the Lord, and their absolute loyalty to the work and to the trust that was placed in them."[32]

Marriage, Family, and Church Service

Of course, Gordon did not think only about work. His courtship with Marjorie Pay continued when he returned from England. His departure had been as difficult for Marjorie as it had been for him. "As anxious as I was for him to serve a mission," Marjorie said later, "I will never forget the feeling of emptiness and loneliness I felt when that train pulled out of the station."[33]

In the fall of 1929, four years before Gordon left for England, Marjorie had registered for classes at the University of Utah, only to find that her father had lost his job due to the Great Depression. She immediately dropped her classes and found a job as a secretary to help support her parents and her five younger siblings—an effort that continued after Gordon returned from his mission in 1935. She never again had the opportunity to obtain a formal education, but she was determined to continue learning, so she educated herself by reading.

Marjorie's cheerful disposition, work ethic, and deep commitment to the gospel endeared her to Gordon, and she was impressed with his goodness and faith. "As we got closer to marriage," she said, "I felt completely confident that Gordon loved me. But I also knew somehow that I would never come first with him. I knew I was going to be second in his life and that the Lord was going to be first. And that was okay." She continued: "It seemed to me that if you understood the gospel and the purpose of our being here, you would want a husband who put the Lord first. I felt secure knowing he was that kind of man."[34]

Gordon and Marjorie were married in the Salt Lake Temple on April 29, 1937, and moved to the Hinckleys' summer home in East Mill Creek. They installed a furnace, made other improvements necessary for year-round living, took care of the orchards and gardens, and began building their own home on a neighboring piece of property. And so the rural area Gordon had loved during the summers of his childhood became the place where he and Marjorie would make their home and rear their children—Kathleen, Richard, Virginia, Clark, and Jane.

Gordon and Marjorie established a home of love, mutual respect, hard work, and gospel living. Daily family prayer provided a window for the children to see their parents' faith and love. As the family prayed together, the children also sensed the nearness of their Father in Heaven.

The Hinckley home was a place of few rules but great expectations. Marjorie spoke about things that were not worth a battle. Describing a parenting approach that she shared with her husband, she said: "I learned that I needed to trust my children, so I tried to never say no if I could possibly say yes. When we were raising a family, it was a matter of getting through every day and having a little fun along the way. As I could see that I wasn't going to be able to make all of my children's decisions anyway, I tried not to worry about every little thing."[35] As a result of their parents' trust, the children felt respected and gained experience and confidence. And when the answer was no, the children understood that it was not an arbitrary restriction.

Marjorie Pay

The Hinckley home was also full of laughter. Marjorie once said: "The only way to get through life is to laugh your way through it. You either have to laugh or cry. I prefer to laugh. Crying gives me a headache."[36] With parents who could laugh at themselves and find humor in everyday life, the children saw their home as a delightful refuge.

Church service was always a part of life for Gordon and Marjorie. Gordon served as the stake Sunday School superintendent and then was called to the Sunday School general board, where he served for nine years. He later served as a counselor in a stake presidency and as stake president, while Marjorie served in Primary, Young Women, and Relief Society. Their children witnessed Church service as a joyful privilege—a model they would each follow in their adult years.

Preparation through Professional Endeavors

For the first six years of Marjorie and Gordon's marriage, Gordon continued to work with the Church Radio, Publicity, and Mission Literature Committee. He was dedicated in his work, and projects and deadlines frequently took him to the edge of his abilities and experience—and beyond. In a letter to a friend, he wrote:

"Much to do. The work of this committee with a long name is growing larger and more complicated and more interesting. . . .

". . . Radio, films, and literature of various kinds . . . serve to keep me praying, humble, busy, and at work for long hours. . . . All of which has served to make me a little more dependent upon glasses, . . . a little more round-shouldered, a little more settled, and a little more full of wonder as to what this all leads to."[37]

In the early 1940s, World War II brought a change in employment for Gordon. Full-time missionary work came to a virtual standstill because of the war, so his job of providing missionary materials became less pressing. Feeling a responsibility to help with the war effort, he applied to officer candidate school in the United States Navy. However, his history of allergies disqualified him. "I was depressed over the rejection," he admitted later. "The war was on, and everybody was doing something to help. I felt that I should participate in some way."[38] This desire led him to apply for a job as an assistant superintendent for the Denver and Rio Grande Railroad. Because trains were critical in moving troops and supplies for the war, Gordon felt that this job would help him serve his country. The company hired him in 1943, and he worked at their depot in Salt Lake City until he and his family were transferred to Denver, Colorado, in 1944.

Supervisors at the railroad were impressed with Gordon's work, and when the war ended in 1945, they offered him a permanent position with a seemingly bright professional future. At the same time, Elder Stephen L Richards called and asked Gordon to return to full-time Church employment. Although the railroad could offer a significantly higher salary than the Church, Gordon followed his heart and returned to Salt Lake City.[39]

Gordon B. Hinckley, 1951

Gordon's employment at Church headquarters soon expanded from his earlier responsibilities. In 1951 he was appointed executive secretary of the General Missionary Committee of the Church and was charged with overseeing the day-to-day operations of the newly formed Missionary Department. This department oversaw everything that had to do with spreading the gospel, including the production, translation, and distribution of materials used by missionaries; training for missionaries and mission presidents; and public relations media used to build bridges and dispel myths about the Church.[40]

In the autumn of 1953, President David O. McKay called Gordon to his office and asked him to consider a question that was not directly related to duties in the Missionary Department. "Brother Hinckley," he began, "as you know, we are building a temple in

Switzerland, and it will be different from our other temples in that it must serve members who speak many languages. I want you to find a way to present the temple instruction in the various languages of Europe while using a minimum number of temple workers."[41]

President McKay provided a place where Gordon could seek inspiration and escape the demands of his workload in the Missionary Department. On weekday evenings, Saturdays, and some Sundays, Gordon worked in a small room on the fifth floor of the Salt Lake Temple. On many Sunday mornings, President McKay joined him to share ideas, look closely at the presentation of the endowment, and pray for direction.

After pondering, praying, and seeking revelation, Gordon recommended that the presentation of the endowment be put on film, with the words of that sacred instruction dubbed in several languages. President McKay and others approved his recommendation and assigned him to produce the film. Gordon worked with a team of talented and faithful professionals who completed the project in September 1955. He then personally carried the films to the Bern Switzerland Temple and oversaw the technical preparations for the initial endowment sessions.[42]

Gordon was touched to see his work bring joy to the Saints in Europe: "As I saw those people gathered from ten nations to participate in the temple ordinances; as I saw elderly people from behind the Iron Curtain who had lost their families in the wars that had washed over them, and witnessed the expressions of joy and tears of gladness which came from their hearts as a result of the opportunities that had been given them; as I saw young husbands and wives with their families—their bright and beautiful children—and saw those families united in an eternal relationship, I knew with a certainty even beyond what I had known before that [President McKay] was inspired and directed of the Lord to bring these priceless blessings into the lives of those men and women of faith gathered from the nations of Europe."[43]

Twenty years had passed since Gordon had returned from his mission, and he had not fulfilled his dream to receive an advanced degree and become a journalist. Instead, he had learned to use new technology to spread the word of God, developed positive relationships with people of other faiths, studied and written works of Church history, and helped prepare the way for thousands of Latter-day Saints to receive the blessings of the temple. These experiences would serve as a foundation for the service he would give for the rest of his life.

Service as an Assistant to the Twelve

On Saturday, April 5, 1958, Gordon and Marjorie's son Richard answered a phone call. The caller did not introduce himself, but Richard recognized the voice of President David O. McKay and hurried to inform his father. After speaking briefly with President McKay, Gordon quickly showered, changed his clothes, and drove to the office of the President of the Church. Because he had received assignments from President McKay before, he expected to be asked to help with something in preparation for the next day's general conference session. He was shocked to find that President McKay had something else in mind. After a friendly greeting, President McKay asked Gordon to serve as an Assistant to the Twelve. Brethren who served in this position, which was discontinued in 1976, were General Authorities of the Church. Gordon was serving as president of the East Mill Creek Stake when President McKay issued this calling.

The next day, Elder Gordon B. Hinckley received a sustaining vote in general conference. Although he admitted in his first conference talk that he was "overwhelmed with a sense of inadequacy," he embraced his new responsibility with characteristic faith and vigor.[44]

One major duty that came to Elder Hinckley as an Assistant to the Twelve was to oversee the work of the Church in all of Asia. He knew little about the people there and spoke none of their languages, but he quickly came to love them, and they came to love him. Kenji Tanaka, a Japanese Latter-day Saint, told of Elder Hinckley's first meeting in Japan: "Elder Hinckley's excitement could be seen in his sparkling eyes. His first word to us was *Subarashii!* ['Wonderful!'] The atmosphere of that meeting changed from stiff and formal to friendliness and closeness to him, and a warm feeling prevailed."[45]

This was the feeling he shared everywhere he went in Asia. He helped the people see that with faith in the Lord, they could accomplish great things and help the Church grow in their homelands. He also stayed close to the full-time missionaries, knowing that their diligence would have a direct impact on the people they served.

A Special Witness of the Name of Christ

Another life-changing phone call came on another Saturday—September 30, 1961. This time it was Marjorie who heard the familiar voice of President McKay on the phone. Again Gordon B. Hinckley hurried to the office of the President of the Church. Again he was surprised and overcome when he learned the reason for the visit. When he arrived, President McKay told him, "I have felt to nominate you to fill the vacancy in the Quorum of the Twelve Apostles, and we would like to sustain you today in conference."[46] Again Elder Hinckley moved forward with faith and enthusiasm despite feelings of inadequacy.

As an Apostle, Elder Hinckley received additional responsibilities. He occasionally met with government leaders and other dignitaries. He was frequently asked to speak publicly for the Church to address criticisms and cultural unrest in the United States. He was at the forefront of efforts to strengthen the Church's broadcasting capabilities and to use technology to spread the gospel throughout the world. Even with these expanding roles, he never lost sight of his responsibility to strengthen the faith of individuals and families. Whether he was speaking to one person or ten thousand people, his was a personal touch, one that became the hallmark of his ministry: to bring people, one by one, to Christ.

Elder Hinckley continued to supervise the work in Asia for the next seven years, and he rejoiced to see the growth of his friends there. He observed, "It is an inspiring experience . . . to witness the manner in which the Lord is weaving the tapestry of his grand design in those . . . parts of the earth."[47]

As assignments changed among the Quorum of the Twelve, Elder Hinckley received opportunities to serve in other parts of the world. Everywhere he went, he showed concern for the individual. In 1970, when he was supervising the work of the Church in South America, he traveled to Chile after presiding over a stake conference in Peru. Two days after arriving in Chile, he learned that a devastating earthquake had hit Peru and that four missionaries were missing. He immediately made plans to return to Peru even though it would delay his return home. "I cannot in good conscience go home while there are missionaries missing," he said.[48]

He arrived in Lima, Peru, the following morning. When the missing missionaries found a ham radio operator, they were able to call Lima, and Elder Hinckley spoke with them. The missionaries were in a small room filled with other survivors, and their conversations were broadcast over a speaker. "As Elder Hinckley's voice came over the speaker in that room crammed with people clamoring to get on the radio, an immediate hush fell across the room. Though he was speaking in English, and these people all spoke Spanish, they began to talk among each other in whispers and ask, 'Who is that man?' There was a sense, even amidst chaos, that that voice belonged to no ordinary man."[49]

During his first two years of supervising the Church in South America, Elder Hinckley toured every mission; created new missions in Colombia and Ecuador; helped create new stakes in Lima, Peru, and São Paulo, Brazil; and helped resolve visa obstructions for missionaries called to serve in Argentina. He was in the midst of doing more when, in May 1971, he was assigned to supervise eight missions in Europe.[50]

Elder Hinckley often felt the fatigue of his unyielding schedule. He was always happy to return home and spend time with Marjorie and the children. However, Marjorie could tell that when he was away from the work too long, he became restless. His calling as an Apostle—one of the "special witnesses of the name of Christ in all the world" (D&C 107:23)—was never far from his mind.

Heavy Responsibilities as a Counselor in the First Presidency

On July 15, 1981, after serving in the Quorum of the Twelve for almost 20 years, Elder Hinckley received another surprising calling. President Spencer W. Kimball, then President of the Church, asked him to serve as a counselor in the First Presidency, in addition to Presidents N. Eldon Tanner and Marion G. Romney. This was an unusual but not unprecedented departure from the pattern of having two counselors. President Kimball and his counselors were not well physically and needed extra support in the Presidency.[51]

At his first general conference in this new capacity, President Hinckley remarked: "My only desire is to serve with loyalty wherever I am called. . . . This sacred calling has made me aware of my weaknesses. If I have offended at any time, I apologize and hope you will forgive me. Whether this assignment be lengthy or brief, I pledge my best effort, given with love and faith."[52]

His best effort was needed as the health of Presidents Kimball, Tanner, and Romney declined. Most of the day-to-day work of the First Presidency fell to President Hinckley. He also shouldered much of the responsibility for larger efforts, such as the dedication of the Jordan River Utah Temple. In addition, he faced some public criticism of the Church and its leaders, both past and present. In the April 1982 general conference he counseled:

"We live in a society that feeds on criticism. . . . I urge you to see the big picture and cease worrying about the little blemishes. . . . These are only incidental to the magnitude of [Church leaders'] service and to the greatness of their contributions."[53]

President Tanner passed away on November 27, 1982, and the health of Presidents Kimball and Romney declined to the point that in the April 1983 general conference, President Hinckley, who by then had been called as Second Counselor in the First Presidency, sat next to empty chairs on the stand. In a deeply personal way, he felt what he had once called "the loneliness of leadership."[54]

President Hinckley proceeded with care and prayer, not wanting to step ahead of the prophet. He called on the senior members of

President Gordon B. Hinckley in general conference at a time when he was the only member of the First Presidency who was healthy enough to attend

the Twelve—particularly Elder Ezra Taft Benson, the quorum president—for assistance in running the daily business of the Church. President Hinckley worked hand in hand with the Quorum of the Twelve, always guided by counsel from President Kimball. Nonetheless, he felt a great burden.

Although President Hinckley's responsibilities in the First Presidency kept him in Salt Lake City much of the time, he occasionally traveled to minister to members and missionaries in other parts of the world. In 1984 he returned to the Philippines. Eighteen years earlier he had dedicated the first chapel there; now he would dedicate the first temple. In the dedicatory prayer, he said:

"This nation of the Philippines is a nation of many islands whose people love freedom and truth, whose hearts are sensitive to the testimony of thy servants, and who are responsive to the message of the eternal gospel. We thank thee for their faith. We thank thee for their spirit of sacrifice. We thank thee for the miracle of the progress of thy work in this land."[55]

The continuing progress of the Church was evident in June 1984 when, on behalf of the First Presidency, President Hinckley announced the calling of Area Presidencies—members of the Seventy who would live around the world and supervise the work of the Church in assigned geographic areas. Working under the direction of the First Presidency and Quorum of the Twelve, these brethren would provide much of the leadership and training needed in their areas. "We can't make every decision in Salt Lake City," he said. "We have to do something about decentralizing authority."[56] About a year later, speaking to Church leaders from around the world, President Hinckley said: "I am confident that it is an inspired and great step forward that we have taken in these last few months. I am confident that the frequent presence of these good men in your midst gives you great reassurance. These Brethren are in effect tying the whole body of the Church together."[57]

After leading the Church through 12 years of remarkable growth, President Spencer W. Kimball died on November 5, 1985. The senior Apostle, President Ezra Taft Benson, was set apart as President of the Church. He asked Gordon B. Hinckley to serve as First Counselor in the First Presidency and Thomas S. Monson to serve as Second Counselor. With three healthy members of the First Presidency, President Hinckley felt his burdens ease and had more opportunities to visit the Saints around the world.

Within a few years, President Benson's health began to fail, and the day-to-day responsibilities of running the Church fell again to President Hinckley. This time, however, he was not alone in the First Presidency. With vitality and energy, Presidents Hinckley and Monson kept the Church on a steady course, always respecting President Benson's calling as prophet, seer, and revelator. They developed a strong, enduring friendship and partnership.

President Benson died on May 30, 1994, and President Howard W. Hunter became President of the Church. Once again, Presidents Hinckley and Monson served as counselors. In June, President and Sister Hinckley accompanied President Hunter and his wife Inis and Elder M. Russell Ballard and his wife, Barbara, to Nauvoo, Illinois, to observe the 150-year commemoration of the martyrdom of Joseph and Hyrum Smith. This would be the only trip President Hunter and

President Ezra Taft Benson (center) *with his counselors,
President Gordon B. Hinckley* (left) *and President
Thomas S. Monson* (right), *in general conference*

President Hinckley would take together. President Hunter had struggled with health problems for years, and his health declined rapidly after this trip. On February 27, 1995, he asked President Hinckley for a priesthood blessing. In the blessing, President Hinckley pleaded for President Hunter's life but also said that he was in the Lord's hands.[58] A few days later, on March 3, 1995, President Hunter passed away.

Prophet, Seer, and Revelator and President of the Church

President Hunter's death, while not surprising, weighed heavily on the Hinckleys. As the senior Apostle, President Hinckley was next in line to become President of the Church. Sister Hinckley recalled the moment they received the news of President Hunter's death: "President Hunter had gone, and we were left to carry on. I felt so sad, so alone. Gordon did, too. He was numb. And he felt very, very lonely. There was no one left who could understand what he was going through."[59]

After President Hunter's funeral, President Hinckley found comfort in the temple. Alone in the meeting room of the First Presidency and Quorum of the Twelve in the Salt Lake Temple, he pored over the scriptures and meditated on what he read. He reflected on the life, ministry, and Atonement of Jesus Christ. Then he studied the portraits on the wall, depicting all the Presidents of the Church from Joseph Smith to Howard W. Hunter. He recorded this experience in his journal:

"I walked around in front of these portraits and looked into the eyes of the men there represented. I felt almost as if I could speak with them. I felt almost as if they were speaking to me and giving me reassurance. . . . I sat down in the chair which I have occupied as first counselor to the President. I spent a good deal of time looking at those portraits. Every one seemed almost to come alive. Their eyes seemed to be upon me. I felt that they were encouraging me and pledging their support. They seemed to say to me that they had spoken in my behalf in a council held in the heavens, that I had no need to fear, that I would be blessed and sustained in my ministry.

"I got on my knees and pleaded with the Lord. I spoke with Him at length in prayer. . . . I am confident that by the power of the Spirit, I heard the word of the Lord, not vocally, but as a warmth that was felt within my heart concerning the questions I had raised in prayer."[60]

After this experience he again recorded his thoughts: "I feel better, and I have a much firmer assurance in my heart that the Lord is working His will with reference to His cause and kingdom, that I will be sustained as President of the Church and prophet, seer, and revelator, and so serve for such time as the Lord wills. With the confirmation of the Spirit in my heart, I am now ready to go forward to do the very best work I know how to do. It is difficult for me to believe that the Lord is placing me in this most high and sacred responsibility. . . . I hope that the Lord has trained me to do what He expects of me. I will give Him total loyalty, and I will certainly seek His direction."[61]

President Gordon B. Hinckley was set apart as President of the Church on March 12, 1995, and the next day he spoke at a press conference and answered reporters' questions. Elder Jeffrey R. Holland reported that "near the end of a warm, often witty, always winning

President Gordon B. Hinckley at the pulpit in general conference

exchange on a wide-ranging number of questions posed in this news conference, President Hinckley was asked by a reporter, 'What will be your focus? What will be the theme of your administration?'

"Instinctively he answered, 'Carry on. Yes. Our theme will be to carry on the great work which has been furthered by our predecessors.'"[62]

President Hinckley was true to that pledge. With respect for the prophets who had gone before him, he carried on with the work they had done. And with faith in God the Father and Jesus Christ, he followed revelation to perform that work in new ways.

Bringing the Church "Out of Obscurity" (D&C 1:30)

Toward the beginning of President Hinckley's ministry, Elder Neal A. Maxwell of the Quorum of the Twelve observed: "President Hinckley is helping to lead the Church out of obscurity. The Church can't move forward as it needs to if we are hidden under a bushel. Someone has to step out, and President Hinckley is willing to do so. He is a man of history and modernity at the same time, and he has marvelous gifts of expression that enable him to present our message in a way that appeals to people everywhere."[63]

President Hinckley's extensive background in media and broad-casting helped prepare him for this effort. As President of the Church, he frequently granted interviews to journalists around the world, answering their questions about Church doctrine and policy and bearing his testimony of the Savior and the restored gospel. Each time, understanding increased and friendships were developed.

Of particular note was a 1996 interview with veteran reporter Mike Wallace of the television program *60 Minutes*. Mr. Wallace was known for being a relentless interviewer, and President Hinckley admitted some initial reservations before the show's airing on national television in the United States. "If it turns out to be favorable, I will be grateful," he said. "Otherwise, I pledge I'll never get my foot in that kind of trap again."[64]

The interview was favorable, showing many positive aspects of the Church. Another result was that Mike Wallace and President Hinckley became friends.

In 2002, Salt Lake City hosted the Winter Olympics, putting the Church in the spotlight internationally. President Hinckley and his counselors were consulted about part of the planning. "We made a deliberate decision that we would not use this as a time or place to proselytize," he said, "but we were confident that out of this significant event would come a wonderful thing for the Church."[65]

He was right. Tens of thousands of people visited the Salt Lake Valley and were greeted by gracious hosts—Latter-day Saints and others working together to create a successful Olympic games. These visitors walked around Temple Square, listened to the Tabernacle Choir, and visited the Family History Library. Billions of people saw the Salt Lake Temple on television and saw the Church presented favorably by reporters. It was, as President Hinckley said, "a wonderful thing for the Church."

In addition to using long-established means of communication, President Hinckley embraced innovations. For example, he saw the Internet as a means of bringing the Church closer to its members and sharing the restored gospel with those of other faiths. During his administration, the Church launched LDS.org, FamilySearch.org, and Mormon.org.

On June 23, 2004, the day President Hinckley turned 94, he was awarded the Presidential Medal of Freedom, the highest civilian award given in the United States. In response he said: "I [am] deeply honored to receive this prestigious award from the President of the United States. I am profoundly grateful. In a larger sense, it recognizes and honors the Church which has given me so many opportunities and whose interests I have tried to serve."[66] He saw this award as symbolic of the growing positive reputation of the Church and evidence that it was indeed being brought out of obscurity.

Traveling among the Latter-day Saints

President Hinckley disliked the rigors of travel, but his desire to serve among the Latter-day Saints was more powerful than his desire to stay home. He said that he wanted to "get out among our people to extend appreciation and encouragement, and to bear testimony of the divinity of the Lord's work."[67] Early in his administration he commented, "I am determined that while I have strength I will get out among the people at home and abroad. . . . I intend to keep moving with energy for as long as I can. I wish to mingle with the people I love."[68]

During his service as President of the Church, he traveled extensively inside the United States and made more than 90 visits to countries outside the United States. In all, he traveled more than a

President Hinckley loved to "get out among the people at home and abroad."

million miles (1.6 million kilometers) as President of the Church, meeting with Saints in all parts of the world.[69]

In some areas, people had to make an even greater effort to see him than he made to see them. For example, in 1996 he and Sister Hinckley visited the Philippines, where Church membership had grown to more than 375,000. President and Sister Hinckley were scheduled to speak one evening at a meeting in Manila's Araneta Coliseum. By mid-afternoon of that day, the coliseum "was filled beyond capacity. Lines had begun to form at 7:00 a.m. for a meeting that wasn't scheduled to begin for twelve hours. The official count later indicated that some 35,000 members had crowded into the coliseum's 25,000 seats as well as the aisles and concourses. Many Saints had traveled twenty hours by boat and bus to reach Manila. For some, the cost of the journey equaled several months' salary. . . .

"When word reached President Hinckley that the coliseum was full and that the building manager wondered if there was any way they could begin the meeting early, he immediately said, 'Let's go.' He and Sister Hinckley entered the vast arena. . . . As if on cue, the congregation spontaneously rose to their feet, applauded, and then began singing an emotional rendition of 'We Thank Thee, O God, for a Prophet.'"[70]

Knowing that he and his brethren could not go everywhere they wanted to go, President Hinckley championed the use of technology to instruct leaders around the world. Using satellite technology, he presided over worldwide leadership training broadcasts, the first one held in January 2003.

Promoting the Importance of Learning and Teaching Spiritual and Secular Truths

President Hinckley stated: "None of us . . . knows enough. The learning process is an endless process. We must read, we must observe, we must assimilate, and we must ponder that to which we expose our minds."[71] He also said: "Effective teaching is the very essence of leadership in the Church. Eternal life will come only as men and women are taught with such effectiveness that they change and discipline their lives. They cannot be coerced into righteousness or into heaven. They must be led, and that means teaching."[72]

President Hinckley desired to provide more spiritual nourishment for Latter-day Saints throughout the world. In 1995 he enthusiastically approved a plan to publish a new series of books that would provide Church members with a gospel library. The Church soon began publishing this series, called *Teachings of Presidents of the Church,* of which this book is a part.

Secular learning was also important to President Hinckley. He was concerned about members of the Church in poverty-stricken areas of the world who could not afford higher education or vocational training. Without such education and training, most of them would remain in poverty. In the priesthood session of the April 2001 general conference, President Hinckley said:

"In an effort to remedy this situation, we propose a plan—a plan which we believe is inspired by the Lord. The Church is establishing a fund largely from the contributions of faithful Latter-day Saints who have and will contribute for this purpose. We are deeply grateful to them. . . . We shall call it the Perpetual Education Fund."[73]

President Hinckley explained that those benefiting from the program would be given loans, taken from funds donated by Church members, for school or vocational training. After completing their education or training, they would be expected to repay their loans so the funds could be used to help others. President Hinckley also explained that the Perpetual Education Fund would be "based on similar principles to those underlying the Perpetual Emigrat[ing] Fund," which the Church had established in the 1800s to help needy Saints emigrate to Zion.[74]

Within six months, Latter-day Saints had donated millions of dollars to the Perpetual Education Fund.[75] A year after introducing the plan, President Hinckley announced: "This endeavor is now on a solid foundation. . . . Young men and women in the underprivileged areas of the world, young men and women who for the most part are returned missionaries, will be enabled to get good educations that will lift them out of the slough of poverty in which their forebears for generations have struggled."[76] This program continues to bless Latter-day Saints, both receivers and givers.

Testifying of the Sanctity of Marriage and Family

In the general Relief Society meeting held on September 23, 1995, President Hinckley said:

"With so much of sophistry that is passed off as truth, with so much of deception concerning standards and values, with so much of allurement and enticement to take on the slow stain of the world, we have felt to warn and forewarn. In furtherance of this, we of the First Presidency and the Council of the Twelve Apostles now issue a proclamation to the Church and to the world as a declaration and reaffirmation of standards, doctrines, and practices relative to the family which the prophets, seers, and revelators of this church have repeatedly stated throughout its history."[77]

With this introduction, President Hinckley read, for the first time in public, "The Family: A Proclamation to the World."

The sanctity of marriage and family was a constant theme in President Hinckley's teachings. He condemned abuse of any kind and encouraged parents and children to be patient with one another, to love one another, to teach one another, and to serve one another.

*"We counsel parents and children to give highest priority
to family prayer, family home evening, gospel study and
instruction, and wholesome family activities."*

In a letter dated February 11, 1999, he and his counselors in the First Presidency said:

"We call upon parents to devote their best efforts to the teaching and rearing of their children in gospel principles which will keep them close to the Church. The home is the basis of a righteous life, and no other instrumentality can take its place or fulfill its essential functions in carrying forward this God-given responsibility.

"We counsel parents and children to give highest priority to family prayer, family home evening, gospel study and instruction, and wholesome family activities. However worthy and appropriate other demands or activities may be, they must not be permitted to displace the divinely appointed duties that only parents and families can adequately perform."[78]

Reaching Out to New Converts

President Hinckley loved to see large numbers of people join the Church, but he was concerned about the individuals represented by those numbers. Early in his administration he said:

"With the ever-increasing number of converts, we must make an increasingly substantial effort to assist them as they find their way. Every one of them needs three things: a friend, a responsibility, and nurturing with 'the good word of God' (Moro. 6:4). It is our duty and opportunity to provide these things."[79]

Strengthening new converts was a constant theme for President Hinckley. Elder Jeffrey R. Holland shared the following account of him emphasizing this theme: "With a twinkle in his eye and a hand smacking the table in front of him, he said to the Twelve recently, 'Brethren, when my life is finished and the final services are concluding, I am going to rise up as I go by, look each of you in the eye, and say, "How are we doing on retention?"'"[80]

Temple Building

In 1910, the year Gordon B. Hinckley was born, there were 4 operating temples in the world, and they were all in Utah. By 1961, when he was ordained an Apostle, the number had increased to 12. This progress was significant, but Elder Hinckley often expressed concern that many people around the world had limited access to temple blessings. In 1973, while serving as chairman of the Church's Temple Committee, he wrote in his journal: "The Church could build [many smaller] temples for the cost of the Washington Temple [then under construction]. It would take the temples to the people instead of having the people travel great distances to get to them."[81]

When he was sustained as President of the Church in 1995, the number of operating temples had increased to 47, but his desire for more temples was still strong. He said, "It has been my consuming desire to have a temple wherever needed so that our people, wherever they might be, could, without too great a sacrifice, come to the House of the Lord for their own ordinances and for the opportunity of doing vicarious work for the dead."[82]

In the October 1997 general conference, President Hinckley made a historic announcement: the Church would begin to build smaller temples around the world.[83] He later said, "The concept of small temples came, I believe, as a direct revelation."[84] In 1998 he announced that 30 new smaller temples, along with other temples

*President Hinckley applies mortar at the coverstone ceremony
prior to dedicating the Nauvoo Illinois Temple in 2002.*

already planned or under construction, would make "a total of 47 new temples in addition to the 51 now in operation." To the delight of all who were listening, President Hinckley then added, "I think we had better add 2 more to make it an even 100 by the end of this century, being 2,000 years 'since the coming of our Lord and Savior Jesus Christ in the flesh' (D&C 20:1)." Then he promised, "There will be more yet to come."[85]

On October 1, 2000, President Hinckley dedicated the Boston Massachusetts Temple, the 100th temple in operation. Before the end of the year 2000, he dedicated two more temples. When he died in 2008, the Church had 124 temples in operation, with 13 more announced. President Hinckley had been involved in the planning and construction of most of them, and he had personally dedicated 85 of them and had rededicated 13 (8 of the rededications were of temples he had previously dedicated).

The Conference Center

In the October 1995 general conference, President Hinckley hinted at an idea that had been on his mind. Speaking from the Tabernacle on Temple Square, he said: "This great Tabernacle seems to grow smaller each year. We now meet with far larger groups gathered under a single roof in some regional conferences."[86] In the April 1996 general conference, President Hinckley said more about his idea:

"I regret that many who wish to meet with us in the Tabernacle this morning are unable to get in. There are very many out on the grounds. This unique and remarkable hall, built by our pioneer forebears and dedicated to the worship of the Lord, comfortably seats about 6,000. Some of you seated on those hard benches for two hours may question the word *comfortably.*

"My heart reaches out to those who wish to get in and could not be accommodated. About a year ago I suggested to the Brethren that perhaps the time has come when we should study the feasibility of constructing another dedicated house of worship on a much larger scale that would accommodate three or four times the number who can be seated in this building."[87]

On July 24, 1997, the 150th anniversary of the pioneers' arrival in the Salt Lake Valley, ground was broken for the new building—to be called the Conference Center—on the block immediately north of Temple Square. Less than three years later, in April 2000, the first sessions of general conference were held there, even though the building was not quite complete. President Hinckley dedicated the Conference Center at the October 2000 general conference. Before offering the dedicatory prayer, he stood at the pulpit, which had been made from a black walnut tree he had grown in his own yard, and said:

"Today we shall dedicate it as a house in which to worship God the Eternal Father and His Only Begotten Son, the Lord Jesus Christ. We hope and we pray that there will continue to go forth to the world from this pulpit declarations of testimony and doctrine, of faith in the Living God, and of gratitude for the great atoning sacrifice of our Redeemer."[88]

*The Conference Center, which President Hinckley
dedicated in the October 2000 general conference*

Testimony of Jesus Christ

On January 1, 2000, President Hinckley, his counselors in the First Presidency, and the Quorum of the Twelve Apostles published a proclamation titled "The Living Christ: The Testimony of the Apostles." Of the Savior, they declared, "None other has had so profound an influence upon all who have lived and will yet live upon the earth."[89]

And none other had so profound an influence on the life of President Gordon B. Hinckley. For more than 46 years he served as a special witness of the name of Jesus Christ. A few months after he and his brethren published "The Living Christ," President Hinckley stood before the Latter-day Saints and said: "Of all the things for which I feel grateful this morning, one stands out preeminently. That is a living testimony of Jesus Christ, the Son of the Almighty God, the Prince of Peace, the Holy One."[90]

Trials and Hope

At the end of the April 2004 general conference, President Hinckley said: "I reluctantly desire a personal indulgence for a moment. Some of you have noticed the absence of Sister Hinckley. For the first time in 46 years, since I became a General Authority, she has not attended general conference. . . . We were on our way home [from Africa in January] when she collapsed with weariness. She's had a difficult time ever since. . . . I guess the clock is winding down, and we do not know how to rewind it.

"It is a somber time for me. We've been married for 67 years this month. She is the mother of our five gifted and able children, the grandmother of 25 grandchildren and a growing number of great-grandchildren. We've walked together side by side through all of these years, coequals and companions through storm and sunshine. She has spoken far and wide in testimony of this work, imparting love, encouragement, and faith wherever she's gone."[91]

Two days later, on April 6, Marjorie Pay Hinckley passed away. Millions of people, who loved her for her caring heart, quick wit, and steady faith, mourned with President Hinckley. He was grateful for letters of support and love that poured in from around the world. These expressions, he said, "shed an aura of comfort in our time of grief."[92] Many people made contributions in Sister Hinckley's name to the Perpetual Education Fund.

As difficult as Marjorie's loss was to him, President Hinckley continued on with the work of the Church, even though his own health declined slightly. He began carrying a cane. Sometimes he used it to support himself, but more often he used it to wave to Church members. President Thomas S. Monson recalled a conversation with President Hinckley's doctor, who was worried about the way President Hinckley used—and did not use—his cane. The doctor said: "The last thing we want is for him to fall and break a hip or worse. Instead, he waves it around and then doesn't use it when he walks. Tell him the cane has been prescribed by his doctor, and he needs to use it as it was meant to be used." President Monson replied, "Doctor, I am President Hinckley's counselor. You are his doctor. *You* tell him!"[93]

In early 2006, at the age of 95, President Hinckley was diagnosed with cancer. At the October general conference that year, he said: "The Lord has permitted me to live; I do not know for how long. But whatever the time, I shall continue to give my best to the task at hand. . . . I feel well; my health is reasonably good. But when it is time for a successor, the transition will be smooth and according to the will of Him whose Church this is."[94]

A year later, in October 2007, President Hinckley closed his final general conference by saying: "We look forward to seeing you again next April. I'm 97, but I hope I'm going to make it. May the blessings of heaven attend you in the meantime is our humble and sincere prayer in the name of our Redeemer, even the Lord Jesus Christ, amen."[95]

President and Sister Hinckley's daughter Virginia described the four years after Sister Hinckley's death as "the capstone years" of President Hinckley's life. She then reflected on a prayer he offered on January 20, 2008, one week before his death, when dedicating a renovated chapel in Salt Lake City:

"In that prayer, in a very unusual way, he petitioned the Lord for himself as prophet. He spoke with gratitude that 'from the days of Joseph Smith to the present Thou hast chosen and appointed a prophet to this people. We thank Thee and plead with Thee that Thou wilt comfort and sustain him and bless him according to his needs and Thy great purposes.'"[96]

On Thursday, January 24, 2008, President Hinckley felt, for the first time, unable to participate with his brethren in their weekly temple meeting. The following Sunday, January 27, President Monson gave him a priesthood blessing, assisted by Presidents Henry B. Eyring and Boyd K. Packer. Later that day, President Gordon B. Hinckley quietly passed away at home, surrounded by his five children and their spouses.

A few days later, thousands paid their respects as they passed by President Hinckley's casket in a public viewing in the Conference Center's Hall of the Prophets. Leaders of other churches and leaders in government and business also sent condolences, expressing gratitude for President Hinckley's influence and teachings.

Funeral services were held in the Conference Center and broadcast to Church buildings around the world. The Tabernacle Choir sang a new hymn as part of the meeting, titled "What Is This Thing That Men Call Death?" The words of the hymn were written by President Hinckley—his final testimony of Jesus Christ to his friends who had looked to him as a prophet:

> *What is this thing that men call death,*
> *This quiet passing in the night?*
> *'Tis not the end, but genesis*
> *Of better worlds and greater light.*
> *O God, touch Thou my aching heart,*
> *And calm my troubled, haunting fears.*
> *Let hope and faith, transcendent, pure,*
> *Give strength and peace beyond my tears.*
> *There is no death, but only change*
> *With recompense for victory won;*
> *The gift of Him who loved all men,*
> *The Son of God, the Holy One.*[97]

Notes

1. See Steve Fidel, "A Temple to Be Built in Ghana," *Church News,* Feb. 21, 1998, 3.

2. Jeffrey R. Holland, "Emerging with Faith in Africa," mormonnewsroom.co.za/article/emerging-with-faith-in-africa; accessed Feb. 11, 2015.

3. Esther Korantemaa Abuyeh, in "Accra Ghana Temple: Commemoration of the Tenth Anniversary," africawest.lds.org/accra-ghana-temple-commemoration-of-the-tenth-anniversary; accessed Feb. 11, 2015.

4. Adney Y. Komatsu, in Sheri L. Dew, *Go Forward with Faith: The Biography of Gordon B. Hinckley* (1996), 288.

5. Russell M. Nelson, "Spiritual Capacity," *Ensign,* Nov. 1997, 15–16.

6. Jeffrey R. Holland, "President Gordon B. Hinckley: Stalwart and Brave He Stands," *Ensign,* June 1995, 4.

7. In Benjamin F. Tibby, Biographical Sketch of Breneman Barr Bitner, Hinckley and Bitner family history collection, Church History Library, Salt Lake City; see also Silas Richards

Company schedule and reports, Sept. 1849, Church History Library.

8. Bryant S. Hinckley, in Sheri L. Dew, *Go Forward with Faith,* 193. Most estimates put the number of *Mayflower* survivors slightly higher than 49.

9. Sheri L. Dew, *Go Forward with Faith,* 24.

10. Sheri L. Dew, *Go Forward with Faith,* 25.

11. Gordon B. Hinckley, "Joseph the Seer," *Ensign,* May 1977, 66; quoting "Praise to the Man," *Hymns,* no. 27.

12. See Sheri L. Dew, *Go Forward with Faith,* 45.

13. *Teachings of Gordon B. Hinckley* (1997), 388.

14. Gordon B. Hinckley, in Sheri L. Dew, *Go Forward with Faith,* 46–47.

15. Gordon B. Hinckley, "God Hath Not Given Us the Spirit of Fear," *Ensign,* Oct. 1984, 4–5.

16. Gordon B. Hinckley, "The Question of a Mission," *Ensign,* May 1986, 40.

17. Gordon B. Hinckley, in Jeffrey R. Holland, "President Gordon B. Hinckley: Stalwart and Brave He Stands," 7–8.

18. Gordon B. Hinckley, "Be Not Afraid, Only Believe," *Ensign,* Feb. 1996, 2.

19. Gordon B. Hinckley, in Sheri L. Dew, *Go Forward with Faith,* 62.

20. Gordon B. Hinckley, in Sheri L. Dew, *Go Forward with Faith,* 64.

21. See Sheri L. Dew, *Go Forward with Faith,* 64.

22. Gordon B. Hinckley, in "His Mission to England Was a Life-Changing Experience," *Deseret Morning News,* Jan. 28, 2008, 11.

23. Gordon B. Hinckley, in Sheri L. Dew, *Go Forward with Faith,* 75.

24. Elders' Labor Record of Liverpool Conference of the British Mission of The Church of Jesus Christ of Latter-day Saints, July 1933 to Feb. 1934; Church History Library, Salt Lake City.

25. See Sheri L. Dew, *Go Forward with Faith,* 69.

26. *Discourses of President Gordon B. Hinckley, Volume 1: 1995–1999* (2005), 348.

27. *Discourses of President Gordon B. Hinckley, Volume 1,* 348.

28. Heber J. Grant, in Sheri L. Dew, *Go Forward with Faith,* 84.

29. For additional details about this experience, see chapter 2 in this book.

30. Gordon B. Hinckley, letter to Parley Giles, Dec. 7, 1936; Church History Library, Salt Lake City.

31. Gordon B. Hinckley, in Sheri L. Dew, *Go Forward with Faith,* 151–52.

32. Gordon B. Hinckley, in Sheri L. Dew, *Go Forward with Faith,* 104.

33. Marjorie Pay Hinckley, in Sheri L. Dew, *Go Forward with Faith,* 59.

34. Marjorie Pay Hinckley, in Sheri L. Dew, *Go Forward with Faith,* 114–15.

35. Marjorie Pay Hinckley, in Sheri L. Dew, *Go Forward with Faith,* 173–74.

36. Marjorie Pay Hinckley, in *Glimpses into the Life and Heart of Marjorie Pay Hinckley,* ed. Virginia H. Pearce (1999), 107.

37. Gordon B. Hinckley, letter to G. Homer Durham, Mar. 27, 1939; Church History Library, Salt Lake City.

38. Gordon B. Hinckley, in Sheri L. Dew, *Go Forward with Faith,* 126.

39. See Sheri L. Dew, *Go Forward with Faith,* 135–36.

40. See Sheri L. Dew, *Go Forward with Faith,* 143–44.

41. David O. McKay, in Sheri L. Dew, *Go Forward with Faith,* 176.

42. See Sheri L. Dew, *Go Forward with Faith,* 177–81.

43. Gordon B. Hinckley, in Conference Report, Apr. 1958, 123–24.

44. Gordon B. Hinckley, in Conference Report, Apr. 1958, 123.

45. Kenji Tanaka, in Sheri L. Dew, *Go Forward with Faith,* 220.

46. David O. McKay, in Sheri L. Dew, *Go Forward with Faith,* 234.

47. Gordon B. Hinckley, in Conference Report, Apr. 1962, 71.

48. See Allen E Litster, in Sheri L. Dew, *Go Forward with Faith,* 313.

49. Allen E Litster, in Sheri L. Dew, *Go Forward with Faith,* 314.

50. See Sheri L. Dew, *Go Forward with Faith,* 315.

51. During the last several years of his service as President of the Church, President David O. McKay also called additional counselors in the First Presidency to assist him.

52. Gordon B. Hinckley, "Faith: The Essence of True Religion," *Ensign,* Nov. 1981, 6.

53. Gordon B. Hinckley, "Five Million Members—A Milestone and Not a Summit," *Ensign,* May 1982, 46.

54. Gordon B. Hinckley, "The Loneliness of Leadership" (Brigham Young University devotional, Nov. 4, 1969), speeches. byu.edu.

55. Gordon B. Hinckley, in Francis M. Orquiola, "Temple Dedication Rewards Faith of Filipino Saints," *Ensign,* Nov. 1984, 106.

56. Gordon B. Hinckley, in "New Mission Presidents Receive Instruction from Church Leaders," *Ensign,* Sept. 1984, 76.

57. Gordon B. Hinckley, in "Leadership Meetings Focus on Missionary Work, Activation, and Strengthening Members," *Ensign,* May 1985, 96.

58. See Sheri L. Dew, *Go Forward with Faith,* 505.

59. Marjorie Pay Hinckley, in Sheri L. Dew, *Go Forward with Faith,* 505.

60. Gordon B. Hinckley, in Sheri L. Dew, *Go Forward with Faith,* 508.

61. Gordon B. Hinckley, in Sheri L. Dew, *Go Forward with Faith,* 508.

62. Jeffrey R. Holland, "President Gordon B. Hinckley: Stalwart and Brave He Stands," 2.

63. Neal A. Maxwell, in Sheri L. Dew, *Go Forward with Faith,* 536.

64. Gordon B. Hinckley, "Remember . . . Thy Church, O Lord," *Ensign,* May 1996, 83.

65. Gordon B. Hinckley, "The Church Goes Forward," *Ensign,* May 2002, 4.

66. Gordon B. Hinckley, in "President Gordon B. Hinckley Awarded Presidential Medal of Freedom," mormonnewsroom.org/article/ president-gordon-b.-hinckley- awarded-presidential-medal-of- freedom; accessed Sept. 21, 2015.

67. Gordon B. Hinckley, "Forgiveness," *Ensign* or *Liahona,* Nov. 2005, 81.

68. Gordon B. Hinckley, "This Glorious Easter Morn," *Ensign,* May 1996, 65–66.

69. See "Milestones in the Presidency of Gordon B. Hinckley," *In Memoriam: President Gordon B. Hinckley, 1910– 2008* (supplement to the *Ensign,* Mar. 2008), 13.

70. Sheri L. Dew, *Go Forward with Faith,* 553–54.

71. *Teachings of Gordon B. Hinckley,* 298.

72. Gordon B. Hinckley, in Jeffrey R. Holland, "A Teacher Come from God," *Ensign,* May 1998, 26.

73. Gordon B. Hinckley, "The Perpetual Education Fund," *Ensign,* May 2001, 52.

74. Gordon B. Hinckley, "The Perpetual Education Fund," 52.

75. See Gordon B. Hinckley, "Reaching Down to Lift Another," *Ensign,* Nov. 2001, 52.

76. Gordon B. Hinckley, "The Church Goes Forward," 6.

77. Gordon B. Hinckley, "Stand Strong against the Wiles of the World," *Ensign,* Nov. 1995, 100.

78. First Presidency letter, Feb. 11, 1999, in "Policies, Announcements, and Appointments," *Ensign,* June 1999, 80. For more on this subject, see chapters 10 and 11.

79. Gordon B. Hinckley, "Converts and Young Men," *Ensign,* May 1997, 47. For more on this subject, see chapter 22.

80. Jeffrey R. Holland, "Abide in Me," *Ensign* or *Liahona,* May 2004, 31.

81. Gordon B. Hinckley, in Sheri L. Dew, *Go Forward with Faith,* 325.

82. *Teachings of Gordon B. Hinckley,* 629.

83. See Gordon B. Hinckley, "Some Thoughts on Temples, Retention of Converts, and Missionary Service," *Ensign,* Nov. 1997, 49–50.

84. Gordon B. Hinckley, "The Quorum of the First Presidency," *Ensign,* Dec. 2005, 50.

85. Gordon B. Hinckley, "New Temples to Provide 'Crowning Blessings' of the Gospel," *Ensign,* May 1998, 88. For more information about the inspiration to build smaller temples, see chapter 23.

86. Gordon B. Hinckley, "As We Gather Together," *Ensign,* Nov. 1995, 4.

87. Gordon B. Hinckley, "This Glorious Easter Morn," 65.

88. Gordon B. Hinckley, "This Great Millennial Year," *Ensign,* Nov. 2000, 68–69.

89. "The Living Christ: The Testimony of the Apostles," *Ensign,* Apr. 2000, 2.

90. Gordon B. Hinckley, "My Testimony," *Ensign,* May 2000, 69. For more on this subject, see chapters 8 and 24.

91. Gordon B. Hinckley, "Concluding Remarks," *Ensign* or *Liahona,* May 2004, 103–4.

92. Gordon B. Hinckley, "The Women in Our Lives," *Ensign* or *Liahona,* Nov. 2004, 82.

93. Thomas S. Monson, "God Be with You Till We Meet Again," *In Memoriam: President Gordon B. Hinckley, 1910– 2008,* 30.

94. Gordon B. Hinckley, "The Faith to Move Mountains," *Ensign* or *Liahona,* Nov. 2006, 82.

95. Gordon B. Hinckley, "Closing Remarks," *Ensign* or *Liahona,* Nov. 2007, 108.

96. Virginia H. Pearce, "A Daughter's Tribute," *In Memoriam: President Gordon B. Hinckley, 1910–2008,* 18–19.

97. Gordon B. Hinckley, "What Is This Thing That Men Call Death?" *In Memoriam: President Gordon B. Hinckley, 1910–2008,* 32.

*The First Vision began "the final chapter in the long chronicle
of God's dealing with men and women upon the earth."*

The Restoration of the Gospel— The Dawning of a Brighter Day

"This glorious gospel was ushered in with the appearance of the Father and the Son to the boy Joseph."

From the Life of Gordon B. Hinckley

Throughout his life, President Gordon B. Hinckley fostered a deep respect for the people and places involved in the restoration of the gospel. He felt special gratitude for Joseph Smith and his role in the Restoration, and he spoke of "an ever-growing compulsion to bear testimony of the divinity of the Lord and of the mission of the Prophet Joseph Smith."[1]

In 1935, when Gordon was traveling home from his mission to England, he and other returning missionaries visited the Sacred Grove and the Hill Cumorah. They also stopped at Carthage Jail, where the Prophet Joseph and Hyrum Smith were martyred. They walked the dusty streets of Nauvoo, where exiled Saints had turned a swampland into a beautiful city. Undoubtedly, reflections on the trials and triumphs of the early Saints pressed upon Gordon's mind while he was in these places and as he continued west along the pioneer route to Salt Lake City.

Gordon B. Hinckley returned to the sacred sites of the Restoration many more times in the following decades. At the First Presidency Christmas devotional on December 3, 2000, he shared this personal experience from a visit to the Sacred Grove:

"Some years ago I was assigned to the Rochester New York Stake conference. On Saturday I said to the brethren who were with me, 'Let us get up early in the morning, early Sunday morning, and go to the Sacred Grove before the conference.' They all agreed. Accordingly, very early on that spring Sabbath, the mission president, the stake president, the regional representative, and I went out to Palmyra and walked into the grove. No one else was there. It was peaceful and beautiful. It had rained during the night. Tiny new leaves were upon the trees.

"We spoke quietly one to another. We knelt upon the damp ground and prayed. We did not hear an audible voice. We did not see a vision. But in an indefinable way we were told in our minds, each of us, that yes, it happened here just as Joseph said it happened. It was here that God our Eternal Father and His Beloved Son, the resurrected Lord Jesus Christ, appeared to the 14-year-old boy and spoke with him. Their matchless light rested upon him, and he was instructed in what he should do.

"That sublime occasion, the First Vision, parted the curtains through which came the restoration to earth of the Church of Christ. It came out of the wilderness of darkness, out of the bleakness of ages past into the glorious dawn of a new day. The Book of Mormon followed as another witness of the Lord Jesus Christ. His holy supernal priesthood was restored under the hands of those who held it anciently. Keys and powers were bestowed upon the Prophet and his associates. The ancient Church was again upon the earth with all of the blessings, powers, doctrines, keys, and principles of previous dispensations. It is [Christ's] Church. It carries His name. It is governed by His priesthood. There is no other name under heaven by which men must be saved. Joseph Smith . . . became His great testator." [2]

Teachings of Gordon B. Hinckley

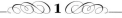

1

Following the Savior's death, the Church He had established drifted into apostasy.

[Jesus Christ] was and is the great central figure of human history, the zenith of the times and seasons of all men.

Before His death, He had ordained His Apostles. They carried on for a period. His Church was set in place.[3]

Following the Savior's death, the Church He had established drifted into apostasy. Fulfilled were the words of Isaiah, who said,

"The earth also is defiled under the inhabitants thereof; because they have transgressed the laws, changed the ordinance, broken the everlasting covenant" (Isaiah 24:5).[4]

Paul's letters cried out for strength among the followers of Christ, lest they fall into the ways of the wicked one. But a spirit of apostasy ultimately prevailed.[5]

The centuries rolled on. A cloud of darkness settled over the earth. Isaiah described it: "For, behold, the darkness shall cover the earth, and gross darkness the people" (Isa. 60:2).

It was a season of plunder and suffering, marked by long and bloody conflict. . . . It was an age of hopelessness, a time of masters and serfs.

The first thousand years passed, and the second millennium dawned. Its earlier centuries were a continuation of the former. It was a time fraught with fear and suffering.[6]

―――――――――――――― 2 ――――――――――――――

The Renaissance and Reformation helped prepare the way for the restoration of the gospel.

Somehow, in that long season of darkness, a candle was lighted. The age of Renaissance brought with it a flowering of learning, art, and science. There came a movement of bold and courageous men and women who looked heavenward in acknowledgment of God and His divine Son. We speak of it as the Reformation.[7]

Reformers worked to change the [Christian] church, notably such men as Luther, Melanchthon, Hus, Zwingli, and Tyndale. These were men of great courage, some of whom suffered cruel deaths because of their beliefs. Protestantism was born with its cry for reformation. When that reformation was not realized, the reformers organized churches of their own. They did so without priesthood authority. Their one desire was to find a niche in which they might worship God as they felt He should be worshiped.

While this great ferment was stirring across the Christian world, political forces were also at work. Then came the American Revolutionary War, resulting in the birth of a nation whose Constitution declared that government should not reach its grasping hand into matters of religion. A new day had dawned, a glorious day. Here there was no longer a state church. No one faith was favored above another.

After centuries of darkness and pain and struggle, the time was ripe for the restoration of the gospel. Ancient prophets had spoken of this long-awaited day.

All of the history of the past had pointed to this season. The centuries with all of their suffering and all their hope had come and gone. The Almighty Judge of the nations, the Living God, determined that the times of which the prophets had spoken had arrived. Daniel had foreseen a stone which was cut out of the mountain without hands and which became a great mountain and filled the whole earth [see Daniel 2:35, 44].[8]

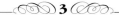

3

The Restoration was ushered in with the appearance of the Father and the Son to Joseph Smith.

After many generations had walked the earth—so many of them in conflict, hatred, darkness, and evil—there arrived the great, new day of the Restoration. This glorious gospel was ushered in with the appearance of the Father and the Son to the boy Joseph.[9]

How truly remarkable was that vision in the year 1820 when Joseph prayed in the woods and there appeared before him both the Father and the Son. One of these spoke to him, calling him by name and, pointing to the other, said, "This is My Beloved Son. Hear Him!" (Joseph Smith—History 1:17).

Nothing like it had ever happened before. One is led to wonder why it was so important that both the Father and the Son appear. I think it was because They were ushering in the dispensation of the fulness of times, the last and final dispensation of the gospel, when there would be gathered together in one the elements of all previous dispensations. This was to be the final chapter in the long chronicle of God's dealing with men and women upon the earth.[10]

Every claim that we make concerning divine authority, every truth that we offer concerning the validity of this work, all finds its root in the First Vision of the boy prophet. Without it we would not

*The authority and keys of the Melchizedek Priesthood were
restored to the earth as part of the Restoration.*

have anything much to say. This was the great curtain-raiser on the
dispensation of the fulness of times, when God promised that He
would restore all the power, the gifts, the blessings, of all previous
dispensations.[11]

4

Priesthood authority and keys were restored.

In restoring the Aaronic Priesthood, the resurrected John the Baptist laid his hands on the heads of Joseph Smith and Oliver Cowdery
and said, "Upon you my fellow servants, in the name of Messiah
I confer the Priesthood of Aaron, which holds the keys of the ministering of angels, and of the gospel of repentance, and of baptism
by immersion for the remission of sins" (D&C 13:1).[12]

This was followed by a visitation of Peter, James, and John, Apostles of the Lord Jesus Christ, who conferred upon Joseph and Oliver
Cowdery the Melchizedek Priesthood, which had been received by
these Apostles under the hands of the Lord Himself.[13]

Three of [the Savior's] Apostles—Peter, James, and John—appeared to Joseph and Oliver somewhere "in the wilderness" along the Susquehanna River (see D&C 128:20). They placed their hands upon their heads and conferred upon them this holy authority. . . .

I can trace my priesthood in a direct line to this event. It goes as follows: I was ordained by David O. McKay; who was ordained by Joseph F. Smith; who was ordained by Brigham Young; who was ordained by the Three Witnesses; who were ordained by Joseph Smith Jr. and Oliver Cowdery; who were ordained by Peter, James, and John; who were ordained by the Lord Jesus Christ.

It has similarly come to [each Melchizedek Priesthood holder]. Each of you brethren who hold this priesthood has also received it in a direct line from the bestowal made by Peter, James, and John.[14]

5

Through Joseph Smith, the Lord revealed truths that distinguish us from other churches.

Permit me to name a few of many doctrines and practices which distinguish us from all other churches, and all of which have come of revelation to the youthful Prophet. They are familiar to you, but they are worth repeating and reflecting on.

The Godhead

The first of these . . . is the manifestation of God Himself and His Beloved Son, the risen Lord Jesus Christ. This grand theophany is, in my judgment, the greatest such event since the birth, life, death, and Resurrection of our Lord in the meridian of time.

We have no record of any other event to equal it.

For centuries men gathered and argued concerning the nature of Deity. Constantine assembled scholars of various factions at Nicaea in the year 325. After two months of bitter debate, they compromised on a definition which for generations has been the doctrinal statement among Christians concerning the Godhead.

I invite you to read that definition and compare it with the statement of the boy Joseph. He simply says that God stood before him and spoke to him. Joseph could see Him and could hear Him. He was in form like a man, a being of substance. Beside Him was the resurrected Lord, a separate being, whom He introduced as His Beloved Son and with whom Joseph also spoke.

I submit that in the short time of that remarkable vision Joseph learned more concerning Deity than all of the scholars and clerics of the past.

In this divine revelation there was reaffirmed beyond doubt the reality of the literal Resurrection of the Lord Jesus Christ.

This knowledge of Deity, hidden from the world for centuries, was the first and great thing which God revealed to His chosen servant.[15]

The Book of Mormon as a companion witness with the Bible

I speak next of another very important thing which God revealed.

The Christian world accepts the Bible as the word of God. Most have no idea of how it came to us.

I have just completed reading a newly published book by a renowned scholar. It is apparent from information which he gives that the various books of the Bible were brought together in what appears to have been an unsystematic fashion. In some cases, the writings were not produced until long after the events they describe. One is led to ask, "Is the Bible true? Is it really the word of God?"

We reply that it is, insofar as it is translated correctly. The hand of the Lord was in its making. But it now does not stand alone. There is another witness of the significant and important truths found therein.

Scripture declares that "in the mouth of two or three witnesses shall every word be established" (2 Corinthians 13:1).

The Book of Mormon has come forth by the gift and power of God. It speaks as a voice from the dust in testimony of the Son of God. It speaks of His birth, of His ministry, of His Crucifixion and Resurrection, and of His appearance to the righteous in the land Bountiful on the American continent.

It is a tangible thing that can be handled, that can be read, that can be tested. It carries within its covers a promise of its divine

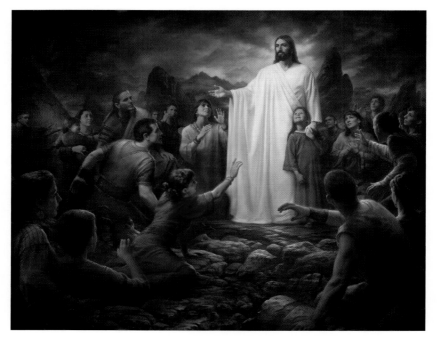

*"The Book of Mormon . . . speaks as a voice from
the dust in testimony of the Son of God."*

origin. Millions now have put it to the test and found it to be a true
and sacred record. . . .

As the Bible is the testament of the Old World, the Book of Mormon is the testament of the New. They go hand in hand in declaration of Jesus as the Son of the Father. . . .

This sacred book, which came forth as a revelation of the Almighty, is indeed another testament of the divinity of our Lord.[16]

Priesthood authority and Church organization

Priesthood is the authority to act in the name of God. . . . I have
read [a] book recently [that] deals with the Apostasy of the primitive Church. If the authority of that Church was lost, how was it to
be replaced?

Priesthood authority came from the only place it could come,
and that is from heaven. It was bestowed under the hands of those
who held it when the Savior walked the earth. . . .

How beautiful is the unfolding of the pattern of restoration which led to the organization of the Church in the year 1830. . . . The very name of the Church came of revelation. Whose Church was it? Was it Joseph Smith's? Was it Oliver Cowdery's? No, it was the Church of Jesus Christ restored to earth in these latter days.[17]

The family

Another great and singular revelation given to the Prophet was the plan for the eternal life of the family.

The family is a creation of the Almighty. It represents the most sacred of all relationships. It represents the most serious of all undertakings. It is the fundamental organization of society.

Through the revelations of God to His Prophet came the doctrine and authority under which families are sealed together not only for this life but for all eternity.[18]

The innocence of little children

The innocence of little children is another revelation which God has given through the instrumentality of the Prophet Joseph. The general practice is the baptism of infants to take away the effects of what is described as the sin of Adam and Eve. Under the doctrine of the Restoration, baptism is for the remission of one's individual and personal sins. It becomes a covenant between God and man. It is performed at the age of accountability, when people are old enough to recognize right from wrong. It is by immersion, in symbolism of the death and burial of Jesus Christ and His coming forth in the Resurrection.[19]

Salvation for the dead

I go on to mention another revealed truth. We are told that God is no respecter of persons, and yet, in no other church of which I am aware, is provision made for those beyond the veil of death to receive every blessing which is afforded the living. The great doctrine of salvation for the dead is unique to this Church. . . . The dead are given the same opportunity as the living. Again, what a glorious and wonderful provision the Almighty has made through His revelation to His Prophet.[20]

The nature, purpose, and potential of God's children

The eternal nature of man has been revealed. We are sons and daughters of God. God is the Father of our spirits. We lived before we came here. We had personality. We were born into this life under a divine plan. We are here to test our worthiness, acting in the agency which God has given to us. When we die we shall go on living. Our eternal life is comprised of three phases: one, our premortal existence; two, our mortal existence; and three, our post-mortal existence. In death we die to this world and step through the veil into the sphere we are worthy to enter. This, again, is a unique, singular, and precious doctrine of this Church which has come through revelation.[21]

Modern revelation

I offer this brief summary of the tremendous outpouring of knowledge and authority from God upon the head of His Prophet. . . . There is one more that I must mention. This is the principle of modern revelation. The article of faith which the Prophet wrote declares:

"We believe all that God has revealed, all that He does now reveal, and we believe that He will yet reveal many great and important things pertaining to the Kingdom of God" (Articles of Faith 1:9).

A growing church, a church that is spreading across the earth in these complex times, needs constant revelation from the throne of heaven to guide it and move it forward.

With prayer and anxious seeking of the will of the Lord, we testify that direction is received, that revelation comes, and that the Lord blesses His Church as it moves on its path of destiny.

On the solid foundation of the Prophet Joseph's divine calling and the revelations of God, which came through him, we go forward.[22]

Standing as the 15th in line from Joseph Smith and bearing the prophetic mantle which came upon him, I solemnly declare my testimony that the Prophet Joseph's account of [the events of the Restoration] is true, that the Father . . . bore witness of the divinity of His Son, that the Son instructed the boy prophet, and that there followed a train of events which led to the organization of "the only true and living church upon the face of the whole earth" [D&C 1:30].[23]

Suggestions for Study and Teaching

Questions

- Why did the people of the world need the Church and gospel of Jesus Christ to be restored? (See section 1.) What are some ways the Lord prepared the way for the restoration of the gospel? (See section 2.)

- Ponder President Hinckley's teachings about the First Vision (see section 3). In what ways has your testimony of the First Vision influenced you?

- Why was it necessary that the priesthood be restored by heavenly messengers? (See section 4.) Why is important that Melchizedek Priesthood holders can trace their priesthood authority to Jesus Christ?

- In section 5, review the summary of some of the truths that came by revelation to the Prophet Joseph Smith. How have these truths blessed your life? How might we help children understand and appreciate these truths?

Related Scriptures

Isaiah 2:1–3; Acts 3:19–21; Revelation 14:6–7; 2 Nephi 25:17–18; D&C 128:19–21

Study Help

"Your gospel study is most effective when you are taught by the Holy Ghost. Always begin your gospel study by praying for the Holy Ghost to help you learn" (*Preach My Gospel* [2004], 18).

Notes

1. In Sheri L. Dew, *Go Forward with Faith: The Biography of Gordon B. Hinckley* (1996), 326.
2. "My Redeemer Lives," *Ensign,* Feb. 2001, 72.
3. "At the Summit of the Ages," *Ensign,* Nov. 1999, 73.
4. "The Stone Cut Out of the Mountain," *Ensign* or *Liahona,* Nov. 2007, 84.
5. "The Dawning of a Brighter Day," *Ensign* or *Liahona,* May 2004, 82.
6. "At the Summit of the Ages," 73.
7. "The Dawning of a Brighter Day," 82–83.

8. "At the Summit of the Ages," 73.

9. "The Dawning of a Brighter Day," 83.

10. "The Stone Cut Out of the Mountain," 84.

11. *Teachings of Gordon B. Hinckley* (1997), 226.

12. "The Things of Which I Know," *Ensign* or *Liahona,* May 2007, 84.

13. "The Great Things Which God Has Revealed," *Ensign* or *Liahona,* May 2005, 82.

14. *Discourses of President Gordon B. Hinckley, Volume 2: 2000–2004* (2005), 411.

15. "The Great Things Which God Has Revealed," 80–81.

16. "The Great Things Which God Has Revealed," 81–82.

17. "The Great Things Which God Has Revealed," 82.

18. "The Great Things Which God Has Revealed," 82.

19. "The Great Things Which God Has Revealed," 82.

20. "The Great Things Which God Has Revealed," 82.

21. "The Great Things Which God Has Revealed," 83.

22. "The Great Things Which God Has Revealed," 83.

23. "Special Witnesses of Christ," *Ensign,* Apr. 2001, 20–21.

An Ensign to the Nations, a Light to the World

"This is a season to be strong. It is a time to move forward without hesitation, knowing well the meaning, the breadth, and the importance of our mission."

From the Life of Gordon B. Hinckley

Soon after returning home from his mission to England, Gordon B. Hinckley fulfilled one last assignment from his mission president, Joseph F. Merrill. President Merrill was also a member of the Quorum of the Twelve Apostles, and he had asked Gordon to make a report to the First Presidency: Presidents Heber J. Grant, J. Reuben Clark Jr., and David O. McKay. Gordon contacted the secretary to the First Presidency and set up an appointment.

When Gordon entered the First Presidency's council room, President Grant and his counselors greeted him warmly. Then President Grant said, "Brother Hinckley, we'll give you fifteen minutes to tell us what Elder Merrill wants us to hear." One hour and fifteen minutes later, Gordon left the room. In his allotted fifteen minutes, he had presented his mission president's concern—that the missionaries needed better printed materials to help them in their work. His short presentation had led to questions from the First Presidency and an hour-long discussion.

Having fulfilled this assignment, Gordon felt that "his mission was now truly over, and it was time to move ahead and plan for the future." He had already graduated from the University of Utah with a degree in English, and he wanted to pursue a graduate degree in journalism at Columbia University in New York City. But a phone call two days after his meeting with the First Presidency changed his plans. The call was from President McKay, who said: "Brother

*"It is the mission of this Church to stand as an ensign
to the nations and a light to the world."*

Hinckley, we discussed in the meeting of the Presidency and the Twelve yesterday what we talked about during your interview with us. And we have organized a committee consisting of six members of the Twelve, with Elder Stephen L Richards as chairman, to address the needs you outlined. We would like to invite you to come and work with that committee."[1]

Gordon accepted the invitation and was hired as executive secretary of the newly formed Church Radio, Publicity, and Mission Literature Committee. He never went to Columbia University, and he never worked as a journalist to publish the news of the world. Instead, he began a lifelong effort to publish the good news of the gospel. These responsibilities were expanded later, when he served as a General Authority.

Having developed the ability to express himself clearly even in difficult situations, Gordon B. Hinckley often received assignments to be interviewed by news reporters. As President of the Church, he continued to welcome such opportunities, doing his part to help bring the Church of Jesus Christ "out of obscurity" (D&C 1:30). He declared:

"I believe and testify that it is the mission of this Church to stand as an ensign to the nations and a light to the world. We have had placed upon us a great, all-encompassing mandate from which we cannot shrink nor turn aside. We accept that mandate and are determined to fulfill it, and with the help of God we shall do it."[2]

Teachings of Gordon B. Hinckley

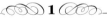 1

Like the stone in Daniel's vision, the Church is rolling forth to fill the whole earth.

This Church began with the humble prayer of the boy Joseph Smith in the grove of his father's farm. From that remarkable experience, which we call the First Vision, has grown this work. . . . It is the very personification of Daniel's vision of a stone cut out of the mountain without hands rolling forth to fill the whole earth (see Daniel 2:44–45).[3]

When the Church was organized in 1830 there were but six members [and] only a handful of believers, all residing in a largely unknown village. . . . Stakes of Zion today flourish in every state of the United States, in every province of Canada, in every state of Mexico, in every nation of Central America and throughout South America.

Congregations are found throughout the British Isles and Europe, where thousands have joined the Church through the years. This work has reached out to the Baltic nations and on down through Bulgaria and Albania and other areas of that part of the world. It reaches across the vast area of Russia. It reaches up into Mongolia and all down through the nations of Asia into the islands of the Pacific, Australia, and New Zealand, and into India and Indonesia. It is flourishing in many of the nations of Africa. . . .

And this is only the beginning. This work will continue to grow and prosper and move across the earth.[4]

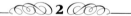 **2**

Early Church leaders had a prophetic view of the destiny of the Lord's work.

On July 24, 1847, the pioneer company of our people came into [the Salt Lake] valley. An advance group had arrived a day or two earlier. Brigham Young arrived on Saturday. The next day, Sabbath services were held both in the morning and in the afternoon. There was no hall of any kind in which to meet. I suppose that in the blistering heat of that July Sunday they sat on the tongues of their wagons and leaned against the wheels while the Brethren spoke. The season was late, and they were faced with a gargantuan and immediate task if they were to grow seed for the next season. But President Young pleaded with them not to violate the Sabbath then or in the future.

The next morning they divided into groups to explore their surroundings. Brigham Young, Wilford Woodruff, and a handful of their associates hiked from their campground. . . . They climbed a dome-shaped peak, President Young having difficulty because of his recent illness.

When the Brethren stood on the summit, they looked over [the] valley to the south of them. It was largely barren, except for the willows and rushes that grew along the streams that carried water from the mountains to the lake. There was no building of any kind, but Brigham Young had said the previous Saturday, "This is the place."

The summit where they stood was named Ensign Peak out of reference to these great prophetic words of Isaiah: "And he [speaking of God] will lift up an ensign to the nations from far, and will hiss unto them from the end of the earth: and, behold, they shall come with speed swiftly." (Isa. 5:26.)

"And he shall set up an ensign for the nations, and shall assemble the outcasts of Israel, and gather together the dispersed of Judah from the four corners of the earth." (Isa. 11:12.) . . .

I think [those Brethren] may also on that occasion have spoken of the building of the temple . . . in fulfillment of the words of Isaiah:

"And it shall come to pass in the last days, that the mountain of the Lord's house shall be established in the top of the mountains, and shall be exalted above the hills; and all nations shall flow unto it.

"And many people shall go and say, Come ye, and let us go up to the mountain of the Lord, to the house of the God of Jacob; and he will teach us of his ways, and we will walk in his paths: for out of Zion shall go forth the law, and the word of the Lord from Jerusalem." (Isa. 2:2–3.)

How foolish, someone might have said, had he heard these men that July morning of 1847. They did not look like statesmen with great dreams. They did not look like rulers poring over maps and planning an empire. They were exiles, driven from their fair city on the Mississippi [River] into this desert region of the West. But they were possessed of a vision drawn from the scriptures and words of revelation.

I marvel at the foresight of that little group. It was both audacious and bold. It was almost unbelievable. Here they were, almost a thousand miles [1,600 kilometers] from the nearest settlement to the east and almost eight hundred miles [1,300 kilometers] from the Pacific Coast. They were in an untried climate. The soil was different from that of the black loam of Illinois and Iowa, where they had

Two days after arriving in the Salt Lake Valley, Brigham Young and several other brethren climbed a dome-shaped hill, which became named Ensign Peak, and surveyed their surroundings.

most recently lived. They had never raised a crop here. They had never experienced a winter. They had not built a structure of any kind. These prophets, dressed in old, travel-worn clothes, standing in boots they had worn for more than a thousand miles from Nauvoo to this valley, spoke of a millennial vision. They spoke out of a prophetic view of the marvelous destiny of this cause. They came down from the peak that day and went to work to bring reality to their dream.[5]

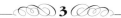

3

We must never lose sight of the divine destiny of God's work and the part we play in it.

Sometimes in our day, as we walk our narrow paths and fill our little niches of responsibility, we lose sight of the grand picture. When I was a small boy, draft horses were common. An important part of the harness was the bridle. On the bridle were blinders, one on each side. They were so placed that the horse could see only straight ahead and not to either side. They were designed to keep him from becoming frightened or distracted and to keep his attention on the road at his feet.

Some of us do our work as if we had blinders on our eyes. We see only our own little narrow track. We catch nothing of the broader vision. Ours may be a small responsibility in the Church. It is good to fulfill that responsibility with diligence. And it is also good to know how that responsibility contributes to the great overall program of the growing kingdom of God.

President Harold B. Lee once said . . . , quoting an unknown writer, "Survey large fields and cultivate small ones."

My interpretation of that statement is that we ought to recognize something of the breadth and depth and height—grand and wonderful, large and all-encompassing—of the program of the Lord, and then work with diligence to meet our responsibility for our assigned portion of that program.

Each of us has a small field to cultivate. While so doing, we must never lose sight of the greater picture, the large composite of the divine destiny of this work. It was given us by God our Eternal Father, and each of us has a part to play in the weaving of its magnificent tapestry. Our individual contribution may be small, but it is not unimportant. . . .

. . . While you are performing the part to which you have been called, never lose sight of the whole majestic and wonderful picture of the purpose of this, the dispensation of the fulness of times. Weave beautifully your small thread in the grand tapestry, the pattern for which was laid out for us by the God of heaven. Hold high the standard under which we walk. Be diligent, be true, be virtuous, be faithful, that there may be no flaw in that banner.

The vision of this kingdom is not a superficial dream in the night that fades with the sunrise. It is veritably the plan and work of God our Eternal Father. It has to do with all of His children.

While grubbing the sagebrush of these western valleys [of Utah] to lay the foundations for a commonwealth, while doing all of the many mundane things they were required to do to stay alive and grow, our [pioneer] forebears ever kept before them the grandeur of the great cause in which they were engaged. It is a work which we must do with the same vision they held. It is a work which will go on after we have left this scene. God help us to do our very best as servants, called under His divine will, to carry forward and build the kingdom with imperfect hands, united together to execute a perfect pattern.[6]

We can become as an ensign to the nations from which the people of the earth may gather strength.

My brethren and sisters, the time has come for us to stand a little taller, to lift our eyes and stretch our minds to a greater comprehension and understanding of the grand millennial mission of this The Church of Jesus Christ of Latter-day Saints. This is a season to be strong. It is a time to move forward without hesitation, knowing well the meaning, the breadth, and the importance of our mission. It is a time to do what is right regardless of the consequences that might follow. It is a time to be found keeping the commandments. It is a season to reach out with kindness and love to those in distress and to those who are wandering in darkness and pain. It is a time to be considerate and good, decent and courteous toward one another in all of our relationships. In other words, to become more Christlike.[7]

Unless the world alters the course of its present trends (and that is not likely); and if, on the other hand, we continue to follow the teachings of the prophets, we shall increasingly become a peculiar and distinctive people of whom the world will take note. For instance, as the integrity of the family crumbles under worldly pressures, our position on the sanctity of the family will become more obvious and even more peculiar in contrast, if we have the faith to maintain that position.

As the growing permissive attitude toward sex continues to spread, the doctrine of the Church, as consistently taught for more than a century and a half, will become increasingly singular and even strange to many.

As the consumption of alcohol and the abuse of drugs increase each year within the mores of our society, our position, set forth by the Lord more than a century and a half ago, will become more unusual before the world. . . .

As the Sabbath increasingly becomes a day of merchandising and entertainment, those who obey the precept of the law, written by the finger of the Lord on Sinai and reinforced by modern revelation, will appear more unusual.

It is not always easy to live in the world and not be a part of it. We cannot live entirely with our own or unto ourselves, nor would we wish to. We must mingle with others. In so doing, we can be gracious. We can be inoffensive. We can avoid any spirit or attitude of self-righteousness. But we can maintain our standards. . . .

As we observe these and other standards taught by the Church, many in the world will respect us and find strength to follow that which they too know is right.

And, in the words of Isaiah, "Many people shall go and say, Come ye, and let us go up to the mountain of the Lord, to the house of the God of Jacob; and he will teach us of his ways, and we will walk in his paths." (Isa. 2:3.)

We need not compromise. We must not compromise. The candle that the Lord has lighted in this dispensation can become as a light unto the whole world, and others seeing our good works can be led to glorify our Father in Heaven and emulate in their own lives the examples they have observed in ours.

Beginning with you and me, there can be an entire people who, by the virtue of our lives in our homes, in our vocations, even in our amusements, can become as a city upon a hill to which men may look and learn, and an ensign to the nations from which the people of the earth may gather strength.[8]

If we are to hold up this Church as an ensign to the nations and a light to the world, we must take on more of the luster of the life of Christ individually and in our own personal circumstances. In standing for the right, we must not be fearful of the consequences. We must never be afraid. Said Paul to Timothy:

"For God hath not given us the spirit of fear; but of power, and of love, and of a sound mind.

"Be not thou therefore ashamed of the testimony of our Lord" (2 Timothy 1:7–8).[9]

You cannot simply take for granted this cause, which is the cause of Christ. You cannot simply stand on the sidelines and watch the play between the forces of good and evil. . . .

. . . I urge you with all the capacity that I have to reach out in a duty that stands beyond the requirements of our everyday lives; that is, to stand strong, even to become a leader in speaking up in behalf of those causes which make our civilization shine and which give comfort and peace to our lives. You can be a leader. You must be a leader, as a member of this Church, in those causes for which this Church stands. Do not let fear overcome your efforts.[10]

We have nothing to fear. God is at the helm. He will overrule for the good of this work. He will shower down blessings upon those who walk in obedience to His commandments. Such has been His promise. Of His ability to keep that promise none of us can doubt.

. . . Our Savior, who is our Redeemer, the Great Jehovah, the mighty Messiah, has promised: "I will go before your face. I will be on your right hand and on your left, and my Spirit shall be in your hearts, and mine angels round about you, to bear you up" (D&C 84:88).

"Therefore," said He, "fear not, little flock; do good; let earth and hell combine against you, for if ye are built upon my rock, they cannot prevail. . . .

"Look unto me in every thought; doubt not, fear not.

"Behold the wounds which pierced my side, and also the prints of the nails in my hands and feet; be faithful, keep my commandments, and ye shall inherit the kingdom of heaven" (D&C 6:34, 36–37).

Unitedly, working hand in hand, we shall move forward as servants of the living God, doing the work of His Beloved Son, our Master, whom we serve and whose name we seek to glorify.[11]

We must stand firm. We must hold back the world. If we do so, the Almighty will be our strength and our protector, our guide and our revelator. We shall have the comfort of knowing that we are doing what He would have us do. Others may not agree with us, but I am confident that they will respect us. We will not be left alone.

"If we are to hold up this Church as an ensign to the nations and a light to the world, we must take on more of the luster of the life of Christ."

There are many [who are] not of our faith but who feel as we do. They will support us. They will sustain us in our efforts.[12]

Let us glory in this wonderful season of the work of the Lord. Let us not be proud or arrogant. Let us be humbly grateful. And let us, each one, resolve within himself or herself that we will add to the luster of this magnificent work of the Almighty, that it may shine across the earth as a beacon of strength and goodness for all the world to look upon.[13]

Suggestions for Study and Teaching

Questions

- As you read section 1, what are your feelings as you consider the growth of the Church from 1830 to the present day?

- Review President Hinckley's account of the first pioneers arriving in the Salt Lake Valley (see section 2). What can we learn from this account? How have we benefited from the prophetic vision of early Church leaders? What do you think it means to be "an ensign to the nations"? (See Isaiah 5:26; 11:12.)

- In section 3, President Hinckley encouraged us to see the "grand picture" and "broader vision" of God's work. Why do we need to see this grand picture? Why do we sometimes lose sight of it? In what ways can our small efforts contribute to the growth of God's kingdom?

- Review the ways President Hinckley says Latter-day Saints are becoming a more "peculiar and distinctive people" (section 4). How can we develop greater vision and courage in moving God's work forward? How can we live in the world without being of the world? How can we "take on more of the luster of the life of Christ"? Why is it important for us to stand for what is right?

Related Scriptures

Matthew 5:14–16; 1 Nephi 14:14; D&C 1:1–6; 65:1–6; 88:81; 115:5–6

Teaching Help

"Be sure you don't believe you are the 'true teacher.' That is a serious mistake. . . . Be careful you do not get in the way. The major role of a teacher is to prepare the way such that the people will have a spiritual experience with the Lord" (Gene R. Cook, quoted in *Teaching, No Greater Call* [1999], 41).

Notes

1. See Sheri L. Dew, *Go Forward with Faith: The Biography of Gordon B. Hinckley* (1996), 83–85.

2. "An Ensign to the Nations, a Light to the World," *Ensign* or *Liahona,* Nov. 2003, 82–83.

3. "Let Virtue Garnish Thy Thoughts Unceasingly," *Ensign* or *Liahona,* May 2007, 115.

4. "The Stone Cut Out of the Mountain," *Ensign* or *Liahona,* Nov. 2007, 84.

5. "An Ensign to the Nations," *Ensign,* Nov. 1989, 51–52.

6. "An Ensign to the Nations," 52–54.

7. "This Is the Work of the Master," *Ensign,* May 1995, 71.

8. "A City upon a Hill," *Ensign,* July 1990, 4–5.

9. "An Ensign to the Nations, a Light to the World," 84.

10. *Teachings of Gordon B. Hinckley* (1997), 138.

11. "This Is the Work of the Master," 71.

12. "An Ensign to the Nations, a Light to the World," 83.

13. "Condition of the Church," *Ensign* or *Liahona,* Nov. 2004, 6.

"We have every reason to be optimistic."

Cultivating an Attitude of Happiness and a Spirit of Optimism

"Be believing. Be happy. Don't get discouraged. Things will work out."

From the Life of Gordon B. Hinckley

President Gordon B. Hinckley's mother, Ada Bitner Hinckley, often said that "a happy attitude and smiling countenance could boost one over almost any misfortune and that every individual was responsible for his own happiness."[1] His father, Bryant S. Hinckley, also had an "inherently positive outlook."[2] President Hinckley recalled, "When I was a young man and was prone to speak critically, my father would say: 'Cynics do not contribute, skeptics do not create, doubters do not achieve.'"[3] Influenced by his parents' counsel and example, young Gordon Hinckley learned to approach life with optimism and faith.

As a missionary in England, Elder Hinckley worked hard to follow his parents' counsel. He and his companions shook hands each morning and told each other, "Life is good."[4] Almost 70 years later, he suggested that a group of missionaries in the Philippines follow the same practice. "Yesterday was a great day in my life," he told them. "Every day is a great day in my life. I hope every day is a great day in your lives—every one of you. I hope you can get ready to go in the morning and shake the hand of your companion and say, 'Brother (Sister), life is good. Let's go out and have a good day.' And when you come in at night, I hope you can say to one another, 'It's been a good day. We've had a good time. We've helped somebody along the way. . . . We'll follow up with them and pray and hope that they will come into the Church.' Every day ought to be a good day in the mission field."[5]

This counsel was representative of President Hinckley's approach to life. President Russell M. Nelson of the Quorum of the Twelve Apostles shared the following observation about President Hinckley and his wife, Marjorie: "They do not waste time pondering the past or fretting about the future. And they persevere in spite of adversity."[6] Elder Jeffrey R. Holland, also of the Quorum of the Twelve, commented: "'Things will work out' may well be President Hinckley's most repeated assurance to family, friends, and associates. 'Keep trying,' he will say. 'Be believing. Be happy. Don't get discouraged. Things will work out.'"[7]

Teachings of Gordon B. Hinckley

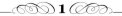

1

Even when many people are negative and pessimistic, we can cultivate a spirit of happiness and optimism.

There is a terrible ailment of pessimism in the land. It's almost endemic. We're constantly fed a steady and sour diet of character assassination, faultfinding, evil speaking of one another. . . .

I come . . . with a plea that we stop seeking out the storms and enjoy more fully the sunlight. I'm suggesting that we accentuate the positive. I'm asking that we look a little deeper for the good, that we still our voices of insult and sarcasm, that we more generously compliment virtue and effort.

I am not asking that all criticism be silent. Growth comes with correction. Strength comes with repentance. Wise is the man or woman who, committing mistakes pointed out by others, changes his or her course. I am not suggesting that our conversation be all honey. Clever expression that is sincere and honest is a skill to be sought and cultivated. What I am suggesting and asking is that we turn from the negativism that so permeates our society and look for the remarkable good in the land and times in which we live, that we speak of one another's virtues more than we speak of one another's faults, that optimism replace pessimism. Let our faith replace our fears.[8]

We have every reason to be optimistic in this world. Tragedy is around, yes. Problems everywhere, yes. But . . . you can't, you don't, build out of pessimism or cynicism. You look with optimism, work with faith, and things happen.[9]

Do not despair. Do not give up. Look for the sunlight through the clouds. Opportunities will eventually open to you. Do not let the prophets of gloom endanger your possibilities.[10]

Cultivate an attitude of happiness. Cultivate a spirit of optimism. Walk with faith, rejoicing in the beauties of nature, in the goodness of those you love, in the testimony which you carry in your heart concerning things divine.[11]

The Lord's plan is a plan of happiness. The way will be lighter, the worries will be fewer, the confrontations will be less difficult if we cultivate a spirit of happiness.[12]

Rather than dwell on our problems, we can let a spirit of thanksgiving guide and bless us.

How magnificently we are blessed! How thankful we ought to be! . . . Cultivate a spirit of thanksgiving for the blessing of life and for the marvelous gifts and privileges each of us enjoy. The Lord has said that the meek shall inherit the earth. (See Matt. 5:5.) I cannot escape the interpretation that meekness implies a spirit of gratitude as opposed to an attitude of self-sufficiency, an acknowledgment of a greater power beyond oneself, a recognition of God, and an acceptance of his commandments. This is the beginning of wisdom. Walk with gratitude before him who is the giver of life and every good gift.[13]

There never was a greater time in the history of the world to live upon the earth than this. How grateful every one of us ought to feel for being alive in this wonderful time with all the marvelous blessings we have.[14]

When I think of the wonders that have come to pass in my lifetime—more than during all the rest of human history together—I stand in reverence and gratitude. I think of the automobile and the airplane, of computers, fax machines, e-mail, and the Internet. It is all so miraculous and wonderful. I think of the giant steps made in medicine and sanitation. . . . And with all of this there has been the restoration of the pure gospel of Jesus Christ. You and I are a part of the miracle and wonder of this great cause and kingdom that is sweeping over the earth blessing the lives of people wherever it reaches. How profoundly thankful I feel.[15]

We live in the fulness of times. Mark that phrase. Mark the word *fulness*. It denotes all of [the] good that has been gathered together [from] the past and restored to earth in this final dispensation.

My heart . . . is filled with thanksgiving unto the Almighty God. Through the gift of His Son, who is the God of this world, we have been so magnificently blessed. My heart rings with the words of our hymn, "Count your blessings; name them one by one. Count your many blessings; see what God hath done" (*Hymns,* no. 241).[16]

With gratitude in our hearts, let us not dwell upon the few problems we have. Let us rather count our blessings and in a great spirit of gratitude, motivated by a great faith, go forth to build the kingdom of God in the earth.[17]

Let a spirit of thanksgiving guide and bless your days and nights. Work at it. You will find it will yield wonderful results.[18]

 3

The gospel of Jesus Christ gives us a reason for gladness.

The Lord said: "Wherefore, lift up thy heart and rejoice, and cleave unto the covenants which thou hast made" [D&C 25:13]. I believe he is saying to each of us, be happy. The gospel is a thing of joy. It provides us with a reason for gladness.[19]

Never forget who you are. . . . You are in very deed a child of God. . . . He is your Eternal Father. He loves you. . . . He wants His sons and daughters to be happy. Sin never was happiness. Transgression never was happiness. Disobedience never was happiness. The way of happiness is found in the plan of our Father in Heaven and in obedience to the commandments of His Beloved Son, the Lord Jesus Christ.[20]

*"In all of living have much of fun and laughter.
Life is to be enjoyed, not just endured."*

Regardless of your way of doing things in the past, I offer you a challenge . . . to square your lives with the teachings of the gospel, to look upon this Church with love and respect and appreciation as the mother of your faith, to live your lives as an example of what the gospel of Jesus Christ will do in bringing happiness to an individual.[21]

Repentance is one of the first principles of the gospel. Forgiveness is a mark of divinity. There is hope for you. Your lives are ahead, and they can be filled with happiness, even though the past may have been marred by sin. This is a work of saving and assisting people with their problems. This is the purpose of the gospel.[22]

I meet so many people who constantly complain about the burden of their responsibilities. Of course the pressures are great. There is much, too much, to do. There are financial burdens to add to all of these pressures, and with all of this we are prone to complain, frequently at home, often in public. Turn your thinking around. The gospel is good news. Man is that he might have joy [see 2 Nephi 2:25]. Be happy! Let that happiness shine through your faces and speak through your testimonies. You can expect problems. There may be occasional tragedies. But shining through all of this is the plea of the Lord:

"Come unto me, all ye that labour and are heavy laden, and I will give you rest.

"Take my yoke upon you, and learn of me; for I am meek and lowly in heart; and ye shall find rest unto your souls.

"For my yoke is easy, and my burden is light." (Matthew 11:28–30.)

I enjoy these words of Jenkins Lloyd Jones which I clipped from a column in the *Deseret News* some years ago. I pass them on to you. . . . Said he:

"Anyone who imagines that bliss is normal is going to waste a lot of time running around shouting that he has been robbed.

"Most putts don't drop. Most beef is tough. Most children grow up to be just people. Most successful marriages require a high degree of mutual toleration. Most jobs are more often dull than otherwise. . . .

"Life is like an old-time rail journey—delays, sidetracks, smoke, dust, cinders, and jolts, interspersed only occasionally by beautiful vistas and thrilling bursts of speed.

"The trick is to thank the Lord for letting you have the ride." (*Deseret News*, 12 June 1973.)

I repeat, my brothers and sisters, the trick is to thank the Lord for letting you have the ride; and really, isn't it a wonderful ride? Enjoy it! Laugh about it! Sing about it! Remember the words of the writer of Proverbs:

"A merry heart doeth good like a medicine: but a broken spirit drieth the bones." (Proverbs 17:22.)[23]

Let there be something of a light tone in your life. Let there be fun and happiness, a sense of humor, the capacity to laugh occasionally at things that are funny.[24]

In all of living have much of fun and laughter. Life is to be enjoyed, not just endured.[25]

The gospel is a message of triumph to be embraced with enthusiasm, affection, and optimism.

I stand here today as an optimist concerning the work of the Lord. I cannot believe that God has established his work in the earth to have it fail. I cannot believe that it is getting weaker. I know that it is getting stronger. . . . I have a simple and solemn faith that right will triumph and that truth will prevail.[26]

The story of Caleb and Joshua and the other spies of Israel has always intrigued me. Moses led the children of Israel into the wilderness. In the second year of their wandering, he chose a representative from each of the twelve tribes to search the land of Canaan and bring back a report concerning its resources and its people. Caleb represented the tribe of Judah, Joshua the tribe of Ephraim. The twelve of them went into the land of Canaan. They found it to be fruitful. They were gone forty days. They brought back with them some of "the firstripe grapes" as evidence of the productivity of the land (Num. 13:20).

They came before Moses and Aaron and all the congregation of the children of Israel and they said concerning the land of Canaan, "Surely it floweth with milk and honey; and this is the fruit of it" (v. 27).

But ten of the spies were victims of their own doubts and fears. They gave a negative report of the numbers and stature of the Canaanites. They concluded that "they are stronger than we" (v. 31). They compared themselves as grasshoppers to the giants they had seen in the land. They were the victims of their own timidity.

Then Joshua and Caleb stood before the people and said, "The land, which we passed through to search it, is an exceeding good land.

"If the Lord delight in us, then he will bring us into this land, and give it us; a land which floweth with milk and honey.

"Only rebel not ye against the Lord, neither fear ye the people of the land; for they are bread for us: their defence is departed from them, and the Lord is with us: fear them not" (14:7–9).

But the people were more willing to believe the ten doubters than to believe Caleb and Joshua.

Then it was that the Lord declared that the children of Israel should wander in the wilderness forty years until the generation of those who had walked with doubt and fear should pass away. The scripture records that "those men that did bring up the evil report upon the land, died by the plague before the Lord.

"But Joshua . . . and Caleb . . . , which were of the men that went to search the land, lived still" (vs. 37–38). They were the only ones of that group who survived through those four decades of wandering and who had the privilege of entering the promised land concerning which they had reported in a positive manner.

We see some around us who are indifferent concerning the future of this work, who are apathetic, who speak of limitations, who express fears, who spend their time digging out and writing about what they regard to be weaknesses which really are of no consequence. With doubt concerning its past, they have no vision concerning its future.

Well was it said of old, "Where there is no vision, the people perish" (Prov. 29:18). There is no place in this work for those who believe only in the gospel of doom and gloom. The gospel is good news. It is a message of triumph. It is a cause to be embraced with enthusiasm.

The Lord never said that there would not be troubles. Our people have known afflictions of every sort as those who have opposed this work have come upon them. But faith has shown through all their sorrows. This work has consistently moved forward and has never taken a backward step since its inception. . . .

. . . This is the work of the Almighty. Whether we as individuals go forward will depend on us. But the Church will never fail to move forward. . . .

When the Lord took Moses unto Himself, He then said to Joshua, "Be strong and of a good courage; be not afraid, neither be thou dismayed: for the Lord thy God is with thee whithersoever thou goest" (Josh. 1:9). This is His work. Never forget it. Embrace it with enthusiasm and affection.[27]

5

With knowledge that we are all children of God, we can stand a little taller, rise a little higher, and be a little better.

There is a sad tendency in our world today for persons to cut one another down. Did you ever realize that it does not take very much in the way of brainpower to make remarks that may wound another? Try the opposite of that. Try handing out compliments. . . .

There is also in our society a sad tendency among many of us to belittle ourselves. Other persons may appear to us to be sure of themselves, but the fact is that most of us have some feelings of inferiority. The important thing is not to talk to yourself about it. . . . The important thing is to make the best of all that we have.

Don't waste your time feeling sorry for yourself. Don't belittle yourself. Never forget that you are a child of God. You have a divine birthright. Something of the very nature of God is within you.[28]

We sing, "I am a child of God" (*Hymns,* no. 301). That isn't just a figment, a poetic figment—that is the living truth. There is something of divinity within each of us that needs cultivation, that needs to come to the surface, that needs to find expression. You fathers and mothers, teach your children that they are, in a very literal way, sons and daughters of God. There is no greater truth in all the world than that—to think that we have something of divinity in us.[29]

Believe in yourself. Believe in your capacity to do great and good things. Believe that no mountain is so high that you cannot climb it. Believe that no storm is so great that you cannot weather it. . . . You are a child of God, of infinite capacity.[30]

Stand a little taller, rise a little higher, be a little better. Make the extra effort. You will be happier. You will know a new satisfaction, a new gladness in your heart.[31]

Of course there will be some problems along the way. There will be difficulties to overcome. But they will not last forever. [God] will not forsake you. . . .

Look to the positive. Know that He is watching over you, that He hears your prayers and will answer them, that He loves you and will make that love manifest.[32]

There is so much of the sweet and the decent and the beautiful to build upon. We are partakers of the gospel of Jesus Christ. The gospel means "good news!" The message of the Lord is one of hope and salvation! The voice of the Lord is a voice of glad tidings! The work of the Lord is a work of glorious accomplishment!

In a dark and troubled hour the Lord said to those he loved: "Let not your heart be troubled, neither let it be afraid." (John 14:27.)

These great words of confidence are a beacon to each of us. In him we may indeed have trust. For he and his promises will never fail.[33]

Suggestions for Study and Teaching

Questions

- Think about President Hinckley's counsel to "look deeper" for the good and to "cultivate an attitude of happiness [and] a spirit of optimism" (section 1). Why do we need this counsel today? How can we cultivate an attitude of happiness?

- President Hinckley said that "wonderful results" come when we "let a spirit of thanksgiving guide [us]" (section 2). Why do you think these "wonderful results" come? How are you blessed when you have a spirit of thanksgiving?

- What are your thoughts about the analogy of life being "like an old-time rail journey"? (See section 3.) How does the "good news" of the gospel influence the way you approach that journey?

- How do you think the story of Caleb and Joshua applies in our lives? (See section 4.) What examples have you seen of people embracing the gospel with enthusiasm? If we find ourselves feeling discouraged, how can we regain our optimism? What experiences have increased your optimism about the Lord's work?

- Why do you think there is a tendency to belittle others and ourselves? How can we overcome this tendency? What can we do, as individuals and families, to help others "stand a little taller" and "rise a little higher"? (See section 5.)

Related Scriptures

John 16:33; Philippians 4:13; Mosiah 2:41; Alma 34:38; Ether 12:4; D&C 19:38–39; 128:19–23

Study Help

"Acting on what you have learned will bring added and enduring understanding (see John 7:17)" (*Preach My Gospel* [2004], 19). Consider asking yourself how you can apply gospel teachings at home, at work, and in your Church responsibilities.

Notes

1. Sheri L. Dew, *Go Forward with Faith: The Biography of Gordon B. Hinckley* (1996), 37.

2. Sheri L. Dew, *Go Forward with Faith,* 37.

3. "The Continuing Pursuit of Truth," *Ensign,* Apr. 1986, 4.

4. See Sheri L. Dew, *Go Forward with Faith,* 76.

5. *Discourses of President Gordon B. Hinckley, Volume 1: 1995–1999* (2005), 343.

6. Russell M. Nelson, "Spiritual Capacity," *Ensign,* Nov. 1997, 15.

7. Jeffrey R. Holland, "President Gordon B. Hinckley: Stalwart and Brave He Stands," *Ensign,* June 1995, 4.

8. "The Lord Is at the Helm" (Brigham Young University devotional, Mar. 6, 1994), 3–4, speeches.byu.edu.

9. Quoted in Jeffrey R. Holland, "President Gordon B. Hinckley: Stalwart and Brave He Stands," 4.

10. "The Continuing Pursuit of Truth," 4.

11. "If Thou Art Faithful," *Ensign,* Nov. 1984, 92.

12. "Each a Better Person," *Ensign,* Nov. 2002, 100.

13. "With All Thy Getting Get Understanding," *Ensign,* Aug. 1988, 3–4.

14. "The Spirit of Optimism," *New Era,* July 2001, 4.

15. "Keep the Chain Unbroken" (Brigham Young University devotional, Nov. 30, 1999), 1–2, speeches.byu.edu.

16. "My Redeemer Lives," *Ensign,* Feb. 2001, 70.

17. "The Lord Is at the Helm," 6.

18. "A Prophet's Counsel and Prayer for Youth," *Ensign,* Jan. 2001, 4.

19. "If Thou Art Faithful," 91–92.

20. "Stand True and Faithful," *Ensign,* May 1996, 93–94.

21. "True to the Faith," *Ensign,* June 1996, 4.

22. "Stand True and Faithful," 94.

23. "Four Imperatives for Religious Educators" (address to religious educators, Sept. 15, 1978), 4.

24. "A Challenging Time—a Wonderful Time" (address to religious educators, Feb. 7, 2003), 4.

25. "Stand True and Faithful," 94.

26. *Teachings of Gordon B. Hinckley* (1997), 410.

27. "Stay the Course—Keep the Faith," *Ensign,* Nov. 1995, 71–72.

28. "Strengthening Each Other," *Ensign,* Feb. 1985, 3–4.

29. *One Bright Shining Hope: Messages for Women from Gordon B. Hinckley* (2006), 90–91.

30. *Discourses of President Gordon B. Hinckley, Volume 2: 2000–2004* (2005), 452.

31. "The Quest for Excellence" (Brigham Young University devotional, Nov. 10, 1998), 5, speeches.byu.edu.

32. "How Can I Become the Woman of Whom I Dream?" *Ensign,* May 2001, 96.

33. "The Continuing Pursuit of Truth," 6.

"The power that moved our gospel forebears was the power of faith in God."

The Pioneer Heritage of Faith and Sacrifice

"Whether you have pioneer ancestry or came into the Church only yesterday, you are a part of this whole grand picture of which those men and women dreamed. . . . They laid the foundation. Ours is the duty to build on it."

From the Life of Gordon B. Hinckley

At the dedication of the Columbus Ohio Temple, President Gordon B. Hinckley reflected on his pioneer ancestors. He later recalled:

"As I sat in the celestial room, I thought of my great-grandfather. . . . I had recently visited his place of burial in Canada just to the north of the New York boundary line. . . . He died at the young age of 38."

When President Hinckley's great-grandfather died, his son Ira, who would become President Hinckley's grandfather, was not quite three years old. Ira's mother soon remarried and within a few years moved to Ohio, then to Illinois. She died in 1842, leaving Ira an orphan at age 13. Continuing this story, President Hinckley said:

"My grandfather [Ira Hinckley] was baptized in Nauvoo and . . . subsequently crossed the plains in the migration of [the pioneers]." During that journey in 1850, Ira's "young wife and his [half brother] both died on the same day. He made rough coffins and buried them and picked up his infant child and carried her to [the Salt Lake] valley.

"At the request of Brigham Young he built Cove Fort, was the first president of the stake in Fillmore, [Utah,] and did a thousand other things to move this work forward.

"Then came my father. . . . He became president of the largest stake in the Church with more than 15,000 members."

President Hinckley's thoughts soon turned from his ancestry to his posterity. He continued:

"Reflecting on the lives of these three men while I was seated in the temple, I looked down at my daughter, at her daughter, who is my grandchild, and at her children, my great-grandchildren. I suddenly realized that I stood right in the middle of these seven generations—three before me and three after me.

"In that sacred and hallowed house there passed through my mind a sense of the tremendous obligation that was mine to pass on all that I had received as an inheritance from my forebears to the generations who have now come after me."[1]

In addition to expressing gratitude for his own pioneer ancestors and the heritage of the early Latter-day Saint pioneers, President Hinckley often emphasized that Church members around the world are pioneers today. In 1997 he told the Saints of Guatemala: "This year we are commemorating the 150th anniversary of the arrival of the Mormon pioneers in the Salt Lake Valley. They came a long way in wagons and handcarts. They were pioneers. But pioneering continues to go on. All over the world we have pioneers, and you are among those pioneers."[2] To the Saints in Thailand he declared, "You are pioneers in carrying forward the work of the Lord in this great nation."[3] While visiting Ukraine in 2002, he spoke similar words: "The Church had its pioneers in early days, and you are now pioneers in this time."[4]

When President Hinckley spoke of the early pioneers, his purpose was much bigger than focusing on those who lived in the past. He looked to the future, hoping that the faith and sacrifices of those Saints would "become a compelling motivation for us all, for each of us is a pioneer in his own life, often in his own family."[5]

Teachings of Gordon B. Hinckley

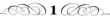

With vision, labor, and confidence in the power of God working through them, the early Latter-day Saint pioneers brought their faith to reality.

It was by faith that a small band of early converts [in the eastern United States] moved from New York to Ohio and from Ohio to Missouri and from Missouri to Illinois in their search for peace and freedom to worship God according to the dictates of conscience.

It was through the eyes of faith that they saw a city beautiful [Nauvoo] when first they walked across the swamps of Commerce, Illinois. With the conviction that faith without works is dead, they drained that swampland, they platted a city, they built substantial homes and houses for worship and education and, crowning all, a magnificent temple, then the finest building in all of Illinois.

. . . Persecution [soon followed], with profane and murderous mobs. Their prophet was killed. Their dreams were shattered. Again it was by faith that they pulled themselves together under the pattern he had previously drawn and organized themselves for another exodus.

With tears and aching hearts they left their comfortable homes and their workshops. They looked back on their sacred temple, and then with faith turned their eyes to the West, to the unknown and to the uncharted, and while the snows of winter fell upon them, they crossed the Mississippi [River] that February of 1846 and plowed their muddy way over the Iowa prairie.

With faith they established Winter Quarters on the Missouri [River]. Hundreds died as plague and dysentery and black canker cut them down. But faith sustained those who survived. They buried their loved ones there on a bluff above the river, and in the spring of 1847 they started . . . toward the mountains of the West.

It was by faith that Brigham Young looked over [the Salt Lake] valley, then hot and barren, and declared, "This is the place." Again by faith, four days later, he touched his cane to the ground . . . and said, "Here will be the temple of our God." The magnificent and sacred [Salt Lake Temple] is a testimony of faith, not only of the faith of those who built it but of the faith of those who now use it in a great selfless labor of love.

Wrote Paul to the Hebrews, "Now faith is the substance of things hoped for, the evidence of things not seen." (Heb. 11:1.) All of the great accomplishments of which I have spoken were once only "the substance of things hoped for, the evidence of things not seen." But with vision, with labor, and with confidence in the power of God working through them, they brought their faith to reality.[6]

The power that moved our gospel forebears was the power of faith in God. It was the same power which made possible the exodus from Egypt, the passage through the Red Sea, the long journey through the wilderness, and the establishment of Israel in the Promised Land. . . .

We need so very, very much a strong burning of that faith in the living God and in his living, resurrected Son, for this was the great, moving faith of our gospel forebears.

Theirs was a vision, transcendent and overriding all other considerations. When they came west they were a thousand miles, a thousand tedious miles [1,600 kilometers], from the nearest settlements to the east and eight hundred miles [1,300 kilometers] from those to the west. A personal and individual recognition of God their Eternal Father to whom they could look in faith was of the very essence of their strength. They believed in that great scriptural mandate: "Look to God and live." (Alma 37:47.) With faith they sought to do his will. With faith they read and accepted divine teaching. With faith they labored until they dropped, always with a conviction that there would be an accounting to him who was their Father and their God.[7]

Behind us is a glorious history. It is bespangled with heroism, tenacity to principle, and unflagging fidelity. It is the product of faith. Before us is a great future. It begins today. We cannot pause. We cannot slow down. We cannot slacken our pace or shorten our stride.[8]

Early Latter-day Saint pioneers looked to the future with a grand dream of Zion.

It is proper that we pause to pay reverent respect to those who laid the foundation of this great work. . . . Their grand objective was Zion [see D&C 97:21; Moses 7:18]. They sang about it. They dreamed of it. It was their great hope. Their epic journey must stand forever as an incomparable undertaking. The movement of tens of thousands to [the] West was fraught with every imaginable hazard, including death, whose grim reality was familiar to every wagon train and every handcart company.

I stand in reverent respect for Brigham Young. He saw the Salt Lake Valley in vision long before he saw it with his natural eyes. Otherwise I doubt he ever would have stopped here. There were greener lands in California and Oregon. There was deeper and richer soil elsewhere. There were great fields of timber in other places, much more water, and climates more equable and pleasant.

There were mountain streams here, it is true, but none of them was very large. The soil was totally untried. No plow had ever broken its hard-baked surface. I marvel, I simply marvel, that President Young would lead a large company . . . to a place where there never before had been a sowing and a harvest. . . .

They were travel-worn, these pioneers. It had taken 111 days to bring them from Winter Quarters to the Salt Lake Valley. They were tired. Their clothes were worn. Their animals were jaded. The weather was hot and dry—the hot weather of July. But here they were, looking down the years and dreaming a millennial dream, a grand dream of Zion.[9]

I stood the other day on the old docks of Liverpool, England. There was practically no activity the Friday morning when we were there. But once this was a veritable beehive. During the 1800s, tens of thousands of our people walked over the same stone paving on which we walked. They came from across the British Isles and from the lands of Europe, converts to the Church. They came with testimony on their lips and faith in their hearts. Was it difficult to leave their homes and step into the unknown of a new world? Of course it was. But they did it with optimism and enthusiasm. They boarded sailing vessels. They knew the crossing at best was hazardous. They soon found out that for the most part it was miserable. They lived in cramped quarters week after week. They endured storms, disease, sickness. Many died on the way and were buried at sea. It was an arduous and fearsome journey. They had doubts, yes. But their faith rose above those doubts. Their optimism rose above their fears. They had their dream of Zion, and they were on their way to fulfill it.[10]

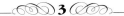

The rescue of the Willie and Martin handcart pioneers speaks of the very essence of the gospel of Jesus Christ.

I take you back to . . . October 1856. On Saturday [October 4,] Franklin D. Richards and a handful of associates arrived in [the Salt Lake] valley. They had traveled from Winter Quarters with strong teams and light wagons and had been able to make good time. Brother Richards immediately sought out President Young. He reported that there were hundreds of men, women, and children scattered over the long trail . . . to [the Salt Lake] valley. Most of them were pulling handcarts. . . . Ahead of them lay a trail that was uphill all the way to the Continental Divide with many, many miles beyond that. They were in desperate trouble. . . . All of them would perish unless they were rescued.

I think President Young did not sleep that night. I think visions of those destitute . . . people paraded through his mind.

The next morning he . . . said to the people:

"I will now give this people the subject and the text for the Elders who may speak. . . . It is this. . . . Many of our brethren and sisters are on the plains with handcarts, and probably many are now seven hundred miles [1,100 kilometers] from this place, and they must be brought here, we must send assistance to them. The text will be, 'to get them here.'

"That is my religion; that is the dictation of the Holy Ghost that I possess. It is to save the people.

"When the rescuers reached the beleaguered Saints, they were like angels from heaven."

"I shall call upon the Bishops this day. I shall not wait until tomorrow, nor until the next day, for 60 good mule teams and 12 or 15 wagons. I do not want to send oxen. I want good horses and mules. They are in this Territory, and we must have them. Also 12 tons of flour and 40 good teamsters, besides those that drive the teams.

"I will tell you all that your faith, religion, and profession of religion, will never save one soul of you in the Celestial Kingdom of our God, unless you carry out just such principles as I am now teaching you. *Go and bring in those people now on the plains"* (in LeRoy R. Hafen and Ann W. Hafen, *Handcarts to Zion* [1960], 120–21).

That afternoon food, bedding, and clothing in great quantities were assembled by the women.

The next morning, horses were shod and wagons were repaired and loaded.

The following morning, Tuesday, 16 mule teams pulled out and headed eastward. By the end of October there were 250 teams on the road to give relief.[11]

When the rescuers reached the beleaguered Saints, they were like angels from heaven. People wept tears of gratitude. The handcart people were transferred into wagons so they could travel more quickly to the Salt Lake community.

Some two hundred died, but a thousand were saved.[12]

Stories of [those] beleaguered Saints and of their suffering and death will be repeated again. . . . Stories of their rescue need to be repeated again and again. They speak of the very essence of the gospel of Jesus Christ.

. . . I am thankful that we do not have brethren and sisters stranded in the snow, freezing and dying, while trying to get to . . . their Zion in the mountains. But there are people, not a few, whose circumstances are desperate and who cry out for help and relief.

There are so many who are hungry and destitute across this world who need help. I am grateful to be able to say that we are assisting many who are not of our faith but whose needs are serious and whom we have the resources to help. But we need not go so far afield. We have some of our own who cry out in pain and suffering and loneliness and fear. Ours is a great and solemn duty to reach out and help them, to lift them, to feed them if they are hungry, to nurture their spirits if they thirst for truth and righteousness.

There are so many young people who wander aimlessly and walk the tragic trail of drugs, gangs, immorality, and the whole brood of ills that accompany these things. There are widows who long for friendly voices and that spirit of anxious concern which speaks of love. There are those who were once warm in the faith, but whose faith has grown cold. Many of them wish to come back but do not know quite how to do it. They need friendly hands reaching out to them. With a little effort, many of them can be brought back to feast again at the table of the Lord.

My brethren and sisters, I would hope, I would pray, that each of us . . . would resolve to seek those who need help, who are in desperate and difficult circumstances, and lift them in the spirit of love into the embrace of the Church, where strong hands and loving hearts will warm them, comfort them, sustain them, and put them on the way of happy and productive lives.[13]

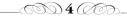

Each of us is a pioneer.

It is good to look to the past to gain appreciation for the present and perspective for the future. It is good to look upon the virtues of those who have gone before, to gain strength for whatever lies ahead. It is good to reflect upon the work of those who labored so hard and gained so little in this world, but out of whose dreams and early plans, so well nurtured, has come a great harvest of which we are the beneficiaries. Their tremendous example can become a compelling motivation for us all, for each of us is a pioneer in his own life, often in his own family, and many of us pioneer daily in trying to establish a gospel foothold in distant parts of the world.[14]

We are still pioneering. We have never ceased pioneering from the time . . . that our people left Nauvoo and came . . . eventually into the valley of the Great Salt Lake. There was adventure in that. But the purpose of it was to find a place where they could establish themselves and worship God according to the dictates of conscience. . . .

Now, we are still reaching out across the world into places that [once] scarcely seemed possible to access. . . . I have witnessed personally the growth of the Church in the Philippines. It was my privilege to open the missionary work there in 1961, when we were able to find one native Filipino member of the Church in a meeting which we held in May of 1961. [In 1996] we were in Manila and had a congregation . . . of some 35,000 in that great Araneta Coliseum. . . . To me it is a miracle [from] when we opened the work in that great land of the Philippines [see pages 29–30 for more about this experience].

We are reaching out everywhere, and that takes pioneering. Our missionaries do not live under the best of circumstances when they go to some of these areas, but they go forward and do their work, and it bears fruit. Before long we have a handful of members, then

"Whether you have pioneer ancestry or came into the Church only yesterday, you are a part of this whole grand picture."

a hundred members, and then five hundred members, and then a thousand members.[15]

The days of pioneering in the Church are still with us; they did not end with covered wagons and handcarts. . . . Pioneers are found among the missionaries who teach the gospel and they are found among the converts who come into the Church. It usually is difficult for each of them. It invariably involves sacrifice. It may involve persecution. But these are costs which are willingly borne, and the price that is paid is as real as was the price of those who crossed the plains in the great pioneering effort more than a century ago.[16]

Whether you have pioneer ancestry or came into the Church only yesterday, you are a part of this whole grand picture of which those men and women dreamed. Theirs was a tremendous undertaking. Ours is a great continuing responsibility. They laid the foundation. Ours is the duty to build on it.

They marked the path and led the way. Ours is the obligation to enlarge and broaden and strengthen that path until it encompasses the whole earth. . . . Faith was the guiding principle in those difficult days. Faith is the guiding principle we must follow today.[17]

5

We honor the sacrifices and heritage of the pioneers by following their example and building on their foundation.

What a marvelous thing it is to have a great heritage, my brothers and sisters. What a grand thing to know that there are those who have gone before and laid out the way we should walk, teaching those great eternal principles that must be the guiding stars of our lives and of those who come after us. We today can follow their example. The pioneers were people of great faith, of tremendous loyalty, of unthinkable industry, and of absolutely solid and unbending integrity.[18]

We stand today as the recipients of [the pioneers'] great effort. I hope we are thankful. I hope we carry in our hearts a deep sense of gratitude for all that they have done for us.

. . . As great things were expected of them, so are they of us. We note what they did with what they had. We have so much more, with an overwhelming challenge to go on and build the kingdom of God. There is so much to do. We have a divine mandate to carry the gospel to every nation, kindred, tongue, and people. We have a charge to teach and baptize in the name of the Lord Jesus Christ. Said the resurrected Savior, "Go ye into all the world, and preach the gospel to every creature" [Mark 16:15]. . . .

Our forebears laid a solid and marvelous foundation. Now ours is the great opportunity to build a superstructure, all fitly framed together with Christ as the chief cornerstone.[19]

You are the fruit of all of [the pioneers'] planning and of all of their labors. . . . What a wonderful people they were. There is nothing like their great effort in all of history. . . . God bless their memory to our good. When the way seems hard, when we are discouraged thinking all is lost, we can turn to them and see how much worse was their condition. When we wonder about the future, we can look to them and their great example of faith. . . .

With so great an inheritance, we must go forward. We must never let down. We must hold our heads high. We must walk with integrity. We must "do what is right [and] let the consequence follow" ("Do What Is Right," *Hymns,* 1985, no. 237).[20]

Suggestions for Study and Teaching

Questions
- Why was faith essential for the pioneers who wanted to gather in the Salt Lake Valley? (See section 1.) How did they put their faith into action? How can we put our faith into action to help bring about the "great future" ahead of us?

- President Hinckley taught that the early pioneers looked to the future, with Zion as their "grand objective," "great hope," and "dream" (section 2). Why do you think this was such a powerful motivating force for the early pioneers? What similar hopes motivate us today?

- What impresses you about President Hinckley's story of the rescue of the Willie and Martin handcart pioneers? (See section 3.) How does Brigham Young's rescue call show his prophetic inspiration? What can we learn from those who responded to his call? What can we do to rescue and lift those who are in need today?

- How does looking to the past help you "gain appreciation for the present and perspective for the future"? (See section 4.) In what ways is each of us a pioneer?

- Why is it good for us to honor the early pioneers? (See section 5.) In what sense are all Church members blessed by the faith and sacrifices of those pioneers? How can the examples of the early pioneers help us as we face challenges?

Related Scriptures
Matthew 25:40; Ether 12:6–9; D&C 64:33–34; 81:5; 97:8–9; 98:1–3

Teaching Help
"Meaningful discussions are fundamental to most gospel teaching. . . . Through well-conducted discussions, learners' interest and attentiveness are increased. Each person present can be encouraged to become actively engaged in the learning process. . . . Ask

questions that encourage thoughtful comments and help individuals truly ponder the gospel" (*Teaching, No Greater Call* [1999], 63).

Notes

1. "Keep the Chain Unbroken" (Brigham Young University devotional, Nov. 30, 1999), 2, speeches.byu.edu.

2. Address given at the Guatemala City North and South Regional Conference, Jan. 26, 1997, 2; Church History Library, Salt Lake City.

3. Address given at a member meeting in Bangkok, Thailand, June 13, 2000, 2; Church History Library, Salt Lake City.

4. *Discourses of President Gordon B. Hinckley, Volume 2: 2000–2004* (2005), 360–61.

5. "The Faith of the Pioneers," *Ensign,* July 1984, 3.

6. "God Grant Us Faith," *Ensign,* Nov. 1983, 52–53.

7. "The Faith of the Pioneers," 5–6.

8. "God Grant Us Faith," 53.

9. "These Noble Pioneers" (Brigham Young University devotional, Feb. 2, 1997), 1–2, speeches.byu.edu.

10. "Stay the Course—Keep the Faith," *Ensign,* Nov. 1995, 72.

11. "Reach with a Rescuing Hand," *Ensign,* Nov. 1996, 85–86.

12. "The Faith to Move Mountains," *Ensign* or *Liahona,* Nov. 2006, 84.

13. "Reach with a Rescuing Hand," 86.

14. "The Faith of the Pioneers," 3.

15. In Sheri L. Dew, *Go Forward with Faith: The Biography of Gordon B. Hinckley* (1996), 592.

16. In Gerry Avant, "Present-Day Pioneers: Many Are Still Blazing Gospel Trails," *Church News,* July 24, 1993, 6.

17. "These Noble Pioneers," 2, 4.

18. "These Noble Pioneers," 2.

19. "True to the Faith," *Ensign,* May 1997, 66–67.

20. "These Noble Pioneers," 2, 6.

"Each of you is a daughter of God. Reflect on all the wondrous meaning of that one paramount fact."

Daughters of God

"Marvelous is the power of women of faith."

From the Life of Gordon B. Hinckley

Throughout his life, Gordon B. Hinckley expressed appreciation for the abilities and contributions of women. He also expressed his strong witness of the importance of women in God's eternal plan. He delighted in women's increasing opportunities, as well as in their faith in the Savior and their devotion to their families and the Church.

Gordon B. Hinckley's mother, Ada, was bright and educated and had a love for literature, music, and art. At the age of 29, she married widower Bryant Hinckley and took on the responsibility of eight children who were mourning the death of their mother. She nurtured them with love, gave them the support they needed, and learned to manage a large household. Gordon was the first of five children born to Ada and Bryant. Although Ada died when Gordon was 20 years old, her teachings and example remained a force for good throughout his life. When he spoke of her, he always mentioned her tremendous influence on him.

Gordon B. Hinckley's wife, Marjorie Pay, also had a profound influence on him. She was a strong woman who was devoted to the gospel of Jesus Christ. She had extraordinary faith, a cheerful disposition, and a love of life. In a tender letter to her, President Hinckley expressed his love and respect:

"We have traveled far and wide together. We have visited every continent. We have held meetings in the great cities of the world and in many smaller ones. . . . We have spoken to millions who have appreciated you so greatly. With your familiar words you have won the love of all who have heard you. Your down-to-earth good sense, your sparkling and refreshing wit, your quiet and unfailing wisdom, and your tremendous and ever constant faith have won the hearts of all who have listened to you. . . . Your voracious appetite for reading and your relentless pursuit of knowledge have kept you alert and refreshing throughout a long and fruitful life."[1]

President Hinckley often spoke about women's divine nature and urged them forward to greater achievement and faith. To young women, he declared: "You are literally a daughter of the Almighty. There is no limit to your potential. If you will take control of your lives, the future is filled with opportunity and gladness. You cannot afford to waste your talents or your time. Great opportunities lie ahead of you."[2] Concerning adult women, he said: "The world needs the touch of women and their love, their comfort, and their strength. Our harsh environment needs their encouraging voices, the beauty that seems to fall within their natures, the spirit of charity that is their inheritance."[3]

At the general conference following the death of his beloved companion, Marjorie, President Hinckley concluded one of his addresses with this heartfelt expression of gratitude: "How thankful I am, how thankful we all must be, for the women in our lives. God bless them. May His great love distill upon them and crown them with luster and beauty, grace and faith."[4]

Teachings of Gordon B. Hinckley

 **1**

Women have a high and sacred place in the eternal plan of God.

Each of you is a daughter of God. Reflect on all the wondrous meaning of that one paramount fact. . . .

I remind you of words spoken by the Prophet Joseph to the women of the Relief Society in April of 1842. Said he: "If you live up to your privileges, the angels cannot be restrained from being your associates" [*Teachings of Presidents of the Church: Joseph Smith* (2007), 454]. What marvelous potential lies within you.[5]

You are very precious, each of you. . . . You occupy a high and sacred place in the eternal plan of God, our Father in Heaven. You are His daughters, precious to Him, loved by Him, and very important to Him. His grand design cannot succeed without you.[6]

Let me say to you sisters that you do not hold a second place in our Father's plan for the eternal happiness and well-being of His children. You are an absolutely essential part of that plan. Without you the plan could not function. Without you the entire program would be frustrated.[7]

There has come to you as your birthright something beautiful and sacred and divine. Never forget that. Your Eternal Father is the great Master of the universe. He rules over all, but He also will listen to your prayers as His daughter and hear you as you speak with Him. He will answer your prayers. He will not leave you alone.[8]

2

The Lord's counsel to Emma Smith applies to all.

The twenty-fifth section of the Doctrine and Covenants . . . is a revelation given through Joseph the Prophet to his wife Emma. . . . Said he to Emma, and to each of us:

"A revelation I give unto you concerning my will; and if thou art faithful and walk in the paths of virtue before me, I will preserve thy life, and thou shalt receive an inheritance in Zion" [D&C 25:2; see also verse 16]. . . .

In very large measure each of us holds the key to the blessings of the Almighty upon us. If we wish the blessing, we must pay the price. A part of that price lies in being faithful. Faithful to what? Faithful to ourselves, to the very best that is within us. No woman can afford to demean herself, to belittle herself, to downgrade her abilities or her capacities. Let each be faithful to the great, divine attributes that are within her. Be faithful to the gospel. Be faithful to the Church. We have all about us those who are seeking to undermine it, to look for weaknesses in its early leaders, to find fault with its programs, to speak critically of it. I give you my testimony that it is the work of God, and those who speak against it are speaking against him.

Be faithful to him. He is the one true source of your strength. He is your Father in Heaven. He lives. He hears and answers prayers. Be faithful to God.

The Lord continued, saying to Emma, "If thou . . . walk in the paths of virtue."

I think every woman . . . understands the meaning of that. I feel those words were given to Emma Smith, and consequently to all of us, as a condition to be observed if we are to receive an inheritance in the kingdom of God. Lack of virtue is totally inconsistent with obedience to the commandments of God. There is nothing more beautiful than virtue. There is no strength that is greater than the strength of virtue. There is no other nobility equal to the nobility of virtue. There is no quality so becoming, no attire so attractive. . . .

Emma was called "an elect lady" [D&C 25:3]. That is, to use another line of scripture, she was a "chosen vessel of the Lord." (See Moro. 7:31.) Each of you is an elect lady. You have come out of the world as partakers of the restored gospel of Jesus Christ. You have made your election, and if you are living worthy of it, the Lord will honor you in it and magnify you. . . .

Emma was to be ordained[9] under the hand of Joseph "to expound scriptures, and to exhort the church, according as it shall be given thee by my Spirit" [D&C 25:7].

She was to be a teacher. She was to be a teacher of righteousness and truth. For the Lord said concerning this calling to her, "Thou shalt receive the Holy Ghost, and thy time shall be given to writing, and to learning much" [D&C 25:8].

She was to study the gospel. She also was to study the things of the world in which she lived. That was made clear in subsequent revelations applicable to all of us. She was to devote her time "to learning much." She was to write, giving expression to her thoughts.

To you women of today, who are old or young, may I suggest that you write, that you keep journals, that you express your thoughts on paper. Writing is a great discipline. It is a tremendous educational effort. It will assist you in various ways, and you will bless the lives of many. . . .

In the language of the revelation, [Emma] was to "expound scriptures, and to exhort the church, according as it shall be given thee by my Spirit."

What a remarkable charge to her and to all of the women of this Church. There must be learning, there must be preparation, there must be organization of thought, there must be an expounding of the scriptures, there must be an exhortation to good works as directed by the Holy Spirit.

The Lord continued, "I say unto thee that thou shalt lay aside the things of this world, and seek for the things of a better" [D&C 25:10].

I feel he was not telling Emma that she should not feel concerned about a place to live, food on her table, and clothing. He was saying to her that she should not be obsessed with these things, as so many of us are wont to be. He was telling her to get her thoughts on the higher things of life, the things of righteousness and goodness, matters of charity and love for others, the things of eternity. . . .

Continuing, the Lord said: "Wherefore, lift up thy heart and rejoice, and cleave unto the covenants which thou hast made" [D&C 25:13].

I believe he is saying to each of us, be happy. The gospel is a thing of joy. It provides us with a reason for gladness. Of course there are times of sorrow. Of course there are hours of concern and anxiety. We all worry. But the Lord has told us to lift our hearts and rejoice.[10]

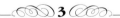 **3**

Mothers have a sacred calling to bring up their children in righteousness and truth.

The true strength of any nation, society, or family lies in those qualities of character that have been acquired for the most part by children taught in the quiet, simple everyday manner of mothers.[11]

It is the home which produces the nursery stock of new generations. I hope that you mothers will realize that when all is said and done, you have no more compelling responsibility, nor any laden

"God bless you, mothers! . . . You will be there, you must be there, as the strength for a new generation."

with greater rewards, than the nurture you give your children in an environment of security, peace, companionship, love, and motivation to grow and do well.[12]

I remind mothers everywhere of the sanctity of your calling. No other can adequately take your place. No responsibility is greater, no obligation more binding than that you rear in love and peace and integrity those whom you have brought into the world.[13]

Rear your children in light and truth. Teach them to pray while they are young. Read to them from the scriptures even though they may not understand all that you read. Teach them to pay their tithes and offerings on the first money they ever receive. Let this practice become a habit in their lives. Teach your sons to honor womanhood. Teach your daughters to walk in virtue. Accept responsibility in the Church, and trust in the Lord to make you equal to any call you may receive. Your example will set a pattern for your children.[14]

God bless you, mothers! When all the victories and defeats of men's efforts are tallied, when the dust of life's battles begins to settle, when all for which we labor so hard in this world of conquest fades before our eyes, you will be there, you must be there, as the strength for a new generation, the ever-improving onward movement of the race. Its quality will depend on you.[15]

Women have great responsibilities in the work of salvation.

There is strength and great capacity in the women of this Church. There is leadership and direction, a certain spirit of independence, and yet great satisfaction in being a part of this, the Lord's kingdom, and of working hand in hand with [holders of] the priesthood to move it forward.[16]

God has given the women of this church a work to do in building his kingdom. That concerns all aspects of our great triad of responsibility—which is, first, to teach the gospel to the world; second, to strengthen the faith and build the happiness of the membership of the Church; and, third, to carry forward the great work of salvation for the dead.[17]

Women in the Church are associates with their brethren in carrying forward this mighty work of the Lord. . . . Women carry tremendous responsibilities and they are accountable for the fulfillment of those responsibilities. They head their own organizations, and those organizations are strong and viable and are significant forces for good in the world. They stand in an associate role to the priesthood, all striving together to build the kingdom of God in the earth. We honor and respect you for your capacity. We expect leadership, and strength, and impressive results from your management of the organizations for which you are responsible. We uphold and sustain you as daughters of God, working in a great partnership to assist him in bringing to pass the immortality and the eternal life of all of the sons and daughters of God.[18]

Relief Society is a source of immeasurable blessings.

The women of the Relief Society are literally encircled eternally in the arms of our Lord. In my judgment, this is the greatest women's organization in all the world. It is a God-given creation. Joseph

Smith spoke and acted as a prophet when he organized the Relief Society in 1842.[19]

It is so tremendously important that the women of the Church stand strong and immovable for that which is correct and proper under the plan of the Lord. I am convinced there is no other organization anywhere to match the Relief Society of this Church. . . . If [its members] will be united and speak with one voice, their strength will be incalculable.[20]

I attended a stake conference where a young woman, president of the Relief Society of a singles ward, spoke of service and the great opportunity afforded the young women in her ward. You have all of this. You have your own organization. You have able leaders to counsel you. You have those who will reach out to you to help you in your times of trouble and distress.[21]

Who can gauge the miraculous effects upon the lives of millions of women whose knowledge has been increased, whose vision has been extended, whose lives have been broadened, and whose understanding of the things of God has been enriched by reason of countless lessons effectively taught and learned in meetings of the Relief Society?

Who can measure the joy that has come into the lives of these women as they have mingled together, socializing in the atmosphere of the ward or branch, enriching the lives of one another through companionships that have been sweet and treasured?

Who, even in the wildest stretch of imagination, can fathom the uncountable acts of charity that have been performed, the food that has been put on barren tables, the faith that has been nurtured in desperate hours of illness, the wounds that have been bound up, the pains that have been ameliorated by loving hands and quiet and reassuring words, the comfort that has been extended in times of death and consequent loneliness? . . .

No one could possibly calculate the projects that have been undertaken and completed by local Relief Societies. No one could possibly estimate the good that has come into the lives of the women belonging to these organizations and those whom they have benefited through their good works. . . .

"I . . . invite women everywhere to rise to the great potential within you."

God bless the Relief Society of The Church of Jesus Christ of Latter-day Saints. May the spirit of love which has motivated its members . . . continue to grow and be felt over the world. May their works of charity touch for good the lives of uncounted numbers wherever they find expression. And may light and understanding, learning and knowledge, and eternal truth grace the lives of generations of women yet to come, throughout the nations of the earth, because of this singular and divinely established institution.[22]

 **6**

Rise to the stature of the divinity within you.

You are a vast concourse of women of The Church of Jesus Christ of Latter-day Saints. . . . No one can calculate the tremendous force for good that you can become. . . . I charge you to stand tall and be strong in defense of those great virtues which have been the backbone of our social progress. When you are united, your power is limitless. You can accomplish anything you wish to accomplish. And oh, how very, very great is the need for you in a world of crumbling values where the adversary seems so very much to be in control.[23]

I feel to invite women everywhere to rise to the great potential within you. I do not ask that you reach beyond your capacity. I hope you will not nag yourselves with thoughts of failure. I hope you will not try to set goals far beyond your capacity to achieve. I hope you will simply do what you can do in the best way you know. If you do so, you will witness miracles come to pass.[24]

I express my gratitude to you faithful Latter-day Saint women, now numbered in the millions and found across the earth. Great is your power for good. Marvelous are your talents and devotion. Tremendous is your faith and your love for the Lord, for His work, and for His sons and daughters. Continue to live the gospel. Magnify it before all of your associates. Your good works will carry more weight than any words you might speak. Walk in virtue and truth, with faith and faithfulness. You are part of an eternal plan, a plan designed by God our Eternal Father. Each day is a part of that eternity.

I know that many of you carry terribly heavy burdens. May your associates in the Church, your brethren and sisters, help you with those burdens. May your prayers ascend to Him who is all powerful, who loves you, and who can bring to bear forces and factors which can help you. This is a work of miracles. You know it, and I know it. It is easy for me to tell you not to become discouraged, but I say it nonetheless, as I urge you to go forward in faith.[25]

Marvelous is the power of women of faith. It has been demonstrated again and again in the history of this church. It goes on among us today. I think it is part of the divinity within you.

Sisters, rise to the stature of that divinity. In that effort make the world in which you live a better place for yourself and for all who will come after you.[26]

God be thanked for the wonderful women of this Church. May he plant in your hearts a sense of pride in your capacities and a conviction of truth which shall be as a rudder to keep you safe through every storm.[27]

Suggestions for Study and Teaching

Questions

- What do we learn from President Hinckley about how Heavenly Father feels about His daughters? (See section 1.) Why is it important for us to understand the "high and sacred place" of women in God's eternal plan?

- What aspects of the Lord's counsel to Emma Smith are especially helpful to you? (See section 2.) What can we learn from section 2 about being faithful? What can we learn about being an "elect lady"? What can we learn about how to apply the scriptures to ourselves?

- What are your impressions as you read President Hinckley's counsel to mothers? (See section 3.) How have you been blessed by a mother's influence? For parents, why is "no obligation more binding" than rearing their children "in love and peace and integrity"?

- What examples have you seen of the "strength and great capacity" of women in the Church? (See section 4.) What are some ways that women can help bring to pass "the immortality and the eternal life of all of the sons and daughters of God"? Why is it important that men and women work together to move the Lord's work forward? What are some examples you have seen of this?

- Review the blessings that come from Relief Society, as President Hinckley outlines in section 5. What blessings have come to you from the efforts of Relief Society sisters, including those who are serving in Young Women and Primary? How can you strengthen the Relief Society in your ward? How can Relief Society help women increase their influence for good?

- Consider President Hinckley's encouragement to "rise to the great potential within you" (section 6). How can we gain a better vision of what God sees our potential to be? How can we progress toward reaching our potential? When have you seen the "marvelous . . . power of women of faith"?

Related Scriptures

Proverbs 31:10–31; Luke 10:38–42; Acts 9:36–40; Romans 16:1–2; 2 Timothy 1:1–5; Alma 56:41–48

Teaching Help

"As you prepare to teach each lesson, pray for the Spirit to help you know when to share your most sacred feelings. You may be prompted to bear testimony several times during a lesson, not just at the conclusion" (*Teaching, No Greater Call* [1999], 44).

Notes

1. In *Glimpses into the Life and Heart of Marjorie Pay Hinckley,* ed. Virginia H. Pearce (1999), 194–95.

2. "Let Virtue Garnish Thy Thoughts Unceasingly," *Ensign* or *Liahona,* May 2007, 115.

3. *Discourses of President Gordon B. Hinckley, Volume 2: 2000–2004* (2005), 509–10.

4. "The Women in Our Lives," *Ensign* or *Liahona,* Nov. 2004, 85.

5. "Stand Strong against the Wiles of the World," *Ensign,* Nov. 1995, 98.

6. "Daughters of God," *Ensign,* Nov. 1991, 97.

7. "Women of the Church," *Ensign,* Nov. 1996, 67.

8. "Stay on the High Road," *Ensign* or *Liahona,* May 2004, 112.

9. President Hinckley's use of *ordained* reflects the use of that word in Doctrine and Covenants 25:7, part of which he quotes in this sentence. In the English edition of the scriptures, the footnote to the word *ordained* in this verse says "or set apart." In the early days of the Restoration, the terms *ordained* and *set apart* were often used interchangeably; *ordained* did not always refer to priesthood offices (see, for example, D&C 63:45).

10. "If Thou Art Faithful," *Ensign,* Nov. 1984, 90–92.

11. *Motherhood: A Heritage of Faith* (pamphlet, 1995), 6.

12. "Stand Strong against the Wiles of the World," 99.

13. "Bring Up a Child in the Way He Should Go," *Ensign,* Nov. 1993, 60.

14. "Stand Strong against the Wiles of the World," 99.

15. *Motherhood: A Heritage of Faith,* 13.

16. "Women of the Church," 68.

17. "Live Up to Your Inheritance," *Ensign,* Nov. 1983, 84.

18. "If Thou Art Faithful," 89.

19. "In the Arms of His Love," *Ensign* or *Liahona,* Nov. 2006, 115.

20. "Standing Strong and Immovable," *Worldwide Leadership Training Meeting,* Jan. 10, 2004, 20.

21. "The BYU Experience" (Brigham Young University devotional, Nov. 4, 1997), 2, speeches.byu.edu.

22. "Ambitious to Do Good," *Ensign,* Mar. 1992, 4–6.

23. "Your Greatest Challenge, Mother," *Ensign,* Nov. 2000, 97.

24. *Teachings of Gordon B. Hinckley* (1997), 696.

25. "Daughters of God," 100.

26. "Rise to the Stature of the Divine within You," *Ensign,* Nov. 1989, 97–98.

27. "Live Up to Your Inheritance," 84.

How Mighty a Thing Is Prayer

"To call upon the Lord for wisdom beyond our
own, for strength to do what we ought to do, for
comfort and consolation, and for the expression of
gratitude is a significant and wonderful thing."

From the Life of Gordon B. Hinckley

"None of us can really make it alone," said President Gordon B.
Hinckley. "We need help, the kind of help that can come in answer
to prayer."[1] President Hinckley practiced this principle in the decisions he faced as President of the Church. Elder Robert D. Hales
of the Quorum of the Twelve Apostles said of him: "He is a bright
man with extraordinary judgment, but when he comes up against
an insoluble problem, he goes to his knees."[2]

President Hinckley and his wife, Marjorie, also practiced this principle in their home. Their son Richard said: "I can't remember a
day when we didn't have family prayer. When it was his turn, Dad
prayed very sincerely but never with a theatrical or emotional air.
We learned much about the depth of his faith by listening to him
pray. He addressed God with great reverence, as he would perhaps
a wise and revered teacher or mentor, and he referred to the Savior with deep feeling. As a child I knew they were real persons to
him—that he loved and revered them."[3] Marjorie observed: "I think
family prayer had a great deal to do with the way our children responded to us. Even though Gordon didn't preach to them, they
heard everything we wanted them to hear in family prayer."[4]

Throughout his service as a General Authority, President Hinckley
encouraged members of the Church to "believe in prayer and the
power of prayer."[5] He testified that "prayer unlocks the powers of
heaven in our behalf."[6] He promised, "Be prayerful and the God of

"Ask, and it shall be given you; seek, and ye shall find; knock,
and it shall be opened unto you" (Matthew 7:7).

heaven will smile upon you and bless you, and give happiness in your hearts and a sense of peace in your lives."[7]

Teachings of Gordon B. Hinckley

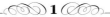

God is our Father, and He invites us to pray to Him individually.

Of all the great and wonderful and inspiring promises I have read, the most reassuring to me are the words of the Savior: "Ask, and it shall be given you; seek, and ye shall find; knock, and it shall be opened unto you." (Matt. 7:7.)[8]

Never forget who you are. . . . You are in very deed a child of God. . . . He is your Eternal Father. He loves you. You can go to Him in prayer. He has invited you to do so. . . . What a wonderful thing this is. He is the Greatest of All. He is the Creator and Governor of the universe. And yet He will listen to your prayer![9]

We can draw nearer to the Lord in our prayers. These can become conversations of thanksgiving. I can never fully understand how the Great God of the Universe, the Almighty, invites us as His children to speak with Him individually. How precious an opportunity is this. How wonderful that it actually happens. I testify that our prayers, offered in humility and sincerity, are heard and answered. It is a miraculous thing, but it is real.[10]

Brethren and sisters, I know that you are a praying people. That is a wonderful thing in this day and time when the practice of prayer has slipped from many lives. To call upon the Lord for wisdom beyond our own, for strength to do what we ought to do, for comfort and consolation, and for the expression of gratitude is a significant and wonderful thing.[11]

I offer a plea that each of us will seek to live closer to the Lord and to commune with Him more frequently and with increased faith.

Fathers and mothers, pray over your children. Pray that they may be shielded from the evils of the world. Pray that they may grow in faith and knowledge. Pray that they may be directed toward lives that will be profitable and good. Husbands, pray for your wives.

Express unto the Lord your gratitude for them and plead with Him in their behalf. Wives, pray for your husbands. Many of them walk a very difficult road with countless problems and great perplexities. Plead with the Almighty that they may be guided, blessed, protected, inspired in their righteous endeavors.

Pray for peace in the earth, that the Almighty who governs the universe will stretch forth His hand and let His Spirit brood upon the people, that the nations may not rage one against another. . . . Pray for wisdom and understanding as you walk the difficult paths of your lives.[12]

The marvelous thing about prayer is that it is personal, it's individual, it's something that no one else gets into, in terms of your speaking with your Father in Heaven in the name of the Lord Jesus Christ. Be prayerful. Ask the Lord to forgive your sins. Ask the Lord for help. Ask the Lord to bless you. Ask the Lord to help you realize your righteous ambitions. . . . Ask the Lord for all of the important things that mean so much to you in your lives. He stands ready to help. Don't ever forget it.[13]

 **2**

Family prayer leads to miracles for individuals, families, and society.

There needs to be a new emphasis on honesty, character, and integrity in our time. Only as we build again into the fiber of our lives the virtues that are the essence of true civilization will the pattern of our times change. The question that confronts us is, Where shall we begin?

I am satisfied that it must begin with recognition of God as our Eternal Father, of our relationship to Him as His children, with communication with Him in recognition of His sovereign position, and with daily supplication for His guidance in our affairs.

I submit that a return to the old pattern of prayer, family prayer in the homes of the people, is one of the basic medications that would check the dread disease that is eroding the character of our society. We could not expect a miracle in a day, but in a generation we would have a miracle. . . .

There is something in the very posture of kneeling that contradicts the attitudes described by Paul: "proud . . . heady, highminded."

There is something in the very practice of father and mother and children kneeling together that evaporates others of those qualities he described: "disobedient to parents, . . . without natural affection."

There is something in the act of addressing Deity that offsets a tendency toward blasphemy and toward becoming lovers of pleasure more than lovers of God. [See 2 Timothy 3:1–4.]

The inclination to be unholy, as Paul described it, to be unthankful, is erased as together family members thank the Lord for life and peace and all they have. And as they thank the Lord for one another, there is developed within the family a new appreciation, a new respect, a new affection one for another. . . .

In remembering together before the Lord the poor, the needy, and the oppressed, there is developed, unconsciously but realistically, a love for others above self, a respect for others, a desire to serve the needs of others. One cannot ask God to help a neighbor in distress without feeling motivated to do something oneself toward helping that neighbor. What miracles would happen in the lives of the children of the world if they would lay aside their own selfishness and lose themselves in the service of others. The seed from which this sheltering and fruitful tree may grow is best planted and nurtured in the daily supplications of the family. . . .

I know of nothing that will so much help to ease family tensions, that in a subtle way will bring about the respect for parents which leads to obedience, that will affect the spirit of repentance which will largely erase the blight of broken homes, than will praying together, confessing weaknesses together before the Lord, and invoking the blessings of the Lord upon the home and those who dwell there. . . .

The family is the basic unit of society. The praying family is the hope of a better society. "Seek ye the Lord while he may be found." (Isa. 55:6.)[14]

I was touched . . . by the heartbreaking statement of a young [missionary]. He said, "I have been here for months. I can't learn the

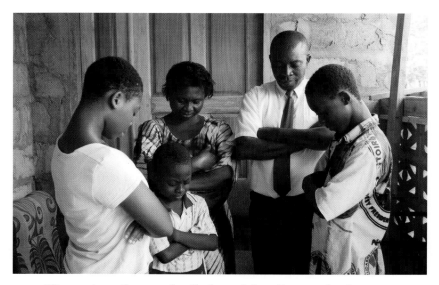

We can strengthen our family through kneeling together in prayer.

language. I dislike the people. I am depressed by day and weep at night. I wanted to die. I wrote my mother and pleaded for an excuse to return home. I have her reply. She says: 'We're praying for you. There is not a day passes that all of us do not kneel together in the morning before we eat and in the evening before we retire and plead with the Lord for his blessing upon you. We have added fasting to our prayer, and when your younger brothers and sisters pray they say, "Heavenly Father, bless Johnny . . . and help him to learn the language and do the work he was called to do." ' "

This young man then went on to say through his tears, "I will try again. I will add my prayers to theirs and my fasting to their fasting."

Now, four months later, I have a letter from him in which he says, "A miracle has happened. The language has come to me as a gift from the Lord. I have learned to love the people in this beautiful land. God be thanked for the prayers of my family." [15]

Can we make our homes more beautiful? Yes, through addressing ourselves as families to the Source of all true beauty. Can we strengthen society and make it a better place in which to live? Yes, by strengthening the virtue of our family life through kneeling together and supplicating the Almighty in the name of his Beloved Son.

This practice, a return to family worship, spreading across the land and over the earth, would in a generation largely lift the blight that is destroying us. It would restore integrity, mutual respect, and a spirit of thankfulness in the hearts of people.[16]

Is prayer such a difficult thing? Would it be so hard to encourage fathers and mothers to get on their knees with their little children and address the throne of Deity to express gratitude for blessings, to pray for those in distress as well as for themselves, and then to ask it in the name of the Savior and Redeemer of the world? How mighty a thing is prayer. Of that I can testify and to that you can testify. How tragic the loss for any family that fails to take advantage of this precious and simple practice.[17]

If there be any among you who are not having family prayer, let that practice start now, to get on your knees together, if you can possibly do it, every morning and every evening, and speak to the Lord and express your thanks, invoke His blessings upon the needy of the earth, and speak to Him concerning your own well-being.[18]

I give you my testimony that if you sincerely apply family prayer, you will not go away unrewarded. The changes may not be readily apparent. They may be extremely subtle. But they will be real, for God "is a rewarder of them that diligently seek him." (Heb. 11:6.)

May we be faithful in setting an example before the world in this practice and in encouraging others to do likewise.[19]

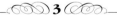 **3**

We need to be prayerful and listen, for our prayers will be answered.

Never assume that you can make it alone. You need the help of the Lord. Never hesitate to get on your knees in some private place and speak with Him. What a marvelous and wonderful thing is prayer. Think of it. We can actually speak with our Father in Heaven. He will hear and respond, but we need to listen to that response. Nothing is too serious and nothing too unimportant to share with Him.[20]

Pray to the Lord with the expectation of answers. . . . The trouble with most of our prayers is that we give them as if we were picking up the telephone and ordering groceries—we place our order and hang up. We need to meditate, contemplate, think of what we are praying about and for and then speak to the Lord as one man speaketh to another. "Come now, and let us reason together, saith the Lord" (Isa. 1:18).[21]

Nothing helps so much as putting a matter in the hands of the Lord. . . . I don't hesitate to say that I have had prayers answered. I know that. I could not deny it. We need to pray for guidance in this difficult age. . . . The marvelous thing is you don't have to be a genius to pray. He will listen to the voice of the most humble. . . . Call upon the Lord. He has extended the invitation, and He will answer.[22]

Believe in the power and majesty of prayer. The Lord answers our prayers. I know that. I have seen it happen again and again and again. Prayer brings us into partnership with God. It offers us an opportunity to speak with Him, to thank Him for His magnificent blessings, and to ask Him for guidance and protection as we walk the paths of life. This great work, which is spreading over the earth, found its roots in the prayer of a boy. He had read in the family Bible, "If any of you lack wisdom, let him ask of God, that giveth to all men liberally, and upbraideth not; and it shall be given him. But let him ask in faith, nothing wavering. For he that wavereth is like a wave of the sea driven with the wind and tossed" (James 1:5–6). That is the promise. Is there any greater promise anywhere in the world than that promise?[23]

Be prayerful, my friends, and listen. You may never hear a voice. You likely will not. But in a manner that you cannot explain, you will be prompted and blessed. For the Lord has promised, "I will tell you in your . . . heart, by the Holy Ghost, which shall come upon you. . . ." (D&C 8:2.)

Be prayerful, and you will know that God hears and answers. Not always as we might wish him to answer, but with the passing of the years, there will come a realization as certain as the sunrise that he heard and responded.[24]

Keep that humility which will cause you to get on your knees in prayer, in acknowledgment of His power and goodness. He will not fail you. He will hear your prayers. He will answer your prayers. In the stillness of the night, you will hear the whisperings of His Spirit to direct you in your times of distress and need. Those times will come to you as they do to all. Keep faith with God, and He will never let you down. He will never turn His back upon you.[25]

Always let your Father in Heaven be your friend, to whom you may go in prayer.[26]

Suggestions for Study and Teaching

Questions

• How has prayer helped you grow closer to your Heavenly Father? Review President Hinckley's counsel about what to include in prayers (see section 1). When has prayer helped you find "wisdom beyond [your] own"? When has prayer brought you "comfort and consolation"? Why should some prayers be "conversations of thanksgiving"?

• Ponder each of the blessings that President Hinckley said can come through family prayer (see section 2). What are some ways that your family has been blessed by praying together? What are some obstacles to consistent family prayer? How can family members work together to overcome these obstacles?

• How can applying President Hinckley's teachings in section 3 help us make our prayers more meaningful? What have you learned about the ways Heavenly Father answers prayers? Why does prayer have the power to bring us "into partnership with God"?

Related Scriptures

Matthew 6:5–15; Luke 18:9–18; 2 Nephi 32:8–9; Alma 34:17–28; 37:36–37; 3 Nephi 18:15–25; D&C 19:28

Study Help

"Get an overview, either by reading the book, chapter, or passage quickly or by reviewing headings. Seek to understand the context and background" (*Preach My Gospel* [2004], 23). Consider reading a chapter or passage more than once so you can understand it more deeply. As you do so, you may discover profound insights.

Notes

1. "Stand True and Faithful," *Ensign,* May 1996, 94.

2. Robert D. Hales, in Sheri L. Dew, *Go Forward with Faith: The Biography of Gordon B. Hinckley* (1996), 444.

3. Richard G. Hinckley, in Sheri L. Dew, *Go Forward with Faith,* 171.

4. Marjorie Pay Hinckley, in Sheri L. Dew, *Go Forward with Faith,* 171.

5. *Teachings of Gordon B. Hinckley* (1997), 469.

6. *Teachings of Gordon B. Hinckley,* 470.

7. "Dedication of Gordon B. Hinckley Building" (Brigham Young University–Idaho, Oct. 22, 2002), byui.edu/ Presentations/transcripts/devotionals/ 2002_10_22_hinckley.htm; accessed Sept. 21, 2015.

8. "Pillars of Truth," *Ensign,* Jan. 1994, 2.

9. "Stand True and Faithful," 93.

10. "An Humble and a Contrite Heart," *Ensign,* Nov. 2000, 89.

11. "The Fabric of Faith and Testimony," *Ensign,* Nov. 1995, 89.

12. "Benediction," *Ensign* or *Liahona,* May 2003, 99–100.

13. *Teachings of Gordon B. Hinckley,* 468.

14. "The Blessings of Family Prayer," *Ensign,* Feb. 1991, 2, 4–5.

15. In Conference Report, Apr. 1963, 128.

16. "The Blessings of Family Prayer," 5.

17. "Four Simple Things to Help Our Families and Our Nations," *Ensign,* Sept. 1996, 8.

18. *Teachings of Gordon B. Hinckley,* 217.

19. "The Blessings of Family Prayer," 5.

20. "Stay on the High Road," *Ensign* or *Liahona,* May 2004, 114.

21. *Teachings of Gordon B. Hinckley,* 469.

22. *Teachings of Gordon B. Hinckley,* 469.

23. "Fear Not; Only Believe," *New Era,* Jan. 2000, 6; bold and italics removed.

24. "Watch the Switches in Your Life," *Ensign,* Jan. 1973, 93.

25. *Discourses of President Gordon B. Hinckley, Volume 2: 2000–2004* (2005), 346.

26. "Daughters of God," *Ensign,* Nov. 1991, 100.

The Whisperings of the Spirit

"I make a plea that we constantly seek the inspiration of the Lord and the companionship of His Holy Spirit to bless us in keeping our efforts on a high spiritual plane."

From the Life of Gordon B. Hinckley

On June 24, 1995, President Gordon B. Hinckley spoke at a meeting for new mission presidents and their wives, giving them counsel to guide their next three years of service. He told of instruction he received when President Harold B. Lee, then a member of the Quorum of the Twelve Apostles, set him apart as a stake president:

"I remember only one thing he said: 'Listen for the whisperings of the Spirit in the middle of the night, and respond to those whisperings.' I don't know why revelation comes sometimes in the night, but it does. It comes in the day as well, of course. But listen to the whisperings of the Spirit, the gift of revelation, to which you are entitled."[1]

Referring to his experiences as he followed this instruction, he said: "The Lord has spoken quietly. . . . In the middle of the night, ideas have come into my head which, I think, have been prophetic in their nature."[2] For example, in July 1992 he was in Hong Kong with other Church leaders, searching for a place to build a temple. He went to bed one night feeling unsettled about the decision he needed to make. Then the whisperings of the Spirit woke him up early the next morning.

"Something very interesting came to my mind," he recorded in his journal. "I did not hear a voice with my natural ears. But into my mind there came the voice of the Spirit. It said, 'Why are you worried about this? You have a wonderful piece of property where the mission home and the small chapel stand. They are in the very heart of Kowloon, in the location with the best transportation. . . .

The Hong Kong China Temple

Build a building of [several] stories. It can include a chapel and classrooms on the first two floors and a temple on the top two or three floors.'" Having received that revelation, President Hinckley said, "I relaxed and went back to sleep."[3]

Today in Kowloon, a densely populated section of Hong Kong, a single building stands where a chapel and mission home once stood. That building, which houses a chapel, a mission home, a mission office, and a sacred temple, is a testament of the whisperings of the Spirit to a prophet of God.

Teachings of Gordon B. Hinckley

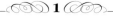

The Holy Ghost is the Comforter and the Testifier of truth.

The Holy Ghost stands as the third member of the Godhead, the Comforter promised by the Savior who would teach His followers all things and bring all things to their remembrance, whatsoever He had said unto them (see John 14:26).[4]

The Holy Ghost bears testimony in our hearts concerning the Father and the Son.[5]

[My] testimony [of Jesus Christ] comes by the power of the Holy Ghost. It is a gift, sacred and wonderful, borne by revelation from the third member of the Godhead.[6]

The Holy Ghost is the Testifier of Truth, who can teach [us] things [we] cannot teach one another. In those great and challenging words of Moroni, a knowledge of the truth of the Book of Mormon is promised "by the power of the Holy Ghost." Moroni then declares, "And by the power of the Holy Ghost ye may know the truth of all things" (Moroni 10:4–5).

I believe this power, this gift, is available to us today.[7]

We need the Holy Ghost to guide us in our service at home and in the Church.

There is no greater blessing that can come into our lives than the gift of the Holy Ghost—the companionship of the Holy Spirit to guide us, protect us, and bless us, to go, as it were, as a pillar before us and a flame to lead us in paths of righteousness and truth. That guiding power of the third member of the Godhead can be ours if we live worthy of it.[8]

We need the Holy Spirit in our many administrative responsibilities. We need it as we teach the gospel in our classes and to the world. We need it in the governance and teaching of our families.

As we direct and teach under the influence of that Spirit, we shall bring spirituality into the lives of those for whom we are responsible. . .

. . . Sweet are the fruits of teaching done under the inspiration of the Holy Spirit. They feed the spirit and nourish the soul.

May I give a special word of counsel to parents who stand as heads of families: we need the direction of the Holy Ghost in the delicate and tremendous task that is ours in strengthening the spirituality of our homes.[9]

Listen to the promptings of the Spirit. Be humble. You may be led to someone by the hand of the Lord because of your spirit, your attitude, your feeling, your humility.[10]

3

Revelation almost always comes to us through a still, small voice—the whispering of the Spirit.

From time to time, I have been interviewed by representatives of the media. Almost invariably they have asked, "How does revelation come to the prophet of the Church?"

I reply that it comes now as it has come in the past. Concerning this, I have recounted to these media representatives the experience of Elijah following his contest with the priests of Baal:

"And, behold, the Lord passed by, and a great and strong wind rent the mountains, and brake in pieces the rocks before the Lord; but the Lord was not in the wind: and after the wind an earthquake; but the Lord was not in the earthquake:

"And after the earthquake a fire; but the Lord was not in the fire: and after the fire a still small voice" (1 Kings 19:11–12).

That is the way it is. There is a still, small voice. It comes in response to prayer. It comes by the whispering of the Spirit. It may come in the silence of the night.

Do I have any question of that? None whatever. I have seen it in instance after instance.[11]

Such almost invariably has been the word of God as it has come to us, not with trumpets, not from the council halls of the learned, but in the still small voice of revelation. Listening to those who seek in vain to find wisdom and who declaim loudly their nostrums [or cures] for the ills of the world, one is prone to reply with the Psalmist, "Be still, and know that I am God: . . ." (Ps. 46:10) and with the Savior, "He that hath ears to hear, let him hear." (Matt. 11:15.)[12]

The things of the Spirit enlighten, build, and uplift us.

How do we know the things of the Spirit? How do we know that it is from God? By the fruits of it. If it leads to growth and development, if it leads to faith and testimony, if it leads to a better way of doing things, if it leads to godliness, then it is of God. If it tears us down, if it brings us into darkness, if it confuses us and worries us, if it leads to faithlessness, then it is of the devil.[13]

You recognize the promptings of the Spirit by the fruits of the Spirit—that which enlighteneth, that which buildeth up, that which is positive and affirmative and uplifting and leads us to better thoughts and better words and better deeds is of the Spirit of God. That which tears down, which leads us into forbidden paths—that is of the adversary. I think it is just that plain, just that simple.[14]

A scholar once expressed the view that the Church is an enemy of intellectualism. If he meant by intellectualism that branch of philosophy which teaches "the doctrine that knowledge is wholly or chiefly derived from pure reason" and "that reason is the final principle of reality," then, yes, we are opposed to so narrow an interpretation as applicable to religion. (Quotations from the *Random House Dictionary of the English Language,* p. 738.) Such an interpretation excludes the power of the Holy Spirit in speaking to and through [us].

"The things of God are understood by the Spirit of God. That Spirit is real."

Of course we believe in the cultivation of the mind, but the intellect is not the only source of knowledge. There is a promise, given under inspiration from the Almighty, set forth in these beautiful words: "God shall give unto you knowledge by his Holy Spirit, yea, by the unspeakable gift of the Holy Ghost." (D&C 121:26.)

The humanists who criticize the Lord's work, the so-called intellectualists who demean, speak only from ignorance of spiritual manifestation. They have not heard the voice of the Spirit. They have not heard it because they have not sought after it and prepared themselves to be worthy of it. Then, supposing that knowledge comes only of reasoning and of the workings of the mind, they deny that which comes by the power of the Holy Ghost.

The things of God are understood by the Spirit of God. That Spirit is real. To those who have experienced its workings, the knowledge so gained is as real as that which is acquired through the operation of the five senses. I testify of this. And I am confident that most members of the Church can so testify. I urge each of us to continue to cultivate a heart in tune with the Spirit. If we will do so, our lives will be enriched. We will feel a kinship with God our Eternal Father. We will taste a sweetness of joy that can be had in no other way.

Let us not be trapped by the sophistry of the world, which for the most part is negative and which so often bears sour fruit. Let us walk with faith in the future, speaking affirmatively and cultivating an attitude of confidence. As we do so, our strength will give strength to others.[15]

I make a plea that we constantly seek the inspiration of the Lord and the companionship of His Holy Spirit to bless us in keeping our efforts on a high spiritual plane. Those prayers will not go unanswered.[16]

The Holy Ghost will be our constant companion as we live for this blessing.

It is the Lord who has said that if we keep the commandments, "the Holy Ghost shall be [our] constant companion" (D&C 121:46) to buoy us up, to teach us, lead us, comfort us, and sustain us. To obtain this companionship, we need to ask for it, to live for it, to be loyal to the Lord.[17]

"How do you keep the Spirit of the Lord with you at all times?" Well, you live worthy of it; you live worthy of the Spirit of the Lord. That is what you do. And you will have it. . . . Just live right. Stay away from the sleaze. Stay away from pornography. Stay away from these things that pull you down. The books you read, the magazines you read, the videos you look at, the television programs you look at, the shows you go to, all have an effect on you and will do if you subject yourself to the influence of those titillating kinds of things which are designed to make you poor and somebody else rich. Stay away from them.[18]

You impose upon yourselves each Sunday a renewal of your pledge and covenant to take upon yourselves the name of the Lord Jesus Christ. Did you ever think of that, of how important that is, of what it means to take upon yourselves the name of the Lord Jesus Christ with a pledge and a promise to keep His commandments? And He makes a pledge and a promise to you that He will give you His Spirit to be with you. What a wonderful thing that is.[19]

How great a blessing it is to have the ministering influence of a member of the Godhead, having received that gift under the hands of those who acted with divine authority. If we continue to walk in virtue, we may enjoy the fulfillment of the promise made by the Lord when He said: "The Holy Ghost shall be thy constant companion, and thy scepter an unchanging scepter of righteousness and truth; and thy dominion shall be an everlasting dominion, and without compulsory means it shall flow unto thee forever and ever." (D&C 121:46.)[20]

Suggestions for Study and Teaching

Questions

- Why do we need the Holy Ghost? (See sections 1 and 2.) When have you felt the Holy Ghost teach and guide you? What have you learned from those experiences?

- What can we learn from President Hinckley's explanation about how revelation comes to the prophet? (See section 3.) Why is it important to know that the Holy Ghost usually communicates in "a still, small voice"? What have you learned from your own experiences about recognizing communications from the Holy Ghost?

- Review the "fruits of the Spirit" that President Hinckley summarizes in section 4. How can these teachings help us recognize the influence of the Spirit? What are the dangers of believing that "the intellect is . . . the only source of knowledge"? What experiences have you had with gaining spiritual knowledge?

- What are your feelings as you ponder President Hinckley's teachings in section 5 about the companionship of the Holy Ghost? In what ways have you been blessed by the Holy Ghost?

Related Scriptures

1 Corinthians 2:9–14; 1 Nephi 10:17; 2 Nephi 31:17–18; Mosiah 3:19; Moroni 8:25–26; D&C 11:12–14

Teaching Help

"When we love those we teach, we pray for each of them. We do all we can to know their interests, achievements, needs, and concerns. We tailor to meet their needs, even if this takes more time and effort. We notice when they are absent and recognize them when they are present. We offer help when it is needed" (*Teaching, No Greater Call* [1999], 32).

Notes

1. *Teachings of Gordon B. Hinckley* (1997), 556.

2. *Discourses of President Gordon B. Hinckley, Volume 1: 1995–1999* (2005), 441.

3. In Sheri L. Dew, *Go Forward with Faith: The Biography of Gordon B. Hinckley* (1996), 481.

4. "The Father, Son, and Holy Ghost," *Ensign,* Nov. 1986, 51.

5. "Latter-day Counsel: Excerpts from Recent Addresses of President Gordon B. Hinckley," *Ensign,* July 1999, 72.

6. "The Father, Son, and Holy Ghost," 51.

7. "The Father, Son, and Holy Ghost," 51.

8. *Teachings of Gordon B. Hinckley,* 259.

9. "Feed the Spirit, Nourish the Soul," *Ensign,* Oct. 1998, 2, 4–5.

10. *Discourses of President Gordon B. Hinckley, Volume 1,* 440.

11. "The Quorum of the First Presidency," *Ensign,* Dec. 2005, 49.

12. In Conference Report, Apr. 1964, 38–39.

13. "Inspirational Thoughts," *Ensign,* July 1998, 5.

14. *Teachings of Gordon B. Hinckley,* 261.

15. "The Continuing Pursuit of Truth," *Ensign,* Apr. 1986, 6.

16. "Feed the Spirit, Nourish the Soul," 2.

17. "Living with Our Convictions," *Ensign,* Sept. 2001, 5.

18. *Discourses of President Gordon B. Hinckley, Volume 1,* 377–78.

19. *Discourses of President Gordon B. Hinckley, Volume 1,* 319.

20. "Priesthood Restoration," *Ensign,* Oct. 1988, 72.

"Absolutely basic to our faith is our testimony of Jesus Christ as the Son of God. . . . He is the chief cornerstone of the church which bears His name."

126

We Look to Christ

"We believe in Christ. We teach of Christ. We look to Christ. He is our Redeemer, our Lord, and our Savior."

From the Life of Gordon B. Hinckley

In the April 1975 general conference, Elder Gordon B. Hinckley, then a member of the Quorum of the Twelve Apostles, shared the following experience:

"We recently held an open house in the [Mesa] Arizona Temple. Following a complete renovation of that building, nearly a quarter of a million people saw its beautiful interior. On the first day of the opening, clergymen of other religions were invited as special guests, and hundreds responded. It was my privilege to speak to them and to answer their questions at the conclusion of their tours. I told them that we would be pleased to answer any queries they might have. Many were asked. Among these was one which came from a Protestant minister.

"Said he: 'I've been all through this building, this temple which carries on its face the name of Jesus Christ, but nowhere have I seen any representation of the cross, the symbol of Christianity. I have noted your buildings elsewhere and likewise find an absence of the cross. Why is this when you say you believe in Jesus Christ?'

"I responded: 'I do not wish to give offense to any of my Christian brethren who use the cross on the steeples of their cathedrals and at the altars of their chapels, who wear it on their vestments, and imprint it on their books and other literature. But for us, the cross is the symbol of the dying Christ, while our message is a declaration of the living Christ.'

"He then asked: 'If you do not use the cross, what is the symbol of your religion?'

"I replied that the lives of our people must become the only meaningful expression of our faith and, in fact, therefore, the symbol of our worship. . . .

". . . No sign, no work of art, no representation of form is adequate to express the glory and the wonder of the Living Christ. He told us what that symbol should be when he said, 'If ye love me, keep my commandments.' (John 14:15.)

"As his followers, we cannot do a mean or shoddy or ungracious thing without tarnishing his image. Nor can we do a good and gracious and generous act without burnishing more brightly the symbol of him whose name we have taken upon ourselves.

"And so our lives must become a meaningful expression, the symbol of our declaration of our testimony of the Living Christ, the Eternal Son of the Living God.

"It is that simple, my brethren and sisters, and that profound and we'd better never forget it."[1]

Teachings of Gordon B. Hinckley

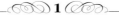 1

Jesus Christ is the living Son of the living God.

Absolutely basic to our faith is our testimony of Jesus Christ as the Son of God. . . . He is the chief cornerstone of the church which bears His name.[2]

We believe in Christ. We teach of Christ. We look to Christ. He is our Redeemer, our Lord, and our Savior.[3]

Earthly ministry

He who was the Son of God, the Only Begotten Son, left His Father's celestial courts to take on mortality. At His birth, angels sang and Wise Men came to bestow gifts. He grew as did other boys in Nazareth of Galilee. There He "increased in wisdom and stature, and in favour with God and man" (Luke 2:52).

With Mary and Joseph, He visited Jerusalem when He was 12. On their journey home, they missed Him. They came back to Jerusalem and found Him in the temple conversing with the learned doctors.

When Mary upbraided Him for not being with them, He answered, "Wist ye not that I must be about my Father's business?" (Luke 2:49). His words were a premonition of His future ministry.

That ministry began with His baptism in the river Jordan at the hands of His cousin John. When He arose from the water, the Holy Ghost descended upon Him in the form of a dove, and His Father's voice was heard, saying, "This is my beloved Son, in whom I am well pleased" (Matt. 3:17). That declaration became the affirmation of His divinity.

He fasted for 40 days and was tempted of the devil, who sought to take Him from His divinely appointed mission. To the adversary's invitation, He responded, "Thou shalt not tempt the Lord thy God" (Matt. 4:7), again declaring His divine sonship.

He walked the dusty roads of Palestine. He had no home that He could call His own, no place to rest His head. His message was the gospel of peace. His teachings were those of generosity and love. "If any man will sue thee at the law, and take away thy coat, let him have thy cloak also" (Matt. 5:40).

He taught with parables. He performed miracles the like of which were never performed before or since. He healed those whose sickness was of long standing. He caused the blind to see, the deaf to hear, the lame to walk. He raised the dead, and they lived again to speak His praises. Surely no man had ever done such before.

A few followed Him, but most hated Him. He spoke of the scribes and Pharisees as hypocrites, as whited sepulchers. They plotted against Him. He drove the money changers from the house of the Lord. They doubtless joined those who planned to destroy Him. But He was not deterred. He "went about doing good" (Acts 10:38).

Was not all of this enough to make His memory immortal? Was it not enough to place His name among, and even above, those of the great men who have walked the earth and who have been remembered for what they said or did? Certainly He would have been ranked among the great prophets of all time.

But all of this was not enough for the Son of the Almighty. It was but prelude to greater things to come. They came in a strange and terrible way.[4]

Arrest, crucifixion, and death

He was betrayed, arrested, condemned to death, to die in awful agony by crucifixion. His living body was nailed to a cross of wood. In unspeakable pain, His life slowly ebbed away. While yet He breathed, He cried out, "Father, forgive them; for they know not what they do" (Luke 23:34).

The earth shook as His spirit passed. The centurion who had seen it all declared in solemnity, "Truly this was the Son of God" (Matt. 27:54).

Those who loved Him took His body from the cross. They dressed it and placed it in a new tomb. . . .

His friends must have wept. The Apostles He loved and whom He had called as witnesses of His divinity wept. The women who loved Him wept. None had understood what He had said about rising the third day. How could they understand? This had never happened before. It was totally unprecedented. It was unbelievable, even for them.

There must have been a terrible sense of dejection and hopelessness and misery as they thought of their Lord taken from them in death.[5]

Resurrection

But that was not the end. On the morning of the third day, Mary Magdalene and the other Mary returned to the tomb. To their utter amazement, the stone was rolled away and the tomb was open. They peered inside. Two beings in white sat at either end of the burial site. An angel appeared to them and said, "Why seek ye the living among the dead?

"He is not here, but is risen: remember how he spake unto you when he was yet in Galilee,

"Saying, The Son of man must be delivered into the hands of sinful men, and be crucified, and the third day rise again" (Luke 24:5–7).

These simple words—"He is not here, but is risen"—have become the most profound in all literature. They are the declaration of

"His message was the gospel of peace. His teachings were those of generosity and love."

the empty tomb. They are the fulfillment of all He had spoken concerning rising again. They are the triumphant response to the query facing every man, woman, and child who was ever born to earth.

The risen Lord spoke to Mary, and she replied. He was not an apparition. This was not imagination. He was real, as real as He had been in mortal life. He did not permit her to touch Him. He had not yet ascended to His Father in Heaven. That would happen shortly. What a reunion it must have been, to be embraced by the Father, who loved Him and who also must have wept for Him during His hours of agony.

He would appear to two men on the road to Emmaus. He would converse with them and eat with them. He would meet with His Apostles behind closed doors and teach them. Thomas was not present on the first occasion. On the second occasion, the Lord invited him to feel of His hands and His side. In utter wonder he exclaimed, "My Lord and my God" (John 20:28). He spoke with 500 at [another] time. . . .

And there is another witness. This biblical companion, the Book of Mormon, testifies that He appeared not only to those of the Old World but also to those of the New. For had He not at one time declared, "Other sheep I have, which are not of this fold: them also I must bring, and they shall hear my voice; and there shall be one fold, and one shepherd"? (John 10:16).

To those of this hemisphere He appeared following His Resurrection. At His descent through the clouds of heaven, the voice of God the Eternal Father was heard again in solemn declaration: "Behold my Beloved Son, in whom I am well pleased, in whom I have glorified my name—hear ye him" (3 Ne. 11:7). . . .

And if all of this is not enough, there is the testimony, sure and certain and unequivocal, of the great prophet of this dispensation, Joseph Smith. As a boy he went into the woods to pray seeking light and understanding. And there appeared before him two Personages, whose brightness and glory defy all description, standing above him in the air. One of them spoke to him, calling him "by name and said, pointing to the other—*This is My Beloved Son. Hear Him!*" [Joseph Smith—History 1:17].

This same Joseph declared on a subsequent occasion: "We beheld the glory of the Son, on the right hand of the Father, and received of his fulness; . . .

"And now, after the many testimonies which have been given of him, this is the testimony, last of all, which we give of him: That he lives!" (D&C 76:20, 22).[6]

To all who may have doubts, I repeat the words given Thomas as he felt the wounded hands of the Lord: "Be not faithless, but believing" [John 20:27]. Believe in Jesus Christ, the Son of God, the greatest figure of time and eternity. Believe that his matchless life reached back before the world was formed. Believe that he was the Creator of the earth on which we live. Believe that he was Jehovah of the Old Testament, that he was the Messiah of the New Testament, that he died and was resurrected, that he visited the western continents and taught the people here, that he ushered in this final gospel dispensation, and that he lives, the living Son of the living God, our Savior and our Redeemer.[7]

Each of us can know that Jesus Christ is the Son of God and the Redeemer of the world, resurrected from the grave.

There is a . . . battle being waged for the faith of men, but the lines are not always . . . clearly drawn, for even among the forces of Christianity there are those who would destroy the divinity of the Christ in whose name they speak. They might be disregarded if their voices were not so seductive, if their influence were not so far-reaching, if their reason were not so subtle.

. . . Multitudes will gather on a thousand hills to welcome the dawn of the Easter day and to remind themselves of the story of the Christ, whose resurrection they will commemorate. In language both beautiful and hopeful, preachers of many faiths will recount the story of the empty tomb. To them—and to you—I raise this question: "Do you actually believe it?"

Do you actually believe that Jesus was the Son of God, the literal offspring of the Father?

Do you believe that the voice of God, the Eternal Father, was heard above the waters of Jordan declaring, "This is my beloved Son, in whom I am well pleased"? (Matt. 3:17.)

Do you believe that this same Jesus was the worker of miracles, the healer of the sick, the restorer of the infirm, the giver of life to the dead?

Do you believe that following his death on Calvary's hill and his burial in Joseph's tomb, he came forth alive the third day?

Do you actually believe that he yet lives—real, vital, and personal—and that he will come again as promised by the angels at his ascension?

Do you actually believe these things? If you do, then you are part of a shrinking body of literalists who more and more are being smiled at by philosophers, who more and more are being ridiculed by certain educators, and who more and more are being considered "out of it" by a growing coterie of ministers of religion and influential theologians.

The resurrected Savior walked with two men on the road to Emmaus.

. . . In the eyes of these intellectuals, these are myths—the birth of Jesus as the Son of God of whom the angels sang on Judea's plains, the worker of miracles who healed the sick and raised the dead, the Christ resurrected from the grave, the ascension and the promised return.

These modern theologians strip him of his divinity and then wonder why men do not worship him.

These clever scholars have taken from Jesus the mantle of godhood and have left only a man. They have tried to accommodate him to their own narrow thinking. They have robbed him of his divine sonship and taken from the world its rightful King. . . .

. . . I give our solemn witness that God is not dead, except as he is viewed with a lifeless interpretation. . . .

. . . There is needed something more than a reasonable belief. There is needed an understanding of his unique and incomparable position as the divine Redeemer and an enthusiasm for him and his message as the Son of God.

That understanding and that enthusiasm are available to all who will pay the price. They are not incompatible with higher education, but they will not come only of reading philosophy. No, they come of a simpler process. The things of God are understood by the Spirit of God. (1 Cor. 2:11.) So declares the word of revelation.

The acquisition of understanding and enthusiasm for the Lord comes from following simple rules. . . . I should like to suggest three, elementary in their concept, almost trite in their repetition, but fundamental in their application and fruitful in their result. . . .

The first is to read—to read the word of the Lord. . . . Read, for instance, the Gospel of John from its beginning to its end. Let the Lord speak for himself to you, and his words will come with a quiet conviction that will make the words of his critics meaningless. Read also the testament of the New World, the Book of Mormon, brought forth as a witness "that Jesus is the Christ, the Eternal God, manifesting himself unto all nations." (Book of Mormon title page.)

The next is to serve—to serve in the work of the Lord. . . . The cause of Christ does not need your doubts; it needs your strength and time and talents; and as you exercise these in service, your faith will grow and your doubts will wane. . . .

The third is to pray. Speak with your Eternal Father in the name of his Beloved Son. "Behold," he says, "I stand at the door, and knock: if any man hear my voice, and open the door, I will come in to him, and will sup with him, and he with me." (Rev. 3:20.)

This is his invitation, and the promise is sure. It is unlikely that you will hear voices from heaven, but there will come a heaven-sent assurance, peaceful and certain. . . .

. . . Shining through all of the confusion of philosophy, so-called higher criticism, and negative theology will come the witness of the Holy Spirit that Jesus is in very deed the Son of God, born in the flesh, the Redeemer of the world resurrected from the grave, the

Lord who shall come to reign as King of kings. It is your opportunity so to know. It is your obligation so to find out.[8]

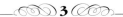

We need to continually ask ourselves, "What shall we do with Jesus who is called Christ?"

I ask anew the question offered by Pilate two thousand years ago, "What shall I do then with Jesus which is called Christ?" (Matt. 27:22.) Indeed, we need continually to ask ourselves, What shall *we* do with Jesus who is called Christ? What shall we do with his teachings, and how can we make them an inseparable part of our lives? . . .

. . . "Behold the Lamb of God, which taketh away the sin of the world." (John 1:29.) How poor indeed would be our lives without the influence of his teachings and his matchless example. The lessons of the turning of the other cheek, going the second mile, the return of the prodigal, and scores of other incomparable teachings have filtered down the ages to become the catalyst to bring kindness and mercy out of much of man's inhumanity to man.

Brutality reigns where Christ is banished. Kindness and forbearance govern where Christ is recognized and his teachings are followed.

What shall we do then with Jesus who is called Christ? "He hath shewed thee, O man, what is good; and what doth the Lord require of thee, but to do justly, and to love mercy, and to walk humbly with thy God?" (Micah 6:8.)

"Wherefore, I say unto you, that ye ought to forgive one another; for he that forgiveth not his brother his trespasses standeth condemned before the Lord; for there remaineth in him the greater sin." (D&C 64:9.) . . .

What shall we do then with Jesus which is called Christ? "For I was an hungred, and ye gave me meat: I was thirsty, and ye gave me drink: I was a stranger, and ye took me in: naked, and ye clothed me: I was sick, and ye visited me: I was in prison, and ye came unto me." (Matt. 25:35–36) . . .

What shall we do with Jesus who is called Christ?

Learn of him. Search the scriptures for they are they which testify of him. Ponder the miracle of his life and mission. Try a little more diligently to follow his example and observe his teachings.[9]

We look to Jesus Christ as the rock of our salvation, our strength, our comfort, and the focus of our faith.

We know not what lies ahead of us. We know not what the coming days will bring. We live in a world of uncertainty. For some, there will be great accomplishment. For others, disappointment. For some, much of rejoicing and gladness, good health, and gracious living. For others, perhaps sickness and a measure of sorrow. We do not know. But one thing we do know. Like the polar star in the heavens, regardless of what the future holds, there stands the Redeemer of the world, the Son of God, certain and sure as the anchor of our immortal lives. He is the rock of our salvation, our strength, our comfort, the very focus of our faith.

In sunshine and in shadow we look to Him, and He is there to assure and smile upon us.[10]

I know that my Redeemer lives,
Triumphant Savior, Son of God,
Victorious over pain and death,
My King, my Leader, and my Lord.

He lives, my one sure rock of faith,
The one bright hope of men on earth,
The beacon to a better way,
The light beyond the veil of death.

Oh, give me thy sweet Spirit still,
The peace that comes alone from thee,
The faith to walk the lonely road
That leads to thine eternity.[11]

Suggestions for Study and Teaching

Questions

- Review President Hinckley's words of testimony in section 1, and take time to ponder your own testimony of Jesus Christ. Why are you grateful for the Savior's ministry and Atonement? What accounts and teachings from the Savior's life have special meaning to you?

- Ask yourself each of the questions in section 2. How do your answers influence your day-to-day living? In the same section, review President Hinckley's three "simple rules" for gaining an understanding of "the things of God." How have these principles helped you deepen your spiritual understanding?

- President Hinckley repeatedly asked, "What shall we do with Jesus who is called Christ?" (section 3). What can we learn from his answers? Consider how you would answer this question. How would your life be different if you did not know of the Savior's teachings and example?

- President Hinckley emphasized that Jesus Christ is our anchor in a world of uncertainty (see section 4). When have you felt the Savior's strength and comfort in a time of need? Ponder each line of President Hinckley's hymn in section 4. In what ways is Christ our "one bright hope"? How is He our "beacon to a better way"?

Related Scriptures

Luke 24:36–39; John 1:1–14; Acts 4:10–12; 2 Nephi 2:8; 25:26; Alma 5:48; D&C 110:3–4

Study Help

"Plan study activities that will build your faith in the Savior" (*Preach My Gospel* [2004], 22). For instance, as you study, you might ask yourself questions such as the following: How might these teachings help me increase my understanding of the Atonement of Jesus Christ? How can these teachings help me become more like the Savior?

Notes

1. "The Symbol of Christ," *Ensign,* May 1975, 92, 94.

2. "Four Cornerstones of Faith," *Ensign,* Feb. 2004, 4.

3. *Teachings of Gordon B. Hinckley* (1997), 280.

4. "He Is Not Here, but Is Risen," *Ensign,* May 1999, 71.

5. "He Is Not Here, but Is Risen," 71.

6. "He Is Not Here, but Is Risen," 71–72.

7. "Be Not Faithless," *Ensign,* Apr. 1989, 2.

8. In Conference Report, Apr. 1966, 85–87.

9. "What Shall I Do Then with Jesus Which Is Called Christ?" *Ensign,* Dec. 1983, 3–5.

10. "We Look to Christ," *Ensign,* May 2002, 90.

11. "My Redeemer Lives," *Hymns,* no. 135; text by Gordon B. Hinckley.

As Latter-day Saints, we are united in our testimony of Jesus Christ.

The Precious Gift of Testimony

"We speak different tongues. We live under a variety of circumstances. But in the heart of each of us beats a common testimony."

From the Life of Gordon B. Hinckley

"The earliest instance of which I have recollection of spiritual feelings," said President Gordon B. Hinckley, "was when I was about five years of age, a very small boy. I was crying from the pain of an earache. . . . My mother prepared a bag of table salt and put it on the stove to warm. My father softly put his hands upon my head and gave me a blessing, rebuking the pain and the illness by authority of the holy priesthood and in the name of Jesus Christ. He then took me tenderly in his arms and placed the bag of warm salt at my ear. The pain subsided and left. I fell asleep in my father's secure embrace. As I was falling asleep, the words of his administration floated through my mind. That is the earliest remembrance I have of the exercise of the authority of the priesthood in the name of the Lord.

"Later in my youth, my brother and I slept in an unheated bedroom in the winter. . . . Before falling into a warm bed, we knelt to say our prayers. There were expressions of simple gratitude. . . . I recall jumping into my bed after I had said amen, pulling the covers up around my neck, and thinking of what I had just done in speaking to my Father in Heaven in the name of His Son. I did not have great knowledge of the gospel. But there was some kind of lingering peace and security in communing with the heavens in and through the Lord Jesus. . . .

"That testimony grew in my heart as a missionary when I read the New Testament and the Book of Mormon, which further bore witness of Him. That knowledge became the foundation of my life, standing on the footings of the answered prayers of my childhood. Since then my faith has grown much further. I have become His Apostle, appointed to do His will and teach His word. I have become His witness to the world."[1]

Teachings of Gordon B. Hinckley

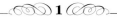

Testimony is the great strength of the Church and the wellspring of faith and activity.

We have become as a great family spread across this vast world. We speak different tongues. We live under a variety of circumstances. But in the heart of each of us beats a common testimony: You and I know that God lives and is at the helm of this His holy work. We know that Jesus is our Redeemer, who stands at the head of this Church which carries His name. We know that Joseph Smith was a prophet and is a prophet who stands at the head of this the dispensation of the fulness of times. We know that the priesthood was restored upon his head and that it has come down to us in this day in an unbroken line. We know that the Book of Mormon is a true testament of the reality and divinity of the Lord Jesus Christ.[2]

This thing which we call testimony is the great strength of the Church. It is the wellspring of faith and activity. . . . It is as real and powerful as any force on the earth. The Lord described it when He spoke to Nicodemus and said, "The wind bloweth where it listeth, and thou hearest the sound thereof, but canst not tell whence it cometh, and whither it goeth: so is every one that is born of the Spirit" (John 3:8). This thing which we call testimony is difficult to define, but its fruits are plainly evident. It is the Holy Spirit testifying through us.[3]

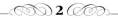

Testimony is a quiet, encouraging voice that sustains us as we walk in faith and impels us to action.

Personal testimony is the factor which turns people around in their living as they come into this Church. This is the element which motivates the membership to forsake all in the service of the Lord.

This is the quiet, encouraging voice which sustains without pause those who walk in faith down to the last days of their lives.

It is a mysterious and wonderful thing, a gift from God to man. It overrides wealth or poverty when one is called to serve. This testimony which is carried in the hearts of our people motivates to an impelling duty. It is found in young and old. It is found in the seminary student, in the missionary, in the bishop and the stake president, in the mission president, in the Relief Society sister, in every General Authority. It is heard from those who hold no office other than membership. It is of the very essence of this work. It is what is moving the work of the Lord forward across the world. It impels to action. It demands that we do what we are asked to do. It brings with it the assurance that life is purposeful, that some things are of far greater importance than others, that we are on an eternal journey, that we are answerable unto God. . . .

It is this element, weak and somewhat feeble at first, which moves every investigator in the direction of conversion. It pushes every convert toward security in the faith. . . .

Wherever the Church is organized its power is felt. We stand on our feet and say that we know. . . . The simple fact is that we *do* know that God lives, that Jesus *is* the Christ, and that this is their cause and their kingdom. The words are simple; the expression comes from the heart. It is at work wherever the Church is organized, wherever there are missionaries teaching the gospel, wherever there are members sharing their faith.

It is something that cannot be refuted. Opponents may quote scripture and argue doctrine endlessly. They can be clever and persuasive. But when one says, "I know," there can be no further argument. There may not be acceptance, but who can refute or deny the quiet voice of the inner soul speaking with personal conviction?[4]

"Light into our lives"

[David Castañeda], his wife, Tomasa, and their children lived on a dry little run-down ranch near Torreón [in Mexico]. They owned 30 chickens, 2 pigs, and 1 thin horse. The chickens provided a few eggs to sustain them and the means whereby to earn an occasional peso. They walked in poverty. Then the missionaries called on them. Sister Castañeda said, "The elders took the blinders from our eyes and brought light into our lives. We knew nothing of Jesus Christ. We knew nothing of God until they came."

She had two years of schooling, her husband none. The elders taught them, and they were eventually baptized. . . . They gradually built a prosperous business in which the father and his five sons worked. With simple faith they paid their tithing. They put their trust in the Lord. They lived the gospel. They served wherever called to do so. Four of their sons and three of their daughters filled missions. . . . They have been taunted by their critics. Their answer is a testimony of the power of the Lord in their lives.

Some 200 of their family and friends have joined the Church due to their influence. Over 30 sons and daughters of family and friends have served missions. They donated the land on which a chapel now stands.

The children, now grown to maturity, and the parents take turns going to Mexico City each month, there to work in the temple. They stand as a living testimony of the great power of this work of the Lord to lift and change people. They are typical of thousands upon thousands throughout the world who experience the miracle of Mormonism as a testimony of the divinity of the work comes into their lives.[5]

"It's true, isn't it? Then what else matters?"

I met a naval officer from a distant nation, a brilliant young man who had been brought to the United States for advanced training. Some of his associates in the United States Navy, whose behavior had attracted him, shared with him at his request their religious beliefs. He was not a Christian, but he was interested. They told him of the Savior of the world, Jesus Christ, born in Bethlehem, who gave his life for all mankind. They told him of the appearance of God, the Eternal Father, and the resurrected Lord to the boy Joseph Smith. They spoke of modern prophets. They taught him the gospel of the Master. The Spirit touched his heart, and he was baptized.

He was introduced to me just before he was to return to his native land. We spoke of these things, and then I said: "Your people are not Christians. What will happen when you return home a Christian, and, more particularly, a Mormon Christian?"

His face clouded, and he replied, "My family will be disappointed. They may cast me out and regard me as dead. As for my future and my career, all opportunity may be foreclosed against me."

I asked, "Are you willing to pay so great a price for the gospel?"

His dark eyes, moistened by tears, shone from his handsome brown face as he answered, "It's true, isn't it?"

Ashamed at having asked the question, I responded, "Yes, it's true."

To which he replied, "Then what else matters?"

These are questions I should like to leave with you: "It's true, isn't it? Then what else really matters?"[6]

A new outlook on life

I once listened to the experience of an engineer who recently had joined the Church. The missionaries had called at his home, and his wife had invited them in. She had eagerly responded to their message, while he felt himself being pulled in against his will. One evening she indicated that she wished to be baptized. He flew into a fit of anger. Didn't she know what this would mean? This would mean time. This would mean the payment of tithing. This would mean giving up their friends. This would mean no more smoking. He threw on his coat and walked out into the night, slamming the door behind him. He walked the streets, swearing at his wife, swearing at the missionaries, swearing at himself for ever permitting them to teach them. As he grew tired his anger cooled, and a spirit of prayer somehow came into his heart. He prayed as he walked. He pleaded with God for an answer to his questions. And then an impression, clear and unequivocal, came almost as if a voice had spoken with words that said, "It's true."

"It's true," he said to himself again and again. "It's true." A peace came into his heart. As he walked toward home, the restrictions, the demands, the requirements over which he had been so incensed began to appear as opportunities. When he opened the door, he found his wife on her knees praying.

"Who can refute or deny the quiet voice of the inner soul speaking with personal conviction?"

. . . Before the congregation to whom he told this, he spoke of the gladness that had come into their lives. Tithing was not a problem. The sharing of their substance with God, who had given them everything, seemed little enough. Time for service was not a problem. This only required a little careful budgeting of the hours of the week. Responsibility was not a problem. Out of it came growth and a new outlook on life. And then this man of intellect and training, this engineer accustomed to dealing with the facts of the physical world in which we live, bore solemn testimony with moistened eyes of the miracle that had come into his life.[7]

"The most precious thing in my life"

Some years ago a brilliant and highly educated young woman spoke in Berchtesgaden, Germany, to a conference of military personnel who were members of the Church. I was there and heard her. She was a major in the army, a medical doctor, a highly respected specialist in her field. She said:

"More than anything else in the world I wanted to serve God. But try as I might I could not find him. The miracle of it all is that he found me. One Saturday afternoon in September 1969 I was at home in Berkeley, California, and heard my doorbell ring. There were two young men there, dressed in suits, with white shirts and ties. Their hair was neatly combed. I was so impressed with them that I said: 'I don't know what you're selling, but I'll buy it.' One of the young men said: 'We aren't selling anything. We're missionaries of The Church of Jesus Christ of Latter-day Saints, and we would like to talk with you.' I invited them to come in, and they spoke about their faith.

"This was the beginning of my testimony. I am thankful beyond words for the privilege and honor of being a member of The Church of Jesus Christ of Latter-day Saints. The joy and peace this glad gospel has brought to my heart is heaven on earth. My testimony of this work is the most precious thing in my life, a gift from my Heavenly Father, for which I will be eternally thankful."[8]

So it is with hundreds of thousands in many lands—men and women of capacity and training, of business and the professions, hard-headed, practical [people] who do things in the work of the world, in whose hearts there burns a silent witness that God lives, that Jesus is the Christ, that this work is divine, that it was restored to earth for the blessing of all who will partake of its opportunities.[9]

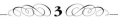

3

Each of us can obtain a testimony of the reality of God and His Beloved Son and the restoration of Their work.

This witness, this testimony, can be the most precious of all the gifts of God. It is a heavenly bestowal when there is the right effort. It is the opportunity, it is the responsibility of every man and woman in this Church to obtain within himself or herself a conviction of the truth of this great latter-day work and of those who stand at its head, even the living God and the Lord Jesus Christ.

Jesus pointed the way for the acquisition of such a testimony when He said: "My doctrine is not mine, but his that sent me.

"If any man will do his will, he shall know of the doctrine, whether it be of God, or whether I speak of myself" (John 7:16–17).

We grow in faith and knowledge as we serve, as we study, as we pray.

When Jesus fed the 5,000 they recognized and wondered at the miracle He had performed. Some came back again. To these He taught the doctrine of His divinity, of Himself as the Bread of Life. He accused them of not being interested in the doctrine but rather only in the satisfaction of the hunger of their bodies. Some, on hearing Him and His doctrine, said, "This is an hard saying; who can hear it?" (John 6:60). Who can believe what this man is teaching?

"From that time many of his disciples went back, and walked no more with him.

"Then said Jesus unto the twelve [I think with some feeling of discouragement], Will ye also go away?

"Then Simon Peter answered him, Lord, to whom shall we go? thou hast the words of eternal life.

"And we believe and are sure that thou art that Christ, the Son of the living God" (John 6:66–69).

This is the great question, and the answer thereto, which we must all face. If not to Thee, then "Lord, to whom shall we go? thou hast the words of eternal life. And we believe and are sure that thou art that Christ, the Son of the living God."

It is this conviction, this quiet inward certainty of the reality of the living God, of the divinity of His Beloved Son, of the restoration of their work in this time, and of the glorious manifestations which have followed which become for each of us the foundation of our faith. This becomes our testimony.

. . . I've recently been in Palmyra, New York [near where Joseph Smith received the First Vision]. Of the events which occurred in that area, one is led to say: "They either happened or they did not. There can be no gray area, no middle ground."

And then the voice of faith whispers: "It all happened. It happened just as he said it happened."

Nearby is the Hill Cumorah. From there came the ancient record from which was translated the Book of Mormon. One must accept or reject its divine origin. Weighing of the evidence must lead every man and woman who has read with faith to say, "It is true."

And so it is with other elements of this miraculous thing which we call the restoration of the ancient gospel, the ancient priesthood, and the ancient Church.

This testimony is now, as it has always been, a declaration, a straightforward assertion of truth as we know it.[10]

We must live up to our testimony and share it with others.

Said Paul to Timothy: "Take heed unto thyself"—listen to this—"and unto the doctrine; continue in them: for in doing this thou shalt both save thyself, and them that hear thee" (1 Timothy 4:16). What a wonderful direction Paul gave to young Timothy.

He went on to say this: "For God hath not given us the spirit of fear; but of power, and of love, and of a sound mind" (2 Timothy 1:7). God hath not given us the spirit of fear, but of power—the power of the message; and of love—love for the people, love for what we have to offer; a sound mind—the simple, understandable principles of the restored gospel of Jesus Christ.

"Be not thou therefore ashamed of the testimony of our Lord" (2 Timothy 1:8). Never, my brothers and sisters, be thou ashamed of the testimony of our Lord. . . . Here is a great charge, a mandate that is laid upon us: "For God hath not given us the spirit of fear; but of power, and of love, and of a sound mind. Be not thou therefore ashamed of the testimony of our Lord."[11]

This is God's holy work. This is His Church and kingdom. The vision that occurred in the Sacred Grove was just as Joseph said it was. There is in my heart a true understanding of the importance of what happened there. The Book of Mormon is true. It testifies of the Lord Jesus Christ. His priesthood has been restored and is among us. The keys of that priesthood, which have come from heavenly beings, are exercised for our eternal blessing. Such is our testimony—yours and mine—a testimony which we must live up to and which we must share with others. I leave this testimony, my blessing, and my love with each of you and my invitation to continue to be part of this great latter-day miracle that is The Church of Jesus Christ of Latter-day Saints.[12]

Suggestions for Study and Teaching

Questions

- In what ways does your personal testimony contribute to the strength of the Church? (See section 1.)

- President Hinckley emphasizes that testimony sustains us and "impels [us] to action" (section 2). How has your testimony sustained you? How has your testimony influenced your actions? What personal applications can you make from the stories in section 2?

- What can we learn from President Hinckley's teachings about obtaining a testimony? (See section 3.) What experiences have helped you gain your testimony? What can we do to strengthen our testimonies?

- Why do you think our testimonies grow stronger when we share them? How have you overcome feelings of fear about sharing your testimony? How have you been blessed by the testimonies of others? (See section 4.)

Related Scriptures

1 Corinthians 12:3; 1 Peter 3:15; Alma 5:43–46; 32:26–30; Moroni 10:3–5; D&C 8:2–3; 80:3–5

Teaching Help

"As you come to know and understand each person, you will be better prepared to teach lessons that speak to their individual situations. This understanding will help you to find ways to help each person participate in discussions and other learning activities" (*Teaching, No Greater Call* [1999], 34).

Notes

1. "My Testimony," *Ensign,* May 2000, 70–71.
2. "Listen by the Power of the Spirit," *Ensign,* Nov. 1996, 5.
3. "Testimony," *Ensign,* May 1998, 69.
4. "Testimony," 69–70.
5. "Testimony," 70.
6. "It's True, Isn't It?" *Ensign,* July 1993, 2.
7. "It's True, Isn't It?" 5.
8. "It's True, Isn't It?" 6.

9. "It's True, Isn't It?" 5.

10. "Testimony," 70–71.

11. *Discourses of President Gordon B. Hinckley, Volume 2: 2000–2004* (2005), 369.

12. "A Perfect Brightness of Hope: To New Members of the Church," *Ensign,* Oct. 2006, 5.

President and Sister Hinckley enjoyed a happy and loving marriage and were strengthened by the "quiet and certain assurance of reunion and eternal companionship."

Nurturing the Eternal Partnership of Marriage

"The sweetest feelings of life, the most generous
and satisfying impulses of the human heart,
find expression in a marriage that stands pure
and unsullied above the evil of the world."

From the Life of Gordon B. Hinckley

One evening when President and Sister Hinckley were sitting quietly together, Sister Hinckley said, "You have always given me wings to fly, and I have loved you for it."[1] Commenting on that expression from his wife, President Hinckley said, "I've tried to recognize [her] individuality, her personality, her desires, her background, her ambitions. Let her fly. Yes, let her fly! Let her develop her own talents. Let her do things her way. Get out of her way, and marvel at what she does."[2] Sister Hinckley was likewise supportive of her husband—as a father, in his personal interests, and in his extensive Church service.

For most of their growing-up years, Gordon B. Hinckley and Marjorie Pay lived in the same ward, and for many years they lived across the street from each other. "I saw her first in Primary," President Hinckley later recalled. "She gave a reading. I don't know what it did to me, but I never forgot it. Then she grew older into a beautiful young woman, and I had the good sense to marry her."[3]

They had their first date—a Church dance—when he was 19 and she was 18. "This young man is going somewhere," Marjorie told her mother afterward.[4] Their relationship continued to grow while Gordon attended the University of Utah. Then in 1933, the year after he graduated, he was called to serve a mission to England. When he returned in 1935, they resumed their courtship, and in 1937 they were married in the Salt Lake Temple. Recalling the early part of their marriage, Sister Hinckley said:

"Money was scarce, but we were full of hope and optimism. Those early days were not all blissful, but they were filled with determination and a great desire to establish a happy home. We loved each other, there was no doubt about that. But we also had to get used to each other. I think every couple has to get used to each other.

"Early on I realized it would be better if we worked harder at getting accustomed to one another than constantly trying to change each other—which I discovered was impossible. . . . There must be a little give and take, and a great deal of flexibility, to make a happy home."[5]

President Hinckley was called as a General Authority in 1958, and during the early years of his service, Sister Hinckley typically stayed home to care for their five children while he traveled on Church assignments. When their children had grown, the Hinckleys often traveled together—something they cherished. In April 1977, their 40th wedding anniversary occurred while they were on a long journey to meet with the Saints in Australia. That day, President Hinckley reflected in his journal:

"We find ourselves today in Perth, Australia, our very presence being representative of what the years have brought to us. We have spent the day meeting with missionaries of the Australia Perth Mission. It has been a wonderful day in which we have heard testimonies and instruction. The missionaries presented Marjorie with a corsage, something I had not time to get for her myself.

"We could write quite a volume on the past 40 years. . . . We have had our struggles and our problems. But by and large, life has been good. We have been marvelously blessed. At this age, one begins to sense the meaning of eternity and the value of eternal companionship. Had we been at home tonight, we likely would have had some kind of a family dinner. As it is, we are far from home in the service of the Lord, and it is a sweet experience."[6]

Twenty-two years later, while serving as President of the Church, President Hinckley wrote a letter to Sister Hinckley expressing his feelings after more than 60 years of marriage. "What a treasured companion you have been," he said. "Now we have grown old together, and it has been a sweet experience. . . . When in some future day the hand of death gently touches one or the other of us there will be tears, yes, but there will also be a quiet and certain assurance of reunion and eternal companionship."[7]

In early 2004 the Hinckleys were on their way home from the dedication of the Accra Ghana Temple when Sister Hinckley collapsed with weariness. She never recovered her strength and passed away on April 6, 2004. Six months later in the October general conference, President Hinckley said:

"As I held her hand and saw mortal life drain from her fingers, I confess I was overcome. Before I married her, she had been the girl of my dreams. . . . She was my dear companion for more than two-thirds of a century, my equal before the Lord, really my superior. And now in my old age, she has again become the girl of my dreams."[8]

In his grief, President Hinckley was sustained by knowing that he and Marjorie had been sealed for eternity. "To lose one's much-loved partner with whom one has long walked through sunshine and shadow is absolutely devastating," he said. "There is a consuming loneliness which increases in intensity. It painfully gnaws at one's very soul. But in the quiet of the night a silent whisper is heard that says, 'All is well. All is well.' And that voice from out of the unknown brings peace, and certainty, and unwavering assurance that death is not the end, that life goes on, with work to do and victories to be gained. That voice quietly, even unheard with mortal ears, brings the assurance that, as surely as there has been separation, there will be a joyful reuniting."[9]

Teachings of Gordon B. Hinckley

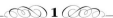 **1**

Heavenly Father designed marriage from the beginning.

How wonderful a thing is marriage under the plan of our Eternal Father, a plan provided in His divine wisdom for the happiness and security of His children and the continuity of the race.

He is our Creator, and He designed marriage from the beginning. At the time of Eve's creation, "Adam said, This is now bone of my bones, and flesh of my flesh: . . . Therefore shall a man leave his father and his mother, and shall cleave unto his wife: and they shall be one flesh." (Gen. 2:23–24.)

Paul wrote to the Corinthian Saints, "Neither is the man without the woman, neither the woman without the man, in the Lord." (1 Cor. 11:11.)

In modern revelation, the Lord has said, "And again, verily I say unto you, that whoso forbiddeth to marry is not ordained of God, for marriage is ordained of God unto man." (D&C 49:15.) . . .

Surely no one reading the scriptures, both ancient and modern, can doubt the divine concept of marriage. The sweetest feelings of life, the most generous and satisfying impulses of the human heart, find expression in a marriage that stands pure and unsullied above the evil of the world.

Such a marriage, I believe, is the desire—the hoped-for, the longed-for, the prayed-for desire—of men and women everywhere.[10]

2

In the temple, a husband and wife can be sealed together for all eternity.

[The] temples . . . offer blessings that are had nowhere else. All that occurs in these sacred houses has to do with the eternal nature of man. Here, husbands and wives and children are sealed together as families for all eternity. Marriage is not "until death do ye part." It is forever, if the parties live worthy of the blessing.[11]

Was there ever a man who truly loved a woman, or a woman who truly loved a man, who did not pray that their relationship might continue beyond the grave? Has a child ever been buried by parents who did not long for the assurance that their loved one would again be theirs in a world to come? Can anyone believing in eternal life doubt that the God of heaven would grant His sons and daughters that most precious attribute of life, the love that finds its most meaningful expression in family relationships? No, reason demands that the family relationship shall continue after death. The human heart longs for it, and the God of heaven has revealed a way whereby it may be secured. The sacred ordinances of the house of the Lord provide for it.[12]

How sweet is the assurance, how comforting is the peace that come from the knowledge that if we marry right and live right, our relationship will continue, notwithstanding the certainty of death and the passage of time. Men may write love songs and sing them. They may yearn and hope and dream. But all of this will be only a romantic longing unless there is an exercise of authority that transcends the powers of time and death.[13]

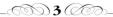

Husbands and wives walk side by side on an eternal journey.

In His grand design, when God first created man, He created a duality of the sexes. The ennobling expression of that duality is found in marriage. One individual is complementary to the other.[14]

In the marriage companionship there is neither inferiority nor superiority. The woman does not walk ahead of the man; neither does the man walk ahead of the woman. They walk side by side as a son and daughter of God on an eternal journey.[15]

Marriage, in its truest sense, is a partnership of equals, with neither exercising dominion over the other, but, rather, with each encouraging and assisting the other in whatever responsibilities and aspirations he or she might have.[16]

Wives, look upon your husbands as your precious companions and live worthy of that association. Husbands, see in your wives your most valued asset in time or eternity, each a daughter of God, a partner with whom you can walk hand in hand, through sunshine and storm, through all the perils and triumphs of life.[17]

I think of two [friends] I knew . . . in the years of high school and university. He was a boy from a country town, plain in appearance, without money or apparent promise. He had grown up on a farm, and if he had any quality that was attractive it was the capacity to work. . . . But with all of his rustic appearance, he had a smile and a personality that seemed to sing of goodness. She was a city girl who had come out of a comfortable home. . . .

Something of magic took place between them. They fell in love. . . . [They] laughed and danced and studied together through those years. They married when people wondered how they could ever earn enough to stay alive. He struggled through his professional school and came out near the top of his class. She scrimped and saved and worked and prayed. She encouraged and sustained and when things were really tough she said quietly, "Somehow we'll make it." Buoyed by her faith in him, he kept going through those difficult years. Their children came, and together they loved them and nourished them and gave them the security that came of their own example of love for and loyalty to one another. Now forty-five years and more have passed. Their children are grown and are a credit to them, to the Church, and to the communities in which they live.

Recently, while riding a plane from New York, I walked down the aisle in the semi-darkness of the cabin and saw a woman, white-haired, her head on her husband's shoulder as she dozed and his hand clasped warmly about hers. He was awake and recognized me. She awakened when we began to talk. They, too, were returning from New York, where he had delivered a paper before one of the great learned societies of the nation. He said little about it, but she proudly spoke of the honors accorded him. . . .

I thought of that as I returned to my seat on the plane. And I said to myself, their friends of those days saw only a farm boy from the country and a smiling girl with freckles on her nose. But these two saw in each other love, loyalty, peace, faith, and the future. Call it chemistry if you will; maybe there was a little of that, but there was much more. There was rather a flowering of something divine, planted there by that Father who is our God. In their school days they had lived worthy of that flowering. They had lived with virtue and faith, with appreciation and respect for self and one another. In the years of their difficult professional and economic struggles, they had found their greatest earthly strength in their companionship. Now in age they were finding their peace, their quiet satisfaction together. And beyond that they were assured of an eternity of joyful association under covenants long since made and promises long since given in the house of the Lord.[18]

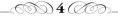

4

God will not withhold any blessings from worthy individuals who are not married.

Somehow we have put a badge on a very important group in the Church. It reads "Singles." I wish we would not do that. You are individuals, men and women, sons and daughters of God, not a mass of "look-alikes" or "do-alikes." Because you do not happen to be married does not make you essentially different from others. All of us are very much alike in appearance and emotional responses, in our capacity to think, to reason, to be miserable, to be happy, to love and be loved.

You are just as important as any others in the scheme of our Father in Heaven, and under His mercy no blessing to which you otherwise might be entitled will forever be withheld from you.[19]

Permit me now to say a word to those who have never had the opportunity to be married. I assure you that we are sensitive to the loneliness that many of you feel. Loneliness is a bitter and painful thing. I suppose all people have felt it at one time or another. Our hearts reach out to you with understanding and love. . . .

. . . This season of your lives can be wonderful. You have maturity. You have judgment. Most of you have training and experience. You have the physical, mental, and spiritual strength to lift and help and encourage.

There are so many out there who need you. . . . Keep your spiritual batteries at full charge and light the lamps of others.[20]

To you who have not married, . . . God has given you talents of one kind or another. He has given you the capacity to serve the needs of others and bless their lives with your kindness and concern. Reach out to someone in need. . . .

Add knowledge to knowledge. Refine your mind and skills in a chosen field of discipline. There are tremendous opportunities for you if you are prepared to take advantage of them. . . . Do not feel that because you are single, God has forsaken you. The world needs you. The Church needs you. So very many people and causes need your strength and wisdom and talents.

Be prayerful, and do not lose hope. . . . Live the very best life of which you are capable, and the Lord in his greater wisdom and in his eternal season will give you answer to your prayers.[21]

To you who are divorced, please know that we do not look down upon you as failures because a marriage failed. . . . Ours is the obligation not to condemn, but to forgive and to forget, to lift and to help. In your hours of desolation turn to the Lord, who said: "Come unto me, all ye that labour and are heavy laden, and I will give you rest. . . . For my yoke is easy, and my burden is light." (Matt. 11:28, 30.)

The Lord will not deny you nor turn you away. The answers to your prayers may not be dramatic; they may not be readily understood or even appreciated. But the time will come when you will know that you have been blessed.[22]

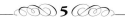 5

Happiness in marriage comes from showing a loving concern for the well-being of one's companion.

Nurture and cultivate your marriage. Guard it and work to keep it solid and beautiful. . . . Marriage is a contract, it is a compact, it is a union between a man and a woman under the plan of the Almighty. It can be fragile. It requires nurture and very much effort.[23]

After dealing with hundreds of divorce situations through the years, I am satisfied that the application of a single practice would do more than all else to solve this grievous problem.

If every husband and every wife would constantly do whatever might be possible to ensure the comfort and happiness of his or her companion, there would be very little, if any, divorce. Argument would never be heard. Accusations would never be leveled. Angry explosions would not occur. Rather, love and concern would replace abuse and meanness. . . .

*"Nurture and cultivate your marriage. Guard it
and work to keep it solid and beautiful."*

The cure for most marital troubles does not lie in divorce. It lies in repentance and forgiveness, in expressions of kindness and concern. It is to be found in application of the Golden Rule.

It is a scene of great beauty when a young man and a young woman join hands at the altar in a covenant before God that they will honor and love one another. Then how dismal the picture when a few months later, or a few years later, there are offensive remarks, mean and cutting words, raised voices, bitter accusations.

It need not be, my dear brothers and sisters. We can rise above these mean and beggarly elements in our lives (see Galatians 4:9). We can look for and recognize the divine nature in one another, which comes to us as children of our Father in Heaven. We can live together in the God-given pattern of marriage in accomplishing that of which we are capable if we will exercise discipline of self and refrain from trying to discipline our companion.[24]

Every marriage is subject to occasional stormy weather. But with patience, mutual respect, and a spirit of forbearance, we can weather these storms. Where mistakes have been made, there can be apology, repentance, and forgiveness. But there must be willingness to do so on the part of both parties. . . .

I have learned that the real essence of happiness in marriage lies . . . in an anxious concern for the comfort and well-being of one's companion. Thinking of self alone and of the gratification of personal desires will build neither trust, love, nor happiness. Only when there is unselfishness will love, with its concomitant qualities, flourish and blossom.[25]

Many of us need to stop looking for faults and begin to look for virtues. . . . Unfortunately, some women want to remake their husbands after their own design. Some husbands regard it as their prerogative to compel their wives to fit their standards of what they think to be the ideal. It never works. It only leads to contention, misunderstanding, and sorrow.

There must be respect for the interests of one another. There must be opportunities and encouragement for the development and expression of individual talent.[26]

Be absolutely true and faithful to your chosen companion. In terms of time and eternity, she or he will be the greatest asset you will ever have. She or he will be deserving of the very best that is within you.[27]

Suggestions for Study and Teaching

Questions

- President Hinckley taught that Heavenly Father designed marriage between a man and a woman "for the happiness and security of His children" (section 1). How can this knowledge influence the relationship between a husband and wife? How can a husband and wife keep their marriage "pure and unsullied above the evil of the world"?

- What are the blessings of an eternal marriage in this life and in eternity? (See section 2.) What experiences have given you greater appreciation for eternal relationships? How can we teach children the importance of eternal marriage?

- Why does marriage need to be "a partnership of equals"? (See section 3.) What do you learn from the story in section 3? How can a husband and wife cultivate this kind of strength in their marriage?

- How can President Hinckley's promises and counsel in section 4 help persons who are not married? How do the teachings in this section apply to all people? Why is it important to use our talents and skills to serve others?

- What are some ways a husband and wife can "nurture and cultivate" their marriage? (See section 5.) What have you learned about how a husband and wife can overcome challenges and find greater happiness together? What examples have you seen?

Related Scriptures

1 Corinthians 11:11; Matthew 19:3–6; D&C 42:22; 132:18–19; Moses 2:27–28; 3:18, 21–24

Study Help

"As you dedicate time every day, personally and with your family, to the study of God's word, peace will prevail in your life. That peace won't come from the outside world. It will come from within your home, from within your family, from within your own heart" (Richard G. Scott, "Make the Exercise of Faith Your First Priority," *Ensign* or *Liahona,* Nov. 2014, 93).

Notes

1. In "The Women in Our Lives," *Ensign* or *Liahona,* Nov. 2004, 85.
2. In "At Home with the Hinckleys," *Ensign,* Oct. 2003, 22.
3. In Jeffrey R. Holland, "President Gordon B. Hinckley: Stalwart and Brave He Stands," *Ensign,* June 1995, 10–11.
4. In *Glimpses into the Life and Heart of Marjorie Pay Hinckley,* ed. Virginia H. Pearce (1999), x.
5. In *Glimpses,* 184.
6. Gordon B. Hinckley journal, Apr. 29, 1977.
7. In Gerry Avant, "A Tender Farewell to an Elect Lady," *Church News,* Apr. 17, 2004, 4.
8. "The Women in Our Lives," 82.
9. In Marjorie Pay Hinckley, *Letters* (2004), 264; see also R. Scott Lloyd, "Apostle's Work Continues beyond Veil," *Church News,* July 31, 2004, 3.
10. "What God Hath Joined Together," *Ensign,* May 1991, 71.
11. "The Things of Which I Know," *Ensign* or *Liahona,* May 2007, 85.
12. "Why These Temples?" *Ensign,* Oct. 2010, 24; see also *Ensign,* Aug. 1974, 39–40.
13. "The Marriage That Endures," *Ensign,* July 2003, 6–7; see also *Ensign,* May 1974, 24.
14. "The Women in Our Lives," 84.
15. "Personal Worthiness to Exercise the Priesthood," *Ensign,* May 2002, 54.

CHAPTER 10

16. "I Believe," *Ensign,* Aug. 1992, 6.

17. "What God Hath Joined Together," 74.

18. "And the Greatest of These Is Love" (Brigham Young University devotional, Feb. 14, 1978), 2–3, speeches.byu.edu.

19. "To Single Adults," *Ensign,* June 1989, 72.

20. "To Single Adults," 72–73.

21. "Live Up to Your Inheritance," *Ensign,* Nov. 1983, 82–83.

22. "To Single Adults," 74.

23. "Walking in the Light of the Lord," *Ensign,* Nov. 1998, 99.

24. "The Women in Our Lives," 84.

25. "I Believe," 5–6.

26. *Cornerstones of a Happy Home* (pamphlet, 1984), 5–6.

27. "Thou Shalt Not Covet," *Ensign,* Mar. 1990, 6.

Home—The Basis of a Righteous Life

"The more surely you rear your children in the ways of the gospel of Jesus Christ, with love and high expectation, the more likely that there will be peace in their lives."

From the Life of Gordon B. Hinckley

In late 1973, Gordon and Marjorie Hinckley reluctantly decided to move from their home in East Mill Creek, Utah, so they could live closer to Church headquarters in Salt Lake City. President Hinckley, who was then a member of the Quorum of the Twelve Apostles, took time on New Year's Eve of that year to write about their home. His words revealed his feelings about the place, but even more, they revealed his feelings about a loving family.

"How sentimentally sad we are about leaving," he wrote. He recalled the family's labor to build the home and to develop its surrounding property. Then his thoughts turned to relationships—with one another and with God:

"Here we played together as our children grew, and here we prayed together. Here we and our children came to know our Heavenly Father, that He lives, and listens, and answers.

"I might go on to write a book . . . not for the world, but for those five children, their spouses and posterity. And if I can get into words the story of that home there will be tears and laughter, and a great, quiet, pervading spirit of love that will touch the hearts of those who read, for those who lived and grew there loved one another, they loved their neighbors, they loved their God and the Lord Jesus Christ."[1]

*"We call upon parents to devote their best efforts to
the teaching and rearing of their children."*

Throughout his ministry, President Hinckley testified of the importance of loving, faithful families. Under his direction, the First Presidency and Quorum of the Twelve Apostles issued "The Family: A Proclamation to the World," which Elder M. Russell Ballard of the Twelve described as "a clarion call to protect and strengthen families."[2] After reading the proclamation in the September 1995 general Relief Society meeting, President Hinckley declared: "The strength of any nation is rooted within the walls of its homes. We urge our people everywhere to strengthen their families in conformity with these time-honored values."[3]

Teachings of Gordon B. Hinckley

 **1**

Family relationships are the most sacred of all relationships.

The family is divine. It was instituted by our Heavenly Father. It encompasses the most sacred of all relationships. Only through its organization can the purposes of the Lord be fulfilled.[4]

We are a church which bears testimony of the importance of the family—the father, the mother, the children—and of the fact that we are all children of God our Eternal Father. Parents who bring children into the world have a responsibility to love those children, to nurture them and care for them, to teach them those values which would bless their lives so that they will grow to become good citizens. . . . I want to emphasize that which is already familiar to you, and that is the importance of binding our families together with love and kindness, with appreciation and respect, and with teaching the ways of the Lord so that your children will grow in righteousness and avoid the tragedies which are overcoming so many families across the world.[5]

It is imperative that you not neglect your families. Nothing you have is more precious.[6]

⟨⟨⟩⟩ **2** *⟨⟨⟩⟩*

Fathers and mothers have the privilege of caring for their children and teaching them the gospel of Jesus Christ.

We call upon parents to devote their best efforts to the teaching and rearing of their children in gospel principles which will keep them close to the Church. The home is the basis of a righteous life, and no other instrumentality can take its place or fulfill its essential functions in carrying forward this God-given responsibility.[7]

I am satisfied that nothing will assure greater success in the hazardous undertaking of parenthood than a program of family life that comes from the marvelous teaching of the gospel: that the father of the home may be clothed with the priesthood of God; that it is his privilege and obligation as a steward of our Heavenly Father's children to provide for their needs; that he is to govern in the home in the spirit of the priesthood "by persuasion, by long-suffering, by gentleness and meekness, and by love unfeigned" (D&C 121:41–42); that the mother in the home is a daughter of God, a soul of intelligence, devotion, and love who may be clothed with the Spirit of God; that it is her privilege and obligation as a steward of our Heavenly Father's children to nurture those children in their daily needs; that she, in companionship with her husband, is also to teach her children to "understand the doctrine of repentance, faith in Christ the Son of the living God, and of baptism and the gift of the Holy Ghost by the laying on of the hands . . . [and] to pray, and to walk uprightly before the Lord." (D&C 68:25, 28.)

In such a home, parents are loved and not dreaded; they are appreciated and not feared. And children are regarded as gifts of the Lord, to be cared for, nurtured, encouraged, and directed.

There may be an occasional disagreement; there may be small quarrels. But if there is prayer in the family, and love, and consideration, there will be a residue of affection that will bind forever and a loyalty that will always guide.[8]

Now a word to the single parents. . . . [You] carry exhausting burdens in fighting the daily battles that go with rearing children and seeing that their needs are met. This is a lonely duty. But you need not be entirely alone. There are many, ever so many in this

Church who would reach out to you with sensitivity and understanding. They do not wish to intrude where they are not wanted. But their interest is genuine and sincere, and they bless their own lives as they bless your lives and those of your children. Welcome their help. They need to give it for their own sakes as well as for your sake.

We have thousands of good bishops in this Church. We have thousands of good quorum officers. We have thousands of wonderful Relief Society women. We have home teachers and visiting teachers. They are your friends, put in place by the Lord to give of their strength to help you. And never forget that the Lord Himself is a source of strength greater than any other. I was touched by an experience recounted by . . . a single parent rearing seven children, when she pleaded to her Father in Heaven that she might go to Him, if only for a night, to find comfort and strength for the trials of tomorrow. Tender was the response that came into her mind almost as a revelation: "You cannot come to me, but I will come to you."[9]

The more surely you rear your children in the ways of the gospel of Jesus Christ, with love and high expectation, the more likely that there will be peace in their lives.[10]

Through family prayer, children grow with faith in the living God.

Behold your little ones. Pray with them. Pray for them and bless them. The world into which they are moving is a complex and difficult world. They will run into heavy seas of adversity. They will need all the strength and all the faith you can give them while they are yet near you. And they also will need a greater strength which comes of a higher power. They must do more than go along with what they find. They must lift the world, and the only levers they will have are the example of their own lives and the powers of persuasion that will come of their testimonies and their knowledge of the things of God. They will need the help of the Lord. While they are young, pray with them that they may come to know that source of strength which shall then always be available in every hour of need.[11]

I know of no other practice that will have so salutary an effect upon your lives as will the practice of kneeling together in prayer. The very words, Our Father in Heaven, have a tremendous effect. You cannot speak them with sincerity and with recognition without having some feeling of accountability to God. . . .

Your daily conversations with him will bring peace into your hearts and a joy into your lives that can come from no other source. . . . Your love will strengthen. Your appreciation for one another will grow.

Your children will be blessed with a sense of security that comes of living in a home where dwells the Spirit of God. They will know and love parents who respect one another, and a spirit of respect will grow in their own hearts. They will experience the security of kind words quietly spoken. They will be sheltered by a father and mother who, living honestly with God, live honestly with one another and with their fellowmen. They will mature with a sense of appreciation, having heard their parents in prayer express gratitude for blessings great and small. They will grow with faith in the living God.[12]

 **4**

Family home evening can draw parents and children together in learning the ways of the Lord.

I can remember when I was a small boy, five years old, President Joseph F. Smith announced to all the Church that they should gather their families together in family home evening. My father said, "The President of the Church has asked that we do it, and we are going to do it."

So we all gathered in family home evening. It was funny. He said, "We'll sing a song." Well, we were not singers. . . . We just tried to sing and laughed at one another. So we did with a lot of other things. But out of that experience there gradually came something that was wonderful—a practice that helped us, that drew us together as a family, that strengthened us, and there grew in our hearts a conviction of the value of family home evening.[13]

I am grateful that we as a Church have as a basic part of our program the practice of a weekly family home evening. It is a significant thing that in these busy days thousands of families across the world are making an earnest effort to consecrate one evening a week to sing together, to instruct one another in the ways of the Lord, to kneel together in prayer, there to thank the Lord for his mercies and to invoke his blessings upon our lives, our homes, our labors, our land. I think we little estimate the vast good that will come of this program.[14]

If you have any doubt about the virtue of family home evening, try it. Gather your children about you, teach them, bear testimony to them, read the scriptures together and have a good time together.[15]

Parents should begin to teach their children when the children are very young.

Not long after we were married, we built our first home. We had little money, and I did a lot of the work. The landscaping was entirely my responsibility. The first of many trees that I planted was a thornless honey locust, and I envisioned the day when its shade would assist in cooling the house in the summer. I put it in a place at the corner where the wind from the canyon to the east blew the hardest. I dug a hole, put in the bare root, put soil around it, poured on water, and largely forgot it. It was only a wisp of a tree, perhaps three-quarters of an inch [2 centimeters] in diameter. It was so supple that I could bend it with ease in any direction. I paid little attention to it as the years passed. Then one winter day when the tree was barren of leaves, I chanced to look out the window at it. I noted that it was leaning to the west, misshapen and out of balance. I could scarcely believe it. I went out and braced myself against it as if to push it upright. But the trunk was now nearly a foot in diameter. My strength was as nothing against it. I took from my toolshed a block and tackle, attaching one end to the tree and the other to a well-set post. I pulled the rope. The pulleys moved just a little, and the trunk of the tree trembled slightly. But that was all. It seemed to say to me, "You can't straighten me. It's too late. I've grown this way because of your neglect, and I will not bend."

Finally in desperation I took my saw and cut off the great heavy branch on the west side. I stepped back and surveyed what I had

"Gather your children about you, teach them, bear testimony to them, read the scriptures together and have a good time together."

done. I had cut off a major part of the tree, leaving a huge scar about eight inches [20 centimeters] across and only one small branch growing skyward.

. . . I recently looked again at the tree. It is large, its shape is better, and it is a great asset to the home. But how serious was the trauma of its youth and how painful the treatment I had used to straighten it. When the tree was first planted, a piece of string would have held it against the forces of the wind. I could have and should have supplied that string with ever so little effort, but I did not. And it bent to the forces that came against it.

Children are like trees. When they are young, their lives can be shaped and directed, usually with ever so little effort. Said the writer of Proverbs, "Train up a child in the way he should go: and when he is old, he will not depart from it" [Proverbs 22:6]. That training finds its roots in the home.[16]

Isaiah said, "All thy children shall be taught of the Lord; and great shall be the peace of thy children" (Isa. 54:13).

So lead your sons and daughters, so guide and direct them from the time they are very small, so teach them in the ways of the Lord, that peace will be their companion throughout life.[17]

 **6**

If children rebel, parents should continue to pray for them, love them, and reach out to them.

I recognize that there are parents who, notwithstanding an outpouring of love and a diligent and faithful effort to teach them, see their children grow in a contrary manner and weep while their wayward sons and daughters willfully pursue courses of tragic consequence. For such I have great sympathy, and to them I am wont to quote the words of Ezekiel: "The son shall not bear the iniquity of the father, neither shall the father bear the iniquity of the son" (Ezekiel 18:20).[18]

Once in a while, notwithstanding all the things you try to do, there is a rebellious child. But keep at it. Do not ever give up. You have never lost as long as you try. Keep at it.[19]

If any of you have a child or loved one in that condition [of rebelliousness], do not give up. Pray for them and love them and reach out to them and help them.[20]

Sometimes it may seem too late. . . . Yet, remember my thornless locust tree [see pages 171–72]. Surgery and suffering brought about something beautiful, whose later life has provided welcome shade from the heat of the day.[21]

 **7**

We strengthen our families as we seek heaven's help and nurture a spirit of love and respect for each other.

[Raising a family] may not be easy. It may be fraught with disappointment and challenge. It will require courage and patience. . . . Love can make the difference—love generously given in childhood and reaching through the awkward years of youth. It will do what money lavished on children will never do.

—And patience, with a bridling of the tongue and self-mastery over anger. . . .

—And encouragement that is quick to compliment and slow to criticize.

These, with prayers, will accomplish wonders. You cannot expect to do it alone. You need heaven's help in raising heaven's child—your child, who is also the child of his or her Heavenly Father.[22]

Every child, with few possible exceptions, is the product of a home, be it good, bad, or indifferent. As children grow through the years, their lives, in large measure, become an extension and a reflection of family teaching. If there is harshness, abuse, uncontrolled anger, disloyalty, the fruits will be certain and discernible, and in all likelihood they will be repeated in the generation that follows. If, on the other hand, there is forbearance, forgiveness, respect, consideration, kindness, mercy, and compassion, the fruits again will be discernible, and they will be eternally rewarding. They will be positive and sweet and wonderful. And as mercy is given and taught by parents, it will be repeated in the lives and actions of the next generation.

I speak to fathers and mothers everywhere with a plea to put harshness behind us, to bridle our anger, to lower our voices, and to deal with mercy and love and respect one toward another in our homes.[23]

It was said of old that "a soft answer turneth away wrath." (Prov. 15:1.) We seldom get into trouble when we speak softly. It is only when we raise our voices that the sparks fly and tiny molehills become great mountains of contention. . . . The voice of heaven is a still small voice [see 1 Kings 19:11–12]; likewise, the voice of domestic peace is a quiet voice.[24]

Of course, there is need for discipline with families. But discipline with severity, discipline with cruelty inevitably leads not to correction but rather to resentment and bitterness. It cures nothing and only aggravates the problem. It is self-defeating.[25]

There is no discipline in all the world like the discipline of love. It has a magic all its own.[26]

Let us continually work to strengthen our families. Let husbands and wives cultivate a spirit of absolute loyalty one to another. Let us not take one another for granted, but let us constantly work to nurture a spirit of love and respect for each other.[27]

O God, our Eternal Father, bless the parents to teach with love and patience and encouragement those who are most precious, the children who have come from Thee, that together they might be safeguarded and directed for good and, in the process of growth, bring blessings to the world of which they will be a part.[28]

Suggestions for Study and Teaching

Questions

- President Hinckley taught that the family "encompasses the most sacred of all relationships" (section 1). How might this truth affect our relationships with family members? How might it affect the way we prioritize our time and activities?

- Why should parents "devote their best efforts to the teaching and rearing of their children in gospel principles"? (See section 2.) How has gospel teaching in your home blessed your family? How can parents improve in their efforts to help their children live the gospel?

- Review President Hinckley's teachings about the blessings of family prayer (see section 3). Why do you think family prayer brings blessings? What blessings have you experienced by having regular family prayer? What do we lose if we neglect family prayer?

- What can we learn from Gordon B. Hinckley's experience with family home evening as a young boy? (See section 4.) What blessings have come to your family through family home evening?

- Review President Hinckley's story of the honey locust tree (see section 5). What applications could this story have for you?

- How can President Hinckley's teachings in section 6 help the parents of a child who is wayward? What are some ways that parents and others can reach out in love?

- Why is it important for parents to discipline their children with love rather than anger? What are some things parents can do to discipline with love? How can family members nurture a spirit of love and respect for each other? (See section 7.)

Related Scriptures

Deuteronomy 11:19; Enos 1:1–5; Mosiah 4:14–15; Alma 56:45–48; 3 Nephi 18:21; see also "The Family: A Proclamation to the World," *Ensign* or *Liahona,* Nov. 2010, 129

Teaching Help

"You may feel that you lack understanding of a certain principle that you are preparing to teach. However, as you prayerfully study it, strive to live it, prepare to teach it, and then share it with others, your own testimony will be strengthened and deepened" (*Teaching, No Greater Call* [1999], 19).

Notes

1. In Sheri L. Dew, *Go Forward with Faith: The Biography of Gordon B. Hinckley* (1996), 333.
2. M. Russell Ballard, in "Today's Family: Proclamation Still a Clarion Call," lds.org/prophets-and-apostles/unto-all-the-world/proclamation-on-family-is-still-a-clarion-call; accessed May 12, 2015.
3. "Stand Strong against the Wiles of the World," *Ensign,* Nov. 1995, 101.
4. "Pillars of Truth," *Ensign,* Jan. 1994, 5.
5. *Teachings of Gordon B. Hinckley* (1997), 208.
6. *Discourses of President Gordon B. Hinckley, Volume 2: 2000–2004* (2005), 387.
7. First Presidency letter, Feb. 11, 1999, in "Policies, Announcements, and Appointments," *Ensign,* June 1999, 80.
8. "Pillars of Truth," 5.
9. "To Single Adults," *Ensign,* June 1989, 74.
10. "Stand Strong against the Wiles of the World," 99.
11. "Behold Your Little Ones," *Ensign,* June 2001, 5.
12. *Cornerstones of a Happy Home* (pamphlet, 1984), 10–11.
13. *Discourses of President Gordon B. Hinckley, Volume 2,* 402.
14. In Conference Report, Oct. 1965, 51.
15. *Teachings of Gordon B. Hinckley,* 212.
16. "Four Simple Things to Help Our Families and Our Nations," *Ensign,* Sept. 1996, 6–7.
17. "Great Shall Be the Peace of Thy Children," *Ensign,* Nov. 2000, 52.
18. "These, Our Little Ones," *Ensign,* Dec. 2007, 8.
19. "Inspirational Thoughts," *Ensign,* Aug. 1997, 4.
20. *Teachings of Gordon B. Hinckley,* 54.
21. "Four Simple Things to Help Our Families and Our Nations," 8.
22. "Bring Up a Child in the Way He Should Go," *Ensign,* Nov. 1993, 60.
23. "Blessed Are the Merciful," *Ensign,* May 1990, 70.
24. "Except the Lord Build the House . . ." *Ensign,* June 1971, 72.
25. "Behold Your Little Ones," 4.
26. "The Environment of Our Homes," *Ensign,* June 1985, 6.
27. "Thanks to the Lord for His Blessings," *Ensign,* May 1999, 88–89.
28. "Bring Up a Child in the Way He Should Go," 60.

Obedience:
Simply Live the Gospel

"The way of the gospel is a simple way. . . .
Humble yourselves and walk in obedience."

From the Life of Gordon B. Hinckley

When Gordon B. Hinckley was about 14 years old, he had an experience in the Salt Lake Tabernacle that stirred him to make an important resolution. He later recalled:

"I [heard] President Heber J. Grant tell of his experience in reading the Book of Mormon when he was a boy. He spoke of Nephi and of the great influence he had upon his life. And then, with a voice ringing with a conviction that I shall never forget, he quoted those great words of Nephi: 'I will go and do the things which the Lord hath commanded, for I know that the Lord giveth no commandments unto the children of men, save he shall prepare a way for them that they may accomplish the thing which he commandeth them' (1 Ne. 3:7).

"There came into my young heart on that occasion a resolution to try to do what the Lord has commanded."[1]

Gordon B. Hinckley always carried that resolution in his heart. Years later, when he was President of the Church, his teachings hearkened back to the message he had heard as a young man. Speaking to a group of Latter-day Saints at a regional conference, he said:

"I have been interviewed by many [news] reporters. The one thing they say is, 'Now what is going to be your theme during your presidency?' I simply say, 'The same theme which I have heard repeated in this Church by the presidents of the Church and the apostles for as far back as I can remember: Simply live the gospel, and

Nephi's example of obedience inspired young Gordon B. Hinckley.

every one who does so will receive in his heart a conviction of the truth of that which he lives.'"[2]

In his first general conference as President of the Church, President Hinckley issued a call for all to try harder to live the gospel:

"Now, my brethren and sisters, the time has come for us to stand a little taller, to lift our eyes and stretch our minds to a greater comprehension and understanding of the grand millennial mission of this The Church of Jesus Christ of Latter-day Saints. This is a season to be strong. It is a time to move forward without hesitation, knowing well the meaning, the breadth, and the importance of our mission. It is a time to do what is right regardless of the consequences that might follow. It is a time to be found keeping the commandments. It is a season to reach out with kindness and love to those in distress and to those who are wandering in darkness and pain. It is a time to be considerate and good, decent and courteous toward one another in all of our relationships. In other words, to become more Christlike."[3]

President Hinckley continued to emphasize this message. Ten years later he repeated these words in general conference and followed up by saying, "You must be the judge of how far we have come in realizing the fulfillment of that invitation given 10 years ago."[4]

Teachings of Gordon B. Hinckley

We are a covenant people, and great are the obligations that go with that covenant.

We are a covenant people, and that is a very serious matter. When this work was restored and the Lord set forth the purposes for that restoration, He said that one reason for the restoration was that His everlasting covenant might be reestablished. That covenant . . . was made between Abraham and Jehovah when the mighty Jehovah made a great and solemn promise to Abraham. He said that his seed should become as the sand upon the seashore, that all nations would be blessed through him. He made this covenant with him, that He would be their God and they would be His people. . . .

"Each time we partake of the sacrament, . . . we take upon ourselves the name of Jesus Christ and pledge ourselves to keep His commandments."

There was established then a relationship that was of eternal consequence in the eternal lives of all who would enter into it. Marvelous are its implications: if we will act as the children of God should act, He will be our God to bless us, to love us, to direct us, to help us.

Now, in this dispensation, that everlasting covenant has been reaffirmed. We, in effect, made that covenant when we were baptized. We became a part of His divine family, as it were. All of God's children are of His family, but in a particular and wonderful way there is a special relationship between God and the children of His covenant. And when we came into the Church, . . . we became a part of a covenant people; and each time we partake of the sacrament, not only do we do it in remembrance of the sacrifice of the Son of God, who gave His life for each of us, but there is the added element that we take upon ourselves the name of Jesus Christ and pledge ourselves to keep His commandments and He pledges with us that He will bless us with His Holy Spirit.

We are a covenant people, and great are the obligations which go with that covenant. We cannot be ordinary people. We must rise above the crowd. We must stand a little taller. We must be a little better, a little kinder, a little more generous, a little more courteous, a little more thoughtful, a little more outreaching to others.[5]

We are a people who have taken upon us a solemn covenant and the name of the Lord Jesus Christ. Let us strive a little harder to keep the commandments, to live as the Lord has asked us to live.[6]

 **2**

The Lord expects us to live the gospel in every aspect.

We live in an age of compromise and acquiescence. In situations with which we are daily confronted, we know what is right, but under pressure from our peers and the beguiling voices of those who would persuade us, we capitulate. We compromise. We acquiesce. We give in, and we are ashamed of ourselves. . . . We must cultivate the strength to follow our convictions.[7]

The way of the gospel is a simple way. Some of the requirements may appear to you as elementary and unnecessary. Do not spurn them. Humble yourselves and walk in obedience. I promise that the results that follow will be marvelous to behold and satisfying to experience.[8]

My great plea is that we all try a little harder to live up to the stature of divinity that is within us. We can do better than we are doing. We can be better than we are. If we would hold before us that image constantly of divine inheritance, of the Fatherhood of God and the brotherhood of man as realities, we would be a little more tolerant, a little more kindly, a little more outreaching to lift and help and sustain those among us. We would be less prone to stoop to those things which clearly are unbecoming [of] us.[9]

The religion of which you are a part is seven days a week, it isn't just Sunday. . . . It's all the time—twenty-four hours a day, seven days a week, 365 days a year.[10]

The Lord expects that we will keep our lives in order, that we will live the gospel in every aspect.[11]

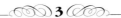

God will shower down blessings upon those who walk in obedience to His commandments.

The Lord told Elijah to go and hide himself by the brook Cherith, that there he should drink of the brook, and that he would be fed by the ravens. The scripture records a simple and wonderful statement about Elijah: "So he went and did according unto the word of the Lord" (1 Kgs. 17:5).

There was no arguing. There was no excusing. There was no equivocating. Elijah simply "went and did according unto the word of the Lord." And he was saved from the terrible calamities that befell those who scoffed and argued and questioned.[12]

The whole story of the Book of Mormon is a story that speaks of the people who, when they were righteous, when they worshipped Jesus Christ, prospered in the land and were richly and abundantly blessed of the Lord; and when they sinned and went astray and forgot their God, they fell into misery and war and trouble. Your safety, your peace, your prosperity lie in obedience to the commandments of the Almighty.[13]

"Keep my commandments continually, and a crown of righteousness thou shalt receive." [D&C 25:15.] That was the promise of the Lord to Emma Hale Smith. It is the promise of the Lord to each of you. Happiness lies in keeping the commandments. For a Latter-day Saint . . . there can be only misery in the violation of those commandments. And for each who observes them, there is the promise of a crown . . . of righteousness and eternal truth.[14]

True freedom lies in obedience to the counsels of God. It was said of old that "the commandment is a lamp; and the law is light." (Prov. 6:23.)

The gospel is not a philosophy of repression, as so many regard it. It is a plan of freedom that gives discipline to appetite and direction to behavior. Its fruits are sweet and its rewards are liberal. . . .

"Stand fast therefore in the liberty wherewith Christ hath made us free, and be not entangled again with the yoke of bondage." (Gal. 5:1.)

"Where the Spirit of the Lord is, there is liberty." (2 Cor. 3:17.)[15]

Our safety lies in repentance. Our strength comes of obedience to the commandments of God. . . . Let us stand firm against evil, both at home and abroad. Let us live worthy of the blessings of heaven, reforming our lives where necessary and looking to Him, the Father of us all.[16]

We have nothing to fear. God is at the helm. He will overrule for the good of this work. He will shower down blessings upon those who walk in obedience to His commandments. Such has been His promise. Of His ability to keep that promise none of us can doubt.[17]

Church leaders point out the way and invite members to live the gospel.

There are those who say, "The Church won't dictate to me how to think about this, that, or the other, or how to live my life."

No, I reply, the Church will not dictate to any man how he should think or what he should do. The Church will point out the way and invite every member to live the gospel and enjoy the blessings that come of such living. The Church will not dictate to any man, but it will counsel, it will persuade, it will urge, and it will expect loyalty from those who profess membership therein.

When I was a university student, I said to my father on one occasion that I felt the General Authorities had overstepped their prerogatives when they advocated a certain thing. He was a very wise and good man. He said, "The President of the Church has instructed us, and I sustain him as prophet, seer, and revelator and intend to follow his counsel."

I have . . . served in the general councils of this Church for [many] years. . . . I want to give you my testimony that although I have sat in literally thousands of meetings where Church policies and programs have been discussed, I have never been in one where the guidance of the Lord was not sought nor where there was any desire on the part of anyone present to advocate or do anything which would be injurious or coercive to anyone.[18]

I say for each and all that we [who sit in the general councils of the Church] have no personal agenda. We have only the Lord's agenda. There are those who criticize when we issue a statement of counsel or warning. Please know that our pleadings are not motivated by any selfish desire. Please know that our warnings are not without substance and reason. Please know that the decisions to speak out on various matters are not reached without deliberation, discussion, and prayer. Please know that our only ambition is to help each of you with your problems, your struggles, your families, your lives. . . . There is no desire to teach anything other than what the Lord would have taught. . . .

Ours is the responsibility outlined by Ezekiel: "Son of man, I have made thee a watchman unto the house of Israel: therefore hear the word at my mouth, and give them warning from me." (Ezek. 3:17.)

We have no selfish desire in any of this, other than the wish that our brethren and sisters will be happy, that peace and love will be found in their homes, that they will be blessed by the power of the Almighty in their various undertakings in righteousness.[19]

God is constantly making known, in his way, his will concerning his people. I give you my witness that the leaders of this church will never ask us to do anything that we cannot perform with the help of the Lord. We may feel inadequate. That which we are asked to do may not be to our liking or fit in with our ideas. But if we will try with faith and prayer and resolution, we can accomplish it.

I give you my testimony that the happiness of the Latter-day Saints, the peace of the Latter-day Saints, the progress of the Latter-day Saints, the prosperity of the Latter-day Saints, and the eternal salvation and exaltation of this people lie in walking in obedience to the counsels of the priesthood of God.[20]

Small decisions can lead to tremendous consequences.

I can describe a principle . . . which, if observed, will greatly increase the probability that our decisions will be correct, and consequently that our progress and happiness in life will be immeasurably increased. This great principle is *keep the faith.* . . .

I cannot tell you in detail how to decide everything. But I can promise that if you will make your decisions according to the standards of the gospel and the teachings of the Church, and if you will keep the faith, your lives will bear fruit of great good and you will know much of happiness and accomplishment.[21]

Many years ago I worked for a railroad. . . . That was in the days when nearly everyone rode passenger trains. One morning I received a call from my counterpart in Newark, New Jersey. He said, "Train number such-and-such has arrived, but it has no baggage car. Somewhere, 300 passengers have lost their baggage, and they are mad."

I went immediately to work to find out where it may have gone. I found it had been properly loaded and properly trained in Oakland, California. It had been moved to our railroad in Salt Lake City [and had eventually arrived in] St. Louis. There it was to be handled by another railroad which would take it to Newark, New Jersey. But some thoughtless switchman in the St. Louis yards moved a small piece of steel just three inches [7.5 centimeters], a switch point, then pulled the lever to uncouple the car. We discovered that a baggage car that belonged in Newark, New Jersey, was in fact in New Orleans, Louisiana—1,500 miles [2,400 kilometers] from its destination. Just the three-inch movement of the switch in the St. Louis yard by a careless employee had started it on the wrong track, and the distance from its true destination increased dramatically. That is the way it is with our lives. Instead of following a steady course, we are pulled by some mistaken idea in another direction. The movement away from our original destination may be ever so small, but, if continued, that very small movement becomes a great gap and we find ourselves far from where we intended to go. . . . It is the little things upon which life turns that make the big difference in our lives.[22]

I approached a large farm gate one day. I lifted the latch and opened the gate. The movement at the hinges was so slight as to be scarcely discernible. But the other end of the gate cut a great arc sixteen feet in radius. Looking at the movement of the hinges alone, one would never dream of the magnified action that came as a result of that tiny movement.

President Hinckley compared our decisions to hinges on a farm gate.

So it is with the decisions in our lives. Some small thought, some small word, some small action can lead to tremendous consequences.[23]

By living the gospel, we strengthen the Church and help God's work grow across the earth.

You can make [the Church] stronger by the manner in which you live. Let the gospel be your sword and your shield. . . .

. . . How magnificent will be the future as the Almighty rolls on His glorious work, touching for good all who will accept and live His gospel.[24]

I see a wonderful future in a very uncertain world. If we will cling to our values, if we will build on our inheritance, if we will walk in obedience before the Lord, if we will simply live the gospel, we will be blessed in a magnificent and wonderful way. We will be looked upon as a peculiar people who have found the key to a peculiar happiness.[25]

Let every man and woman and child resolve to make the work of the Lord better and stronger and greater than it has ever been before. It is the quality of our lives that makes the difference. It is our resolution to live the gospel of Jesus Christ that makes the difference. This is an individual matter. If we all pray, the Church is so much the stronger. And so it is with every principle of the gospel. Let us be part of this great forward-moving cause that is growing across the entire earth. We cannot stand still; we have to move forward. It is imperative that we do so. The personal conviction that dwells in each of our hearts is the real strength of the Church. Without it, we have very little of anything; with it, we have everything.[26]

I invite every one of you, wherever you may be as members of this church, to stand on your feet and with a song in your heart move forward, living the gospel, loving the Lord, and building the kingdom. Together we shall stay the course and keep the faith, the Almighty being our strength.[27]

Suggestions for Study and Teaching

Questions

- Why is it that we, as the Lord's covenant people, "cannot be ordinary people"? (See section 1.) What are some ways the covenants you have made with God influence your daily living?

- President Hinckley taught that "we must cultivate the strength to follow our convictions" (section 2). How do we sometimes compromise our convictions? How can we strengthen ourselves to resist temptation?

- What applications does President Hinckley's telling of the story of Elijah have for us? (See section 3.) How would you respond to someone who feels that the commandments are too restricting? How have you seen that obeying the commandments brings freedom, safety, and peace?

- Review President Hinckley's explanation of how Church leaders give counsel and warnings (see section 4). How have you been blessed by following the counsel of Church leaders?

- What can we learn from President Hinckley's story of the lost luggage car? (See section 5.) Why do small decisions or actions make such a big difference in our lives? What is a small decision that has made a big difference in your life? How can we better recognize small deviations that could lead us away from God's path?

• How can living the gospel help us cope with uncertainties in the world? (See section 6.) How can living the gospel simplify our lives? Consider how you could more actively strengthen the Church and help God's work grow across the earth.

Related Scriptures

Deuteronomy 4:39–40; Hebrews 5:8–9; D&C 64:33–34; 93:26–28; 98:22; Abraham 3:24–26; Articles of Faith 1:3

Study Help

"Reading, studying, and pondering are not the same. We read words and we may get ideas. We study and we may discover patterns and connections in scripture. But when we ponder, we invite revelation by the Spirit. Pondering, to me, is the thinking and the praying I do after reading and studying in the scriptures carefully" (Henry B. Eyring, "Serve with the Spirit," *Ensign* or *Liahona,* Nov. 2010, 60).

Notes

1. "If Ye Be Willing and Obedient," *Ensign,* July 1995, 2.

2. *Teachings of Gordon B. Hinckley* (1997), 404.

3. "This Is the Work of the Master," *Ensign,* May 1995, 71.

4. "Opening Remarks," *Ensign* or *Liahona,* May 2005, 4.

5. *Teachings of Gordon B. Hinckley,* 148–49.

6. *Teachings of Gordon B. Hinckley,* 146.

7. "Building Your Tabernacle," *Ensign,* Nov. 1992, 52.

8. "Everything to Gain—Nothing to Lose," *Ensign,* Nov. 1976, 96.

9. *Teachings of Gordon B. Hinckley,* 160–61.

10. *Teachings of Gordon B. Hinckley,* 404.

11. *Discourses of President Gordon B. Hinckley, Volume 2: 2000–2004* (2005), 412.

12. "If Ye Be Willing and Obedient," 4.

13. *Teachings of Gordon B. Hinckley,* 406–7.

14. "If Thou Art Faithful," *Ensign,* Nov. 1984, 92.

15. In Conference Report, Apr. 1965, 78.

16. "The Times in Which We Live," *Ensign,* Nov. 2001, 74.

17. "This Is the Work of the Master," 71.

18. "Loyalty," *Ensign* or *Liahona,* May 2003, 60.

19. "The Church Is on Course," *Ensign,* Nov. 1992, 59–60.

20. "If Ye Be Willing and Obedient," *Ensign,* Dec. 1971, 125.

21. "Keep the Faith," *Ensign,* Sept. 1985, 3, 6.

22. "A Prophet's Counsel and Prayer for Youth," *Ensign,* Jan. 2001, 5–7.

23. "Keep the Faith," 3.

24. "Stay the Course—Keep the Faith," *Ensign,* Nov. 1995, 72.

25. "Look to the Future," *Ensign,* Nov. 1997, 69.

26. *Teachings of Gordon B. Hinckley,* 138–39.

27. "Stay the Course—Keep the Faith," 72.

Peace and Contentment through Temporal Self-Reliance

*"We teach self-reliance as a principle of
life, that we ought to provide for ourselves
and take care of our own needs."*

From the Life of Gordon B. Hinckley

As a child, Gordon B. Hinckley learned principles of self-reliance while he worked with his parents and siblings. He later recalled:

"We lived in what I thought was a large home. . . . There was a big lawn, with many trees that shed millions of leaves, and an immense amount of work to be done constantly.

". . . We had a stove in the kitchen and a stove in the dining room. A furnace was later installed, and what a wonderful thing that was. But it had a voracious appetite for coal, and there was no automatic stoker. The coal had to be shoveled into the furnace and carefully banked each night.

"I learned a great lesson from that monster of a furnace: if you wanted to keep warm, you had to work the shovel.

"My father had an idea that his boys ought to learn to work, in the summer as well as in the winter, and so he bought a five-acre farm [about 20,000 square meters], which eventually grew to include more than thirty acres. We lived there in the summer and returned to the city when school started.

"We had a large orchard, and the trees had to be pruned each spring. Father took us to pruning demonstrations put on by experts from the agriculture college. We learned a great truth—that you could pretty well determine the kind of fruit you would pick in September by the way you pruned in February."[1]

*"There is no substitute under the heavens for productive labor.
It is the process by which dreams become realities."*

With these truths as part of his personal foundation, President Hinckley often taught practical lessons of gospel living. He testified of the blessings that come through hard work, and he encouraged Latter-day Saints to live within their means and prepare themselves for calamities that could come in the future.

In addition to teaching these principles, President Hinckley helped provide ways for the Saints to follow them. For example, in April 2001 he introduced the Perpetual Education Fund, which he said was inspired by the Lord.[2] Through this program, people could donate to a fund that would provide short-term loans to help qualified Church members, mostly returned missionaries, gain education or vocational training that would lead to meaningful employment. When people repaid those loans, that money would be included in the fund to help future participants. The Perpetual Education Fund has helped tens of thousands of people become self-reliant. It provides, as President Hinckley once said, a "bright ray of hope."[3]

Teachings of Gordon B. Hinckley

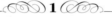

As we work with integrity, our lives are blessed forever.

I believe in the gospel of work. There is no substitute under the heavens for productive labor. It is the process by which dreams become realities. It is the process by which idle visions become dynamic achievements.[4]

A little play and a little loafing are good. But it is work that spells the difference in the life of a man or woman. It is work that provides the food we eat, the clothing we wear, the homes in which we live. We cannot deny the need for work with skilled hands and educated minds if we are to grow and prosper individually and collectively.[5]

I have discovered that life is not a series of great heroic acts. Life at its best is a matter of consistent goodness and decency, doing without fanfare that which needed to be done when it needed to be done. I have observed that it is not the geniuses that make the difference in this world. I have observed that the work of the world

"Children need to work with their parents. . . . They will learn that labor is the price of cleanliness and progress and prosperity."

is done largely by men and women of ordinary talent who have worked in an extraordinary manner.[6]

Children need to work with their parents—to wash dishes with them, to mop floors with them, to mow lawns, to prune trees and shrubbery, to paint and fix up and clean up and do a hundred other things where they will learn that labor is the price of cleanliness and progress and prosperity.[7]

The great genius of this Church is work. Everybody works. You do not grow unless you work. Faith, testimony of the truth, is just like the muscle of my arm. If you use it, it grows strong. If you put it in a sling, it grows weak and flabby. We put people to work. We expect great things of them, and the marvelous and wonderful thing is they come through. They produce.[8]

Nothing happens in this Church unless you work. It is like a wheelbarrow. It doesn't move until you get ahold of the two handles and push. Hard work moves the work of the Lord forward, and if you have learned to work with real integrity it will bless your lives forever. I mean that with all my heart. It will bless your lives forever.[9]

2

We have a responsibility to help others lift themselves and become self-reliant.

There is an old saying that if you give a man a fish, he will have a meal for a day. But if you teach him how to fish, he will eat for the remainder of his life. . . .

May the Lord grant us vision and understanding to do those things which will help our members not only spiritually but also temporally. We have resting upon us a very serious obligation. President Joseph F. Smith said . . . that a religion which will not help a man in this life will not likely do much for him in the life to come (see "The Truth about Mormonism," *Out West* magazine, Sept. 1905, 242).

Where there is widespread poverty among our people, we must do all we can to help them to lift themselves, to establish their lives upon a foundation of self-reliance that can come of training. Education is the key to opportunity. . . .

It is our solemn obligation . . . to "succor the weak, lift up the hands which hang down, and strengthen the feeble knees" (D&C 81:5). We must help them to become self-reliant and successful.

I believe the Lord does not wish to see His people condemned to live in poverty. I believe He would have the faithful enjoy the good things of the earth. He would have us do these things to help them.[10]

The individual, as we teach, ought to do for himself all that he can. When he has exhausted his resources, he ought to turn to his family to assist him. When the family can't do it, the Church takes over. And when the Church takes over, our great desire is to first take care of his immediate needs and then to help him for so long as he needs to be helped, but in that process to assist him in training, in securing employment, in finding some way of getting on his feet again. That's the whole objective of [the Church's] great welfare program.[11]

Those who have participated as the recipients of this program have been spared "the curse of idleness and the evils of the dole." Their dignity and self-respect have been preserved. And those myriads of men and women who have not been direct recipients, but who have participated in the growing and processing of food and in scores of associated undertakings, bear testimony of the joy to be found in unselfish service to others.

No one witnessing this program in its vast implications and in its tremendous consequences can reasonably doubt the spirit of revelation that brought it about and that has enlarged its practical power for good.[12]

We shall go on in this work. There will always be a need. Hunger and want and catastrophes will ever be with us. And there will always be those whose hearts have been touched by the light of the gospel who will be willing to serve and work and lift the needy of the earth.

As a correlated effort we have established the Perpetual Education Fund. It has come about through your generous contributions. . . . Loans are extended to worthy young men and women for education. Otherwise, they would be trapped in the stagnated poverty their parents and forebears have known for generations. . . .

The Spirit of the Lord guides this work. This welfare activity is secular activity, expressing itself in terms of rice and beans, of blankets and tents, of clothing and medicine, of employment and education for better employment. But this so-called secular work is but an outward expression of an inward spirit—the Spirit of the Lord, of whom it was said, He "went about doing good" (Acts 10:38).[13]

_____ ⟨⟨⟩⟩ 3 ⟨⟨⟩⟩ _____

Prophets have encouraged us to prepare ourselves spiritually and temporally for catastrophes to come.

We teach self-reliance as a principle of life, that we ought to provide for ourselves and take care of our own needs. And so we encourage our people to have something, to plan ahead, keep . . . food on hand, to establish a savings account, if possible, against a rainy day. Catastrophes come to people sometimes when least expected—unemployment, sickness, things of that kind.[14]

This old world is no stranger to calamities and catastrophes. Those of us who read and believe the scriptures are aware of the warnings of prophets concerning catastrophes that have come to pass and are yet to come to pass. . . .

How portentous are the words of revelation found in the 88th section of the Doctrine and Covenants concerning the calamities that should befall after the testimonies of the elders. The Lord says:

"For after your testimony cometh the testimony of earthquakes, that shall cause groanings in the midst of her, and men shall fall upon the ground and shall not be able to stand.

"And also cometh the testimony of the voice of thunderings, and the voice of lightnings, and the voice of tempests, and the voice of the waves of the sea heaving themselves beyond their bounds.

"And all things shall be in commotion; and surely, men's hearts shall fail them; for fear shall come upon all people" (D&C 88:89–91). . . .

. . . Just as there have been calamities in the past, we expect more in the future. What do we do?

Someone has said it was not raining when Noah built the ark. But he built it, and the rains came.

The Lord has said, "If ye are prepared ye shall not fear" (D&C 38:30).

The primary preparation is also set forth in the Doctrine and Covenants, wherein it says, "Wherefore, stand ye in holy places, and be not moved, until the day of the Lord come" (D&C 87:8). . . .

We can so live that we can call upon the Lord for His protection and guidance. This is a first priority. We cannot expect His help if we are unwilling to keep His commandments. We in this Church have evidence enough of the penalties of disobedience in the examples of both the Jaredite and the Nephite nations. Each went from glory to utter destruction because of wickedness.

We know, of course, that the rain falls on the just as well as the unjust (see Matthew 5:45). But even though the just die they are not lost, but are saved through the Atonement of the Redeemer. Paul wrote to the Romans, "For whether we live, we live unto the Lord; and whether we die, we die unto the Lord" (Romans 14:8). . . .

Our people . . . have been counseled and encouraged to make such preparation as will assure survival should a calamity come.

We can set aside some water, basic food, medicine, and clothing to keep us warm. We ought to have a little money laid aside in case of a rainy day.[15]

We have a great welfare program with facilities for such things as grain storage in various areas. It is important that we do this. But the best place to have some food set aside is within our homes, together with a little money in savings. The best welfare program is our own welfare program. Five or six cans of wheat in the home are better than a bushel in the welfare granary. . . .

We can begin ever so modestly. We can begin with a one week's food supply and gradually build it to a month, and then to three months. I am speaking now of food to cover basic needs. As all of you recognize, this counsel is not new. But I fear that so many feel that a long-term food supply is so far beyond their reach that they make no effort at all.

Begin in a small way . . . and gradually build toward a reasonable objective. Save a little money regularly, and you will be surprised how it accumulates.[16]

⟨∞⟩ 4 ⟨∞⟩

We enjoy independence and freedom as we avoid debt to the extent possible and set aside money for times of need.

We have been counseled again and again concerning self-reliance, concerning debt, concerning thrift. So many of our people are heavily in debt for things that are not entirely necessary. . . . I urge you as members of this Church to get free of debt where possible and to have a little laid aside against a rainy day.[17]

The time has come to get our houses in order. . . .

President J. Reuben Clark Jr., in the priesthood meeting of the conference in 1938, [said]: "Once in debt, interest is your companion every minute of the day and night; you cannot shun it or slip away from it; you cannot dismiss it; it yields neither to entreaties, demands, or orders; and whenever you get in its way or cross its course or fail to meet its demands, it crushes you" (in Conference Report, Apr. 1938, 103).

I recognize that it may be necessary to borrow to get a home, of course. But let us buy a home that we can afford and thus ease the payments which will constantly hang over our heads without mercy or respite. . . .

Since the beginnings of the Church, the Lord has spoken on this matter of debt. To Martin Harris through revelation He said: "Pay the debt thou hast contracted with the printer. Release thyself from bondage" (D&C 19:35).

President Heber J. Grant spoke repeatedly on this matter. . . . He said: "If there is any one thing that will bring peace and contentment into the human heart, and into the family, it is to live within our means. And if there is any one thing that is grinding and discouraging and disheartening, it is to have debts and obligations that one cannot meet" (*Gospel Standards,* comp. G. Homer Durham [1941], 111).

We are carrying a message of self-reliance throughout the Church. Self-reliance cannot obtain when there is serious debt hanging over a household. One has neither independence nor freedom from bondage when he is obligated to others.

In managing the affairs of the Church, we have tried to set an example. We have, as a matter of policy, stringently followed the practice of setting aside each year a percentage of the income of the Church against a possible day of need.

I am grateful to be able to say that the Church in all its operations, in all its undertakings, in all of its departments, is able to function without borrowed money. If we cannot get along, we will curtail our programs. We will shrink expenditures to fit the income. We will not borrow. . . .

What a wonderful feeling it is to be free of debt, to have a little money against a day of emergency put away where it can be retrieved when necessary. . . .

I urge you . . . to look to the condition of your finances. I urge you to be modest in your expenditures; discipline yourselves in your purchases to avoid debt to the extent possible. Pay off debt as quickly as you can, and free yourselves from bondage.

This is a part of the temporal gospel in which we believe. May the Lord bless you . . . to set your houses in order. If you have paid your debts, if you have a reserve, even though it be small, then should storms howl about your head, you will have shelter for your [family] and peace in your hearts.[18]

Suggestions for Study and Teaching

Questions
- President Hinckley taught that "there is no substitute . . . for productive labor" (section 1). How has work been a blessing in your life? What have you learned through hard work? How can parents help their children learn to work?

- What are our responsibilities toward those who have temporal needs? (See section 2.) How can we help others become self-reliant? How has your life been influenced by service you have given and received?

- Review the preparations that President Hinckley counseled us to make for times of need (see section 3). When have you seen the importance of preparing for times of need? What are some small, gradual things we can do to prepare ourselves?

• Review President Hinckley's counsel about debt and thrift (see section 4). Why is it important to be disciplined in the way we spend money? How can debt affect us temporally and spiritually? How can parents teach their children to use money wisely?

Related Scriptures

1 Thessalonians 4:11–12; D&C 1:11–13; 78:13–14; 104:13–18; Moses 5:1

Teaching Help

"Be careful not to end good discussions too soon in an attempt to present all the material you have prepared. Although it is important to cover the material, it is more important to help learners feel the influence of the Spirit, resolve their questions, increase their understanding of the gospel, and deepen their commitment to keep the commandments" (*Teaching, No Greater Call* [1999], 64).

Notes

1. "Some Lessons I Learned as a Boy," *Ensign,* May 1993, 52.
2. See "The Perpetual Education Fund," *Ensign,* May 2001, 52.
3. "Reaching Down to Lift Another," *Ensign,* Nov. 2001, 54.
4. "I Believe," *New Era,* Sept. 1996, 6.
5. "I Believe," 6.
6. *One Bright Shining Hope: Messages for Women from Gordon B. Hinckley* (2006), 24.
7. *Teachings of Gordon B. Hinckley* (1997), 707.
8. *Discourses of President Gordon B. Hinckley, Volume 2: 2000–2004* (2005), 532.
9. "Inspirational Thoughts," *Ensign,* Aug. 2000, 5.
10. "The Perpetual Education Fund," 52–53.
11. "This Thing Was Not Done in a Corner," *Ensign,* Nov. 1996, 50.
12. "President Harold B. Lee: An Appreciation," *Ensign,* Nov. 1972, 8; see also Heber J. Grant, in Conference Report, Oct. 1936, 3.
13. "I Was an Hungred, and Ye Gave Me Meat," *Ensign* or *Liahona,* May 2004, 61.
14. "This Thing Was Not Done in a Corner," 50.
15. "If Ye Are Prepared Ye Shall Not Fear," *Ensign* or *Liahona,* Nov. 2005, 61–62.
16. "To Men of the Priesthood," *Ensign* or *Liahona,* Nov. 2002, 58.
17. "The Times in Which We Live," *Ensign,* Nov. 2001, 73.
18. "To the Boys and to the Men," *Ensign,* Nov. 1998, 53–54.

"If we would claim to worship and follow the Master,
must we not strive to emulate his life of service?"

Losing Ourselves in the Service of Others

"May the real meaning of the gospel distill into our hearts that we may realize that our lives, given us by God our Father, are to be used in the service of others."

From the Life of Gordon B. Hinckley

Young Elder Gordon B. Hinckley struggled through his first few weeks as a full-time missionary in England. He was sick when he arrived, and his attempts to preach the gospel were repeatedly rejected. During that difficult time, he was blessed with what he later called his "day of decision"—an experience that influenced his service for the rest of his life.

"I was discouraged," he recalled. "I wrote a letter home to my good father and said that I felt I was wasting my time and his money. He was my father and my stake president, and he was a wise and inspired man. He wrote a very short letter to me which said, 'Dear Gordon, I have your recent letter. I have only one suggestion: forget yourself and go to work.' Earlier that morning in our scripture class my companion and I had read these words of the Lord: 'Whosoever will save his life shall lose it; but whosoever shall lose his life for my sake and the gospel's, the same shall save it.' (Mark 8:35.)

"Those words of the Master, followed by my father's letter with his counsel to forget myself and go to work, went into my very being. With my father's letter in hand, I went into our bedroom in the house at 15 Wadham Road, where we lived, and got on my knees and made a pledge with the Lord. I covenanted that I would try to forget myself and lose myself in His service.

"That July day in 1933 was my day of decision. A new light came into my life and a new joy into my heart."[1]

That light never left Gordon B. Hinckley's life. From that day, he dedicated himself to the Lord in the service of others. At President Hinckley's funeral, President Henry B. Eyring listed a few of President Hinckley's contributions: building temples across the earth, establishing smaller temples to accelerate temple work, establishing the Perpetual Education Fund, and building the Conference Center. Then he said:

"His personal legacy goes beyond that brief list and my power to describe. But his accomplishments have at least one thing in common. Always they were to bless individuals with opportunity. And always he thought of those with the least opportunity, the ordinary person struggling to cope with the difficulties of everyday life and the challenge of living the gospel of Jesus Christ. More than once he tapped his finger on my chest when I made a suggestion and said, 'Hal, have you remembered the person who is struggling?'"[2]

"I wish to be up and doing," President Hinckley said. "I wish to face each day with resolution and purpose. I wish to use every waking hour to give encouragement, to bless those whose burdens are heavy, to build faith and strength of testimony."[3]

Teachings of Gordon B. Hinckley

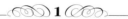 **1**

Our lives are gifts from God and are to be used in the service of others.

There is . . . much of poverty and stark want across the world, so much of rebellion and meanness, so much of sleaze and filth, so many broken homes and destroyed families, so many lonely people living colorless lives without hope, so much of distress everywhere.

And so I make a plea to you. I plead with you that with all your getting you will also give to make the world a little better.[4]

If the world is to be improved, the process of love must make a change in the hearts of men. It can do so when we look beyond self to give our love to God and others, and do so with all our heart, with all our soul, and with all our mind.

The Lord has declared in modern revelation, "If your eye be single to my glory, your whole bodies shall be filled with light, and there shall be no darkness in you." (D&C 88:67.)

As we look with love and gratitude to God, as we serve him with an eye single to his glory, there goes from us the darkness of sin, the darkness of selfishness, the darkness of pride. There will come an increased love for our Eternal Father and for his Beloved Son, our Savior and our Redeemer. There will come a greater sense of service toward our fellowmen, less of thinking of self and more of reaching out to others.

This principle of love is the basic essence of the gospel of Jesus Christ.[5]

If we would claim to worship and follow the Master, must we not strive to emulate his life of service? None of us may rightly say that his life is his own. Our lives are gifts of God. We come into the world not of our own volition. We leave not according to our wish. Our days are numbered not by ourselves, but according to the will of God.

So many of us use our lives as if they were entirely our own. Ours is the choice to waste them if we wish. But that becomes a betrayal of a great and sacred trust. As the Master made so abundantly clear, "For whosoever will save his life shall lose it; but whosoever shall lose his life for my sake and the gospel's, the same shall save it." (Mark 8:35.)[6]

My beloved brethren and sisters, the challenge is great. The opportunities are all about us. God would have us do His work—and do it with energy and cheerfulness. That work, as He has defined it, is to "succor the weak, lift up the hands which hang down, and strengthen the feeble knees." (D&C 81:5.)

It is to minister to those in need. It is to comfort the bereaved. It is to visit the widow and the fatherless in their affliction. It is to feed the needy, to clothe the naked, to shelter those who have not a roof over their heads. It is to do as the Master did, who "went about doing good." (Acts 10:38.)[7]

My message to you today . . . is that you resolve to dedicate a part of your time, as you map out your life's work, to those in distress and need, with no consideration of recompense. Your skills are needed, whatever they may be. Your helping hands will lift someone out of the mire of distress. Your steady voice will give encouragement to some who might otherwise simply give up. Your skills can change the lives, in a remarkable and wonderful way, of those who walk in need. If not now, when? If not you, who?[8]

May the real meaning of the gospel distill into our hearts that we may realize that our lives, given us by God our Father, are to be used in the service of others.

If we will give such service, our days will be filled with joy and gladness. More important, they will be consecrated to our Lord and Savior, Jesus Christ, and to the blessing of all whose lives we touch.[9]

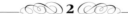 **2**

Service is the best medicine for self-pity, selfishness, despair, and loneliness.

I recall visiting a college campus where I heard the usual, commonplace complaining of youth: complaints about the pressures of school—as if it were a burden rather than an opportunity to partake of the knowledge of the earth—complaints about housing and about food. . . .

I counseled those youth that if the pressures of school were too heavy, if they felt to complain about their housing and their food, then I could suggest a cure for their problems. I suggested that they lay their books aside for a few hours, leave their rooms, and go visit someone who is old and lonely, or someone sick and discouraged. By and large, I have come to see that if we complain about life, it is because we are thinking only of ourselves.

For many years there was a sign on the wall of a shoe repair shop I patronized. It read, "I complained because I had no shoes until I saw a man who had no feet." The most effective medicine for the sickness of self-pity is to lose ourselves in the service of others.[10]

I believe that for most of us the best medicine for loneliness is work and service in behalf of others. I do not minimize your

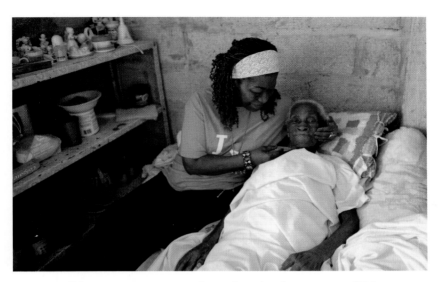

"There are so many out there whose burdens you can lift."

problems, but I do not hesitate to say that there are many others whose problems are more serious than yours. Reach out to serve them, to help them, to encourage them. There are so many boys and girls who fail in school for want of a little personal attention and encouragement. There are so many elderly people who live in misery and loneliness and fear for whom a simple conversation would bring a measure of hope and brightness. . . .

There are so many who have been injured and who need a good Samaritan to bind up their wounds and help them on their way. A small kindness can bring a great blessing to someone in distress and a sweet feeling to the one who befriends him.[11]

There are so many out there whose burdens you can lift. There are the homeless, there are the hungry, there are the destitute all around us. There are the aged who are alone in rest homes. There are handicapped children, and youth on drugs, and the sick and the homebound who cry out for a kind word. If you do not do it, who will?

The best antidote I know for worry is work. The best medicine for despair is service. The best cure for weariness is the challenge of helping someone who is even more tired.[12]

Why are missionaries happy? Because they lose themselves in the service of others.

Why are those who labor in the temples happy? Because their labor of love is in very deed harmonious with the great vicarious work of the Savior of mankind. They neither ask for nor expect thanks for what they do. For the most part, they know nothing more than the name of him or her in whose behalf they labor.[13]

Give expression to the noble desires that lie within your hearts to reach out to comfort, sustain, and build others. As you do so, the cankering poison of selfishness will leave you, and it will be replaced by a sweet and wonderful feeling that seems to come in no other way.[14]

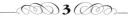

3

When we reach out to help others, we find our true selves.

One Sunday morning several years ago, I was in the home of a stake president in a small Idaho town. Before morning prayer, the family read together a few verses of scripture. Among these were the words of Jesus as recorded in John 12:24: "Verily, verily, I say unto you, Except a corn of wheat fall into the ground and die, it abideth alone: but if it die, it bringeth forth much fruit."

No doubt the Master was referring to his own forthcoming death, declaring that except he die his mission in life would be largely in vain. But I see in these words a further meaning. It seems to me that the Lord is saying to each of us that unless we lose ourselves in the service of others, our lives are largely lived to no real purpose, for he went on to say, "He that loveth his life shall lose it; and he that hateth his life in this world shall keep it unto life eternal." (John 12:25.) Or, as recorded in Luke, "Whosoever shall seek to save his life shall lose it; and whosoever shall lose his life shall preserve it." (Luke 17:33.) In other words, he who lives only unto himself withers and dies, while he who forgets himself in the service of others grows and blossoms in this life and in eternity.

That morning in stake conference, the president with whom I had stayed was released after thirteen years of faithful service. There was a great outpouring of love and appreciation, not because of his wealth, not because of his stature in the business community, but because of the great service he had unselfishly given. Without thought of personal interest, he had driven tens of thousands of miles in all kinds of weather. He had spent literally thousands of hours in the interest of others. He had neglected his personal affairs to assist those who needed his help. And in so doing he had come alive and had become great in the eyes of those he had served.[15]

Years ago I read the story of a young woman who went into a rural area as a schoolteacher. Among those in her class was a girl who had failed before and who was failing again. The student could not read. She came from a family without means to take her to a larger city for examination to determine whether she had a problem that could be remedied. Sensing that the difficulty might lie with the girl's eyes, the young teacher arranged to take the student, at the teacher's own expense, to have her eyes tested. A deficiency was discovered that could be corrected with glasses. Soon an entire new world opened to the student. For the first time in her life, she saw clearly the words before her. The salary of that country schoolteacher was meager, but out of the little she had, she made an investment that completely changed the life of a failing student, and in doing so she found a new dimension in her own life.[16]

As you so serve, a new dimension will be added to your life. You will find new and stimulating associations. You will find friendship and sociality. You will grow in knowledge and understanding and wisdom, and in your capacity to do.[17]

I testify that as each of you reach out to help others, you will find your true selves and bless greatly the world in which you live.[18]

The Church provides many opportunities for unselfish service.

Brothers and sisters, you will never be happy if you go through life thinking only of yourself. Get lost in the best cause in the world —the cause of the Lord. The work of the quorums, and of the auxiliary organizations, temple work, welfare service work, missionary work. You will bless your own life as you bless the lives of others.[19]

"As you . . . serve, a new dimension will be added to your life."

There is no other work in all the world so fraught with happiness as is this work. That happiness is peculiar. It comes of serving others. It is real. It is unique. It is wonderful.[20]

Let the Church be your dear friend. Let it be your great companion. Serve wherever you are called to serve. Do what you are asked to do. Every position you hold will add to your capacity. I have served in many responsibilities in this great organization. Every service brought its own reward.

This . . . will require your unselfish devotion, your unyielding loyalty and faith. You will serve in many capacities before your lives are complete. Some of them may seem small, but there is no small or unimportant calling in this Church. Every calling is important. Every calling is necessary to the advancement of the work. Never demean a responsibility in the Church. . . .

Make room for the Church in your life. Let your knowledge of its doctrine grow. Let your understanding of its organization increase. Let your love for its eternal truths become ever and ever stronger.

The Church may call upon you to make sacrifice. It may call upon you to give of the very best that you have to offer. There will be no cost in this, because you will discover that it will become an investment that will pay you dividends for as long as you live. The Church is the great reservoir of eternal truth. Embrace it and hold fast to it.[21]

Do you want to be happy? Forget yourself and get lost in this great cause. Lend your efforts to helping people. Cultivate a spirit of forgiveness in your heart against any who might have offended you. Look to the Lord and live and work to lift and serve His sons and daughters. You will come to know a happiness that you have never known before if you will do that. I do not care how old you are, how young you are, whatever. You can lift people and help them. Heaven knows there are so very, very, very many people in this world who need help. Oh, so very, very many. Let's get the cankering, selfish attitude out of our lives, my brothers and sisters, and stand a little taller and reach a little higher in the service of others. . . . Stand taller, stand higher, lift those with feeble knees, hold up the arms of those that hang down. Live the gospel of Jesus Christ. Forget yourself.[22]

Suggestions for Study and Teaching

Questions

- President Hinckley taught that our lives are gifts from God, to be used in serving others (see section 1). How can we make serving others a way of life? What do you think it means to serve with an eye single to the glory of God? How has someone else's service blessed you?

- Why does service help us overcome self-pity, selfishness, and loneliness? (See section 2.) How has service brought you happiness? As you read President Hinckley's descriptions of people who are in need, determine how you and your family can reach out to serve.

- Why does losing ourselves in the service of others help us "find [our] true selves"? (See section 3.) What can we learn from the stories in section 3?

- President Hinckley counseled, "Get lost in the best cause in the world—the cause of the Lord" (section 4). What blessings has Church service brought into your life?

Related Scriptures

Matthew 20:25–28; 25:34–40; John 13:35; Mosiah 2:16–18; 18:8–9; D&C 64:33

Study Help

"As you study, pay careful attention to ideas that come to your mind and feelings that come to your heart" (*Preach My Gospel* [2004], 18). Consider recording the impressions you receive, even if they seem unrelated to the words you are reading. They may be the very things the Lord wants you to learn.

Notes

1. "Taking the Gospel to Britain: A Declaration of Vision, Faith, Courage, and Truth," *Ensign,* July 1987, 7.

2. Henry B. Eyring, "Things Will Work Out," *In Memoriam: President Gordon B. Hinckley, 1910–2008* (supplement to the *Ensign,* Mar. 2008), 27; see also page 26.

3. "Testimony," *Ensign,* May 1998, 69.

4. *Discourses of President Gordon B. Hinckley, Volume 1: 1995–1999* (2005), 543.

5. "And the Greatest of These Is Love," *Ensign,* Mar. 1984, 5.

6. "The Gift of Self," *Tambuli,* Dec. 1986, 3; see also lds.org/liahona/1986/12/the-gift-of-self.

7. "To Single Adults," *Ensign,* June 1989, 75.

8. *Discourses of President Gordon B. Hinckley, Volume 1,* 544–45.

9. "Giving Ourselves to the Service of the Lord," *Ensign,* Mar. 1987, 5.

10. "Whosoever Will Save His Life," *Ensign,* Aug. 1982, 5.

11. "A Conversation with Single Adults," *Ensign,* Mar. 1997, 61.

12. "To Single Adults," 73–74.

13. "Giving Ourselves to the Service of the Lord," 5.

14. "To a Man Who Has Done What This Church Expects of Each of Us" (Brigham Young University devotional, Oct. 17, 1995), 6, speeches.byu.edu.

15. "Whosoever Will Save His Life," 3–4.

16. "And the Greatest of These Is Love," 4.

17. "Women of the Church," *Ensign,* Nov. 1996, 69.

18. "Whosoever Will Save His Life," 6.

19. "Pillars of Truth," *Ensign,* Jan. 1994, 7.

20. "Rejoicing in the Privilege to Serve," *Worldwide Leadership Training Meeting,* June 21, 2003, 23.

21. "Life's Obligations," *Ensign,* Feb. 1999, 4.

22. *Teachings of Gordon B. Hinckley* (1997), 597.

"With [the priesthood], nothing is impossible in carrying forward the work of the kingdom of God."

The Holy Priesthood

"I love the priesthood of this Church. It is a vital, living thing. It is the very heart and strength of this work. It is the power and authority by which God, our Eternal Father, accomplishes His work in the earth."

From the Life of Gordon B. Hinckley

In 1980, Elder Gordon B. Hinckley and his wife, Marjorie, participated in a three-week tour in Asia, speaking at area conferences and participating in the dedication of the Tokyo Japan Temple. Before returning home, they traveled to the Japan Sendai Mission, where Elder Hinckley presided over the creation of the first stake in the mission. Just before a meeting with the new stake presidency, Elder Hinckley approached the mission president, Kiyoshi Sakai. "He asked a surprised President Sakai if he had any consecrated oil and then added, 'I am so exhausted; would you give me a blessing?' President Sakai remembered, 'I was so afraid and felt too weak to bless an Apostle of the Lord. I told him I could not give the blessing in English. Elder Hinckley said Japanese would be fine. So Elder Hitoshi Kashikura, the Regional Representative, and I proceeded.' After the blessing had been pronounced, Elder Hinckley said simply, 'Thank you, thank you. Now I can go home tomorrow.'

"The next morning Elder Hinckley looked strong and healthy, and when President Sakai asked how he felt he responded, '*Dai Jobu,* more than fine. I am well.' A few days later President Sakai received a letter of thanks from Elder Hinckley, who wrote: '. . . I so much appreciate the blessing which you gave me. I immediately began to feel better after that. My recovery was quick and total. Sister Hinckley and I are deeply grateful for the privilege of staying in your mission home.'"[1]

President Hinckley frequently testified of the blessings of the priesthood, from miraculous but temporary blessings of physical healing to eternal, binding blessings through temple ordinances. He declared, "I believe that in His priesthood rests divine authority—the power to bless, the power to heal, the power to govern in the earthly affairs of God, the power to bind in the heavens that which is bound upon the earth."[2]

Teachings of Gordon B. Hinckley

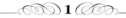 1

God has restored the priesthood and the keys of the kingdom of heaven.

Priesthood power and authority [were] given to men anciently. The lesser authority was given to the sons of Aaron to administer in things temporal as well as in some sacred ecclesiastical ordinances. The higher priesthood was given by the Lord Himself to His Apostles, in accordance with His declaration to Peter: "And I will give unto thee the keys of the kingdom of heaven: and whatsoever thou shalt bind on earth shall be bound in heaven: and whatsoever thou shalt loose on earth shall be loosed in heaven" (Matthew 16:19).

The full restoration of the priesthood involved the coming of John the Baptist . . . and of Peter, James, and John. . . . It involved Moses, Elias, and Elijah, each bringing priesthood keys to complete the work of restoring all of the acts and ordinances of previous dispensations in this, the great, final dispensation of the fulness of times.

The priesthood is here. . . . We know, for we have seen, the power of this priesthood. We have seen the sick healed, the lame made to walk, and the coming of light and knowledge and understanding to those who have been in darkness.[3]

The Prophet Joseph Smith described [the priesthood] on one occasion in these words: "The Priesthood is an everlasting principle, and existed with God from eternity, and will [exist] to eternity, without beginning of days or end of years." (*History of the Church,* 3:386.)

It is veritably the power of the Almighty given to man to act in His name and in His stead. It is a delegation of divine authority, different from all other powers and authorities on the face of the earth. Small wonder that it was restored to man by resurrected beings who held it anciently, that there might be no question concerning its authority and validity. Without it there could be a church in name only, lacking authority to administer in the things of God. With it, nothing is impossible in carrying forward the work of the kingdom of God. It is divine in its nature. It is both temporal and eternal in its authority. It is the only power on the earth that reaches beyond the veil of death.[4]

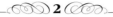

2

The priesthood is the power and authority by which God accomplishes His work.

I love the priesthood of this Church. It is a vital, living thing. It is the very heart and strength of this work. It is the power and authority by which God, our Eternal Father, accomplishes His work in the earth.[5]

The holy priesthood carries with it the authority to govern in the affairs of the kingdom of God on the earth. Under the revelations of the Lord, the Church is to be presided over by three presiding high priests. They are to be assisted by a council of Twelve Apostles, who in turn are to be assisted by . . . the Seventy. A Presiding Bishopric of three are responsible for temporal affairs under the direction of the Presidency. All of these are priesthood officers. That power divinely given is the authority by which they govern. It is so in the stakes and the wards with presidencies and bishoprics. It is so in the quorums. The auxiliary officers carry forth their work under direction and delegation from the priesthood. Without the priesthood there might be the form of a church, but not the true substance. This is the church of Jesus Christ, and it is governed by that authority which is "after the Order of the Son of God." (D&C 107:3.)[6]

―――――――――― ∞ **3** ∞ ――――――――――

The blessings of the priesthood are to be enjoyed by all.

[The priesthood] . . . is a part of the plan of God our Eternal Father to bless the lives of His sons and daughters of all generations.[7]

The holy priesthood includes the power to bless. For those of the Aaronic Priesthood, it carries with it the authority to administer to the congregation the emblems of the flesh and blood of the Lord, who gave His life as a sacrifice for all. The sacrament and the partaking of these emblems is the very heart of our sabbath worship. It includes a renewal of covenants with God. It carries with it a promise of His Holy Spirit to be with us. It is a blessing without peer to be enjoyed by all and made possible by the authority given to worthy young men. . . .

The Melchizedek Priesthood carries with it the authority to bestow the Holy Ghost. How great a blessing it is to have the ministering influence of a member of the Godhead, having received that gift under the hands of those who acted with divine authority. If we continue to walk in virtue, we may enjoy the fulfillment of the promise made by the Lord when He said: "The Holy Ghost shall be thy constant companion, and thy scepter an unchanging scepter of righteousness and truth; and thy dominion shall be an everlasting dominion, and without compulsory means it shall flow unto thee forever and ever." (D&C 121:46.)

The priesthood includes the power to bless the sick. Is there anyone within my hearing who has not exercised or felt that divine power? Can any of us have any doubt concerning its efficacy? We could tell of miracles, sacred and wonderful, that we have witnessed within our own experience. . . .

This holy Melchizedek Priesthood carries with it the power to bless with prophecy, to comfort, to sustain, to direct. We have patriarchs in our midst who, under the authority that they hold, declare lineage and pronounce blessings for our guidance. These blessings may become as an anchor to which we may hold to keep us steady through the storms of life.

In its ultimate expression the holy priesthood carries with it the authority to seal on the earth and have that sealing effective in the heavens. It is unique and wonderful. It is the authority exercised in the temples of God. It concerns both the living and the dead. It is of the very essence of eternity. It is divine power bestowed by the Almighty as a part of His great plan for the immortality and eternal life of man.

How precious is the gift of God that has come to us.[8]

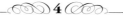

Sons of God who hold His divine authority must be true to the very best that is in them.

Every worthy man, regardless of nationality, ethnic background, or any other factor, is eligible to receive the priesthood. His obedience to the commandments of God becomes the determining factor. Its bestowal is based only on worthiness before the Lord. . . .

Such is the wonder of this priesthood. Wealth is not a factor. Education is not a factor. The honors of men are not a factor. The controlling factor is acceptability unto the Lord.[9]

The time has come for all of us who have been ordained to either the Aaronic or the Melchizedek Priesthood, and to any of the offices therein, to reflect upon our lives, to assess our shortcomings, and to repent of those matters of conduct which are at variance with the high and holy commission we have received. . . .

No man, young or old, . . . who has been . . . ordained, can regard lightly that which he holds. He is in partnership with God and has resting upon him a solid and sacred obligation so to live as one worthy to speak and act in the name of God as his qualified representative.[10]

Even though those in authority lay hands upon our heads and we are ordained, we may through our behavior nullify and forfeit any right to exercise this divine authority.

. . . "No power or influence can or ought to be maintained by virtue of the priesthood, only by persuasion, by long-suffering, by gentleness and meekness, and by love unfeigned;

"By kindness, and pure knowledge, which shall greatly enlarge the soul without hypocrisy, and without guile" (D&C 121:41–42).

Now, my brethren, those are the parameters within which this priesthood must find expression. It is not as a cloak that we put on and take off at will. It is, when exercised in righteousness, as the very tissue of our bodies, a part of us at all times and in all circumstances.[11]

We must be true to the very best that is in us. We are sons of God honored to hold His divine authority. But we live in a world of evil. There is a constant power, pulling us down, inviting us to partake of those things which are totally inconsistent with the divine priesthood which we hold. . . .

To you men I issue a challenge. Run from the tide of sleaze that would overcome you. Flee the evils of the world. Be loyal to your better self. Be loyal to the best that is in you. Be faithful and true to the covenants that are associated with the priesthood of God.[12]

To every officer, to every teacher in this Church who acts in a priesthood office, there comes the sacred responsibility of magnifying that priesthood calling. Each of us is responsible for the welfare and the growth and development of others. We do not live only unto ourselves. If we are to magnify our callings, we cannot live only unto ourselves.[13]

Many men seem to think that because they have been ordained, the priesthood is theirs in perpetuity to exercise as they choose. They feel they can break a covenant and a commandment here and there, and sin in this way or that, and yet still have within themselves the power of the priesthood and that God will ratify that which they speak in His holy name and in the name of the Redeemer. This becomes mockery, and I believe that in such an exercise, they take the name of God in vain. They profane the name of His Beloved Son. They desecrate the sacred gift which came through ordination, and the authority which they have lost because of transgression. . . .

. . . I lift a warning voice to all, boys and men, to shun sin. Transgression is incompatible with divine authority. Avoid pornography as you would avoid the plague. Avoid sexual sin of any degree. Shun dishonesty and deceit. I plead with you to rein in any element of pride or vain ambition. I ask you to look into yourselves to see that there is no attitude of dominion or compulsion over your wives or your children. . . .

. . . I am satisfied that our Father in Heaven is not pleased with any man or boy who accepts ordination and then indulges in evil. In the very process of accepting ordination he enters into an oath and covenant between himself and his God.[14]

No man, be he youth or elder, is living up to the standards of the priesthood who demeans or degrades womanhood, who fails to accord that measure of respect to the daughters of God which our Father in heaven would have them accorded.[15]

Let us be good husbands and fathers. Any man who is a tyrant in his own home is unworthy of the priesthood. He cannot be a fit instrument in the hands of the Lord when he does not show respect and kindness and love toward the companion of his choice. Likewise, any man who is a bad example for his children, who cannot control his temper, or who is involved in dishonest or immoral practices will find the power of his priesthood nullified.[16]

The wife you choose will be your equal. . . . She is not your servant, your chattel, nor anything of the kind. How tragic and utterly disgusting a phenomenon is wife abuse. Any man in this Church who abuses his wife, who demeans her, who insults her, who exercises unrighteous dominion over her is unworthy to hold the priesthood. Though he may have been ordained, the heavens will withdraw, the Spirit of the Lord will be grieved, and it will be amen to the authority of the priesthood of that man. Any man who engages in this practice is unworthy to hold a temple recommend. . . .

. . . If there be any . . . who are guilty of such behavior, I call upon you to repent. Get on your knees and ask the Lord to forgive you. Pray to Him for the power to control your tongue and your heavy hand. Ask for the forgiveness of your wife and your children. . . .

I am confident that when we stand before the bar of God, there will be little mention of how much wealth we accumulated in life or of any honors which we may have achieved. But there will be searching questions concerning our domestic relations. And I am convinced that only those who have walked through life with love and respect and appreciation for their companions and children will receive from our eternal judge the words, "Well done, thou good and faithful servant: . . . enter thou into the joy of thy lord" (Matt. 25:21).[17]

A priesthood quorum can be an anchor of strength for its members.

I am confident that the Lord intended that a priesthood quorum should be far more than a class in theology on Sunday mornings. Of course, the building of spirituality and the strengthening of testimony through effective gospel teaching is an important priesthood responsibility. But this is only a segment of the quorum function. Each quorum must be a working brotherhood for every member if its purpose is to be realized. . . .

. . . The priesthood quorum is the Lord's organization for men of the Church, just as the Relief Society is the Lord's organization for women of the Church. Each has among its responsibilities, basic to its reason for being, the assisting of those in need.

When the Relief Society was organized the Prophet Joseph said of the women of the Society: "They will fly to the relief of the stranger; they will pour in the wine and oil to the wounded heart of the distressed; they will dry up the tears of the orphan and make the widow's heart to rejoice" [*Teachings of Presidents of the Church: Joseph Smith* (2007), 452]. I would hope that the same might be said of the men of the priesthood.

It will be a marvelous day . . . when our priesthood quorums become an anchor of strength to every man belonging thereto, when each such man may appropriately be able to say, "I am a member of a priesthood quorum of The Church of Jesus Christ of Latter-day Saints. I stand ready to assist my brethren in all of their needs, as I am confident they stand ready to assist me in mine. Working together, we shall grow spiritually as covenant sons of God. Working together, we can stand, without embarrassment and without fear, against every wind of adversity that might blow, be it economic, social, or spiritual."[18]

Church leaders and members—both men and women—work together to "carry forth their work under direction and delegation from the priesthood."

 **6**

In homes and in the Church, men and women work together to move the Lord's kingdom forward.

The men hold the priesthood, yes. But my wife is my companion. In this Church the man neither walks ahead of his wife nor behind his wife but at her side. They are co-equals in this life in a great enterprise.[19]

There is strength and great capacity in the women of this Church. There is leadership and direction, a certain spirit of independence, and yet great satisfaction in being a part of this, the Lord's kingdom, and of working hand in hand with [holders of] the priesthood to move it forward.[20]

I thank my Eternal Father for the restoration of the holy priesthood, that "every man might speak in the name of God the Lord, even the Savior of the world" (D&C 1:20). I have seen the beauty and wonder of that priesthood in the governance of this remarkable church. I have felt its power flow through me to the blessing and the healing of the sick. I have seen the ennoblement it has given to humble men who have been called to great and serious responsibility. I have seen it as they have spoken with power and authority from on high as if the voice of God were speaking through them.

I thank the Lord for the testimony he has given me of the wholeness of the gospel, of its breadth and reach and depth. It is designed to bless the sons and daughters of all generations of time—both the living and the dead.[21]

Suggestions for Study and Teaching

Questions

- Review President Hinckley's teachings in section 1 about the restoration of the priesthood. What experiences have helped you gain a testimony of these truths?

- President Hinckley taught, "The holy priesthood carries with it the authority to govern in the affairs of the kingdom of God on the earth" (section 2). How does this truth apply in stakes and wards? in quorums? in Relief Society? How does priesthood authority strengthen your service in God's kingdom?

- In section 3, review the blessings we all can receive through the priesthood. In what ways have you experienced the power and blessings of the priesthood?

- What can we learn from President Hinckley's teachings about the difference between priesthood authority and priesthood power? (See section 4.) What do you think it means for a priesthood holder to "be true to the very best that is in [him]"? Why must priesthood holders "not live only unto [them]selves"?

- In section 5, what impresses you about President Hinckley's descriptions of priesthood quorums and Relief Society? What can we do in our ward or branch to follow his counsel?

- Why do men and women need to work together as "co-equals" to accomplish the Lord's work? (See section 6.)

Related Scriptures

Hebrews 5:1–4; 1 Nephi 14:12–14; Alma 13:1–9; D&C 84:33–44; 88:133; 112:30–32

Teaching Help

"Ask questions that require learners to find answers in the scriptures and the teachings of latter-day prophets" (*Teaching, No Greater Call* [1999], 62).

Notes

1. Sheri L. Dew, *Go Forward with Faith: The Biography of Gordon B. Hinckley* (1996), 377.

2. "The Father, Son, and Holy Ghost," *Ensign,* Mar. 1998, 5.

3. "Four Cornerstones of Faith," *Ensign,* Feb. 2004, 6–7.

4. "Priesthood Restoration," *Ensign,* Oct. 1988, 71.

5. "Why We Do Some of the Things We Do," *Ensign,* Nov. 1999, 54.

6. "Priesthood Restoration," 72.

7. *Teachings of Gordon B. Hinckley* (1997), 475.

8. "Priesthood Restoration," 72.

9. "The Stake President," *Ensign,* May 2000, 49.

10. In "News of the Church: Priesthood Restoration Honored," *Ensign,* July 1983, 76.

11. "Personal Worthiness to Exercise the Priesthood," *Ensign,* May 2002, 52.

12. "Loyalty," *Ensign* or *Liahona,* May 2003, 58–59.

13. "Magnify Your Calling," *Ensign,* May 1989, 47.

14. "Only upon Principles of Righteousness," *Ensign,* Sept. 1992, 70.

15. In "News of the Church: Priesthood Restoration Honored," 76.

16. "Reaching Down to Lift Another," *Ensign,* Nov. 2001, 52.

17. "Personal Worthiness to Exercise the Priesthood," 53–54.

18. "Welfare Responsibilities of the Priesthood Quorums," *Ensign,* Nov. 1977, 86.

19. "This Thing Was Not Done in a Corner," *Ensign,* Nov. 1996, 49.

20. "Women of the Church," *Ensign,* Nov. 1996, 68.

21. "My Testimony," *Ensign,* Nov. 1993, 52.

"The evidence for [the Book of Mormon's] truth and validity lies within the covers of the book itself. The test of its truth lies in reading it."

The Power of the Book of Mormon

"To a world wavering in its faith, the Book of Mormon is [a] powerful witness of the divinity of the Lord."

From the Life of Gordon B. Hinckley

When Gordon B. Hinckley was a young man, he established a pattern for scripture study. "As a missionary, I read each evening before going to bed a few chapters of the Book of Mormon," he said, "and there came into my heart a conviction which has never left: that this is the word of God, restored to the earth by the power of the Almighty, translated by the gift and power of God to the convincing of the Jew and the Gentile that Jesus is the Christ."[1]

His knowledge and testimony of the Book of Mormon influenced many people after his mission, when he worked as an employee of the Church's Radio, Publicity, and Mission Literature Committee. He received an assignment to write scripts for a radio series titled *A New Witness for Christ*. The series brought Book of Mormon passages to life for radio listeners. At the time, he commented to an associate: "I have always thought that we will do our best work when we get people interested in the Book of Mormon to the point where they will read it. It is then that the Spirit can bear witness of its divinity."[2]

Throughout his ministry, President Hinckley emphasized the importance of the Book of Mormon. In August 2005, as President of the Church, he challenged Latter-day Saints to read the entire book before the end of the year. He later reported: "It is amazing how many met that challenge. Everyone who did so was blessed for his or her effort. As they became immersed in this added witness of our Redeemer, their hearts were quickened and their spirits touched."[3]

Teachings of Gordon B. Hinckley

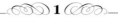 **1**

Hand in hand with the Bible, the Book of Mormon testifies of Jesus Christ.

It was said of old, it was said by the Savior, that in the mouths of two or more witnesses shall all things be established.[4]

As the Bible is the testament of the Old World, the Book of Mormon is the testament of the New. They go hand in hand in declaration of Jesus as the Son of the Father.[5]

The Book of Mormon . . . testifies of Him who was born in Bethlehem of Judea and who died on the hill of Calvary. To a world wavering in its faith, the Book of Mormon is another and powerful witness of the divinity of the Lord. Its very preface, written by a prophet who walked the Americas a millennium and a half ago, categorically states that it was written "to the convincing of the Jew and Gentile that Jesus is the Christ, the Eternal God, manifesting himself unto all nations."[6]

There is nothing we could do of greater importance than to have fortified in our individual lives an unshakable conviction that Jesus is the Christ. . . . And, my brothers and sisters, that is the purpose of the coming forth of this remarkable and wonderful book.[7]

 **2**

By the power of the Holy Ghost, we can receive a witness of the divine origin of the Book of Mormon.

I have read the Book of Mormon, which [Joseph Smith] translated by the gift and power of God. By the power of the Holy Ghost I have received a testimony and a witness of the divine origin of this sacred record.[8]

Its origin is miraculous; when the story of that origin is first told to one unfamiliar with it, it is almost unbelievable. But the book is here to be felt and handled and read. No one can dispute its presence. All efforts to account for its origin, other than the account given by Joseph Smith, have been shown to lack substance.[9]

The evidence for its truth, for its validity in a world that is prone to demand evidence, lies not in archaeology or anthropology, though these may be helpful to some. It lies not in word research or historical analysis, though these may be confirmatory. The evidence for its truth and validity lies within the covers of the book itself. The test of its truth lies in reading it. It is a book of God. Reasonable people may sincerely question its origin; but those who have read it prayerfully have come to know by a power beyond their natural senses that it is true, that it contains the word of God, that it outlines saving truths of the everlasting gospel, that it "[came] forth by the gift and power of God . . . to the convincing of the Jew and Gentile that Jesus is the Christ." [10]

[Moroni] wrote his last testament in the book which carries his name and which concludes the Nephite record. He wrote as one with a certain knowledge that his record would eventually come to light. . . .

In the final chapter of his own composition he bore testimony of the record of his people and categorically promised that those who would read it could know by the power of the Holy Ghost of its truth [see Moroni 10:3–5].

No other book contains such a promise. If Moroni had written nothing else, this promise in his concluding testimony would mark him forever as an eloquent witness of eternal truth. For, said he, "by the power of the Holy Ghost ye may know the truth of all things" (Moroni 10:5). [11]

 **3**

A testimony of the Book of Mormon leads to a conviction of other truths.

Each time we encourage others to read the Book of Mormon, we do them a favor. If they read it prayerfully and with a sincere desire to know the truth, they will know by the power of the Holy Ghost that the book is true.

From that knowledge there will flow a conviction of the truth of many other things. For if the Book of Mormon is true, then God lives. Testimony upon testimony runs through its pages of the solemn fact that our Father is real, that he is personal, that he loves his children and seeks their happiness.

If the Book of Mormon is true, then Jesus is the Son of God, the Only Begotten of the Father in the flesh, born of Mary, "a virgin, most beautiful . . . above all other virgins" (see 1 Ne. 11:13–21), for the book so testifies in a description unexcelled in all literature.

If the Book of Mormon is true, then Jesus is verily our Redeemer, the Savior of the world. . . .

If the Book of Mormon is true, Joseph Smith was a Prophet of God, for he was the instrument in the hands of God in bringing to light this testimony of the divinity of our Lord.

If this book is true, [the President of the Church] is a prophet, for he holds all of the keys, gifts, powers, and authority held by the Prophet Joseph, who brought forth this latter-day work.

If the Book of Mormon is true, the Church is true, for the same authority under which this sacred record came to light is present and manifest among us today. It is a restoration of the Church set up by the Savior in Palestine. It is a restoration of the Church set up by the Savior when he visited [the American] continent as set forth in this sacred record.

If the Book of Mormon is true, the Bible is true. The Bible is the Testament of the Old World; the Book of Mormon is the Testament of the New. One is the record of Judah; the other is the record of Joseph, and they have come together in the hand of the Lord in fulfillment of the prophecy of Ezekiel. (See Ezek. 37:19.) Together they declare the Kingship of the Redeemer of the world and the reality of his kingdom.[12]

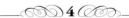

The Book of Mormon offers teachings that can help us find solutions to the problems of today's society.

[The Book of Mormon] narrative is a chronicle of nations long since gone. But in its descriptions of the problems of today's society, it is as current as the morning newspaper and much more definitive, inspired, and inspiring concerning the solutions to those problems.[13]

I open its pages and read, and it has language both beautiful and uplifting. The ancient record from which it was translated came out of the earth as a voice speaking from the dust. It came as the testimony of generations of men and women who lived their lives upon the earth, who struggled with adversity, who quarreled and fought, who at various times lived the divine law and prospered and at other times forsook their God and went down to destruction.[14]

I know of no other writing that sets forth with such clarity the tragic consequences to societies that follow courses contrary to the commandments of God. Its pages trace the stories of two distinct civilizations that flourished on the Western Hemisphere. Each began as a small nation, its people walking in the fear of the Lord. Each prospered, but with prosperity came growing evils. The people succumbed to the wiles of ambitious and scheming leaders who oppressed them with burdensome taxes, who lulled them with hollow promises, who countenanced and even encouraged loose and lascivious living, who led them into terrible wars that resulted in the death of millions and the final extinction of two great civilizations in two different eras.

No other written testament so clearly illustrates the fact that when men and nations walk in the fear of God and in obedience to his commandments, they prosper and grow, but when they disregard him and his word, there comes a decay which, unless arrested by righteousness, leads to impotence and death. The Book of Mormon is an affirmation of the Old Testament proverb, "Righteousness exalteth a nation: but sin is a reproach to any people." (Prov. 14:34.)[15]

5

The Book of Mormon has the power to change our lives and our perspective.

In August 1830, as a lay preacher, Parley Parker Pratt was traveling from Ohio to eastern New York. At Newark, along the Erie Canal, he left the boat and walked ten miles [16 kilometers] into the country, where he met a Baptist deacon by the name of Hamlin, who told him "of a *book*, a STRANGE BOOK, a VERY STRANGE BOOK! . . . This book, he said, purported to have been originally written on plates either of gold or brass, by a branch of the tribes

*The Book of Mormon had a profound effect on Parley P. Pratt,
who later became an Apostle.*

of Israel; and to have been discovered and translated by a young man near Palmyra, in the State of New York, by the aid of visions, or the ministry of angels. I inquired of him how or where the book was to be obtained. He promised me the perusal of it, at his house the next day. . . . Next morning I called at his house, where, for the first time, my eyes beheld the 'BOOK OF MORMON'—that book of books . . . which was the principal means, in the hands of God, of directing the entire course of my future life.

"I opened it with eagerness, and read its title page. I then read the testimony of several witnesses in relation to the manner of its being found and translated. After this I commenced its contents by course. I read all day; eating was a burden, I had no desire for food; sleep was a burden when the night came, for I preferred reading to sleep.

"As I read, the spirit of the Lord was upon me, and I knew and comprehended that the book was true, as plainly and manifestly as a man comprehends and knows that he exists." (*Autobiography of Parley P. Pratt,* 3rd ed., Salt Lake City: Deseret Book Co., 1938, pp. 36–37.)

Parley Pratt was then twenty-three years of age. Reading the Book of Mormon affected him so profoundly that he was soon baptized into the Church and became one of its most effective and powerful advocates. . . .

Parley Pratt's experience with the Book of Mormon was not unique. As the volumes of the first edition were circulated and read, strong men and women by the hundreds were so deeply touched that they gave up everything they owned, and in the years that followed, not a few gave their lives for the witness they carried in their hearts of the truth of this remarkable volume.

Today . . . it is more widely read than at any time in its history. . . . Its appeal is as timeless as truth, as universal as mankind.[16]

[The Book of Mormon] has touched for good the lives of millions who have prayerfully read it and pondered its language. May I tell you of one such. . . .

He was a businessman, successful in his undertakings. In the course of his travels he met two of our missionaries. They tried to set up an appointment to teach him. He put them off, but finally agreed to listen. He somewhat perfunctorily accepted what they had to say. He became convinced in his mind that they spoke the truth, but he was not moved in his heart.

He decided that he would read the Book of Mormon. He said that he had been a man of the world, never given to crying. But as he read the book, tears coursed his cheeks. It did something to him. He read it again and felt the same emotions. What had been conversion of the mind became conversion of the heart.

His way of life was altered, his perspective changed. He threw himself into the work of the Lord. Today he fills a high and holy calling in the cause he has come to love.[17]

Let me tell you [another] story about the Book of Mormon. I heard a man who was a banker in California tell this story. He said his secretary smoked, constantly smoked. She was addicted to smoking. She could not set it aside. She said to him one day, "How can I stop smoking?"

He reached down in his desk and took out a copy of the Book of Mormon and handed it to her. He said, "Now, you read this."

She said, "All right, I'll read it."

She came back a couple of days later and said, "I've read 200 pages, and I didn't see the word *smoking* anywhere. I didn't see the word *tobacco* anywhere. I saw nothing that referred to it."

He said, "Keep reading."

So she came back another couple of days later and said, "I've read 200 more pages—no mention of smoking, no mention of nicotine, no mention of anything associated with tobacco."

He said, "Keep reading."

She came back three or four days later. She said, "I've read the entire book. I didn't see tobacco anywhere; I didn't see smoking anywhere. But," she said, "there has come into my heart as a result of reading that book some influence, some power, that has taken from me the desire to smoke, and it is wonderful."[18]

Let me tell you of a letter which we received. . . . A man wrote, saying, "I am in a federal prison. I recently came across a copy of the Book of Mormon in the prison library. I have read it, and when I read Mormon's lamentation over his fallen people—'O ye fair ones, how could ye have departed from the ways of the Lord! O ye fair ones, how could ye have rejected that Jesus, who stood with open arms to receive you! Behold, if ye had not done this, ye would not have fallen' (Morm. 6:17–18)—I felt that Mormon was talking to me. Can I get a copy of that book?"

We sent him a copy. Some time later, he walked into my office a changed man. He was touched by the spirit of the Book of Mormon and today is a successful man, rehabilitated, earning a living honestly for himself and his family.

Such is the power of this great book in the lives of those who read it prayerfully.

Brothers and sisters, without reservation I promise you that if you will prayerfully read the Book of Mormon, regardless of how many times you previously have read it, there will come into your hearts an added measure of the Spirit of the Lord. There will come a strengthened resolution to walk in obedience to his commandments, and there will come a stronger testimony of the living reality of the Son of God.[19]

Suggestions for Study and Teaching

Questions

- Why do we need the Book of Mormon? What are some passages in the Book of Mormon that have strengthened your testimony of Jesus Christ? What examples have you seen of the Book of Mormon and the Bible going "hand in hand" in testifying of the Savior? (See section 1.)

- Why do you think the promise in Moroni 10:3–5 is more important than physical evidence of the Book of Mormon? (See section 2.) What experiences have you had with this promise?

- As you review section 3, note the truths we can know when we have a testimony of the Book of Mormon. How does the Book of Mormon testify of these truths?

- Think about some of the "problems of today's society" (section 4). In what ways can the Book of Mormon help us find solutions to those problems? What are some passages in the Book of Mormon that have helped you in times of personal challenge?

- Ponder the stories in section 5. If someone asked you about the Book of Mormon, what could you say about how it has influenced your life?

Related Scriptures

Isaiah 29:9–18; 1 Nephi 13:35–41; 2 Nephi 29:6–9; Moroni 10:27–29; D&C 20:8–12; 42:12–13

Study Help

"I am grateful for emphasis on reading the scriptures. I hope that for you this will become something far more enjoyable than a duty; that, rather, it will become a love affair with the word of God. I promise you that as you read, your minds will be enlightened and your spirits will be lifted. At first it may seem tedious, but that will change into a wondrous experience with thoughts and words of things divine" (Gordon B. Hinckley, "The Light within You," *Ensign,* May 1995, 99).

Notes

1. "Gifts to Bring Home from the Mission Field," *New Era,* Mar. 2007, 2.

2. In Sheri L. Dew, *Go Forward with Faith: The Biography of Gordon B. Hinckley* (1996), 100.

3. "Let Virtue Garnish Thy Thoughts Unceasingly," *Ensign* or *Liahona,* May 2007, 116.

4. "Inspirational Thoughts," *Ensign,* July 1998, 2.

5. "The Great Things Which God Has Revealed," *Ensign* or *Liahona,* May 2005, 82.

6. "The Symbol of Our Faith," *Ensign,* Apr. 2005, 4; quoting the title page of the Book of Mormon.

7. "Excerpts from Recent Addresses by President Gordon B. Hinckley," *Ensign,* July 1997, 72.

8. "Believe His Prophets," *Ensign,* May 1992, 51.

9. "An Angel from on High, the Long, Long Silence Broke," *Ensign,* Nov. 1979, 7.

10. "Four Cornerstones of Faith," *Ensign,* Feb. 2004, 6; quoting the title page of the Book of Mormon.

11. In *Heroes from the Book of Mormon* (1995), 198.

12. "The Power of the Book of Mormon," *Ensign,* June 1988, 6.

13. "The Power of the Book of Mormon," 4.

14. "Four Cornerstones of Faith," 5.

15. "The Power of the Book of Mormon," 5.

16. "The Power of the Book of Mormon," 2, 4.

17. "*Mormon* Should Mean 'More Good,'" *Ensign,* Nov. 1990, 52.

18. *Discourses of President Gordon B. Hinckley, Volume 2: 2000–2004* (2005), 402–3.

19. "The Power of the Book of Mormon," 6.

Continue in the Great
Process of Learning

"We must go on growing. We must continually learn. It is a divinely given mandate that we go on adding to our knowledge."

From the Life of Gordon B. Hinckley

"I love to learn," President Gordon B. Hinckley said. "I relish any opportunity to acquire knowledge. Indeed, I believe in and have vigorously supported, throughout my life, the pursuit of education—for myself and for others. . . . From my point of view, learning is both a practical matter and a spiritual one."[1]

President Hinckley's fellow servants in Church leadership marveled at his gift for accumulating knowledge and applying it in his work. Elder Robert D. Hales of the Quorum of the Twelve Apostles observed: "I have never met an individual who can become so well informed through reading and through contact with people. When he spends an evening at dinner with someone, he leaves knowing something about that individual's expertise." Elder Neal A. Maxwell, also of the Quorum of the Twelve, said: "What makes President Hinckley unique is that he remembers what he has read and distills that which he wishes to retain. His is an integrated intellect. He can draw upon what he knows to make prudent decisions."[2]

In his lifelong efforts to learn and improve himself, President Hinckley followed the example of his parents. He related the following account of how his father, Bryant S. Hinckley, was committed to learning:

"When he was about the age that I am now, he was fully retired. But he was active. He lived in a rather simple but comfortable home in a rural area. He had an orchard around him and enjoyed giving

"Seek learning, even by study and also by faith" (D&C 88:118).

away the fruit. The yard of his home included lawns and shrubs and trees. It had a rock wall about two feet high separating one level from another. Whenever the weather was good he would sit on the wall, an old hat on his head to shade his eyes from the summer sun. When we went to visit him, I would sit at his side. With a little prompting he would talk of his life. . . .

"He was an educator. He was a successful businessman. He presided over the largest stake in the Church with more than 15,000 members. He served as a mission president and in many other capacities. And now he was retired, and he sat on the wall. He was a great reader with a wonderful library. He was an excellent speaker and writer. Almost to the time he died, just short of the age of 94, he read and wrote and contemplated the knowledge that had come to him.

"I discovered that when he sat on the wall, hours at a time on a warm day, he would reflect on the things he had read from his library.

"I think he grew old gracefully and wonderfully. He had his books with the precious treasures they contained of the thoughts of great men and women of all the ages of time. He never ceased to learn, and as he sat on the wall he thought deeply of what he had read the night before. . . .

". . . Why am I telling you of an old man and the wall on which he sat? I am telling you because I think it has a lesson for each of us. We must never cease to learn. We believe in eternal progression and that this life is a part of eternity to be profitably lived until the very end."[3]

Teachings of Gordon B. Hinckley

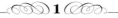 1

The Lord wants us to educate ourselves so we can progress individually and contribute to society.

You belong to a church that teaches the importance of education. You have a mandate from the Lord to educate your minds and your hearts and your hands. The Lord has said, "Teach ye diligently . . . of things both in heaven and in the earth, and under the earth; things which have been, things which are, things which must shortly come to pass; things which are at home, things which are abroad; the wars and the perplexities of the nations, and the judgments which are on the land; and a knowledge also of countries and of king-doms—that ye may be prepared in all things" (D&C 88:78–80).[4]

We of this Church have been given a marvelous promise by the Lord. Said He: "That which is of God is light; and he that receiveth light, and continueth in God, receiveth more light; and that light groweth brighter and brighter until the perfect day" (D&C 50:24).

What a remarkable statement that is. It is one of my favorite verses of scripture. It speaks of growth, of development, of the march that leads toward godhood. It goes hand in hand with these great decla-rations: "The glory of God is intelligence, or, in other words, light and truth" (D&C 93:36); "If a person gains more knowledge and intelligence in this life through his diligence and obedience than another, he will have so much the advantage in the world to come" (D&C 130:19). . . .

What a profound challenge is found in these marvelous state-ments. We must go on growing. We must continually learn. It is a divinely given mandate that we go on adding to our knowledge. . . .

. . . Said the Lord to you and to me: "Seek ye out of the best books words of wisdom; seek learning, even by study and also by faith. . . . Organize yourselves. . . . Cease to be idle" (D&C 88:118–119, 124).[5]

The Lord wants you to educate your minds and hands, whatever your chosen field. Whether it be repairing refrigerators, or the work of a skilled surgeon, you must train yourselves. Seek for the best schooling available. Become a workman of integrity in the world that lies ahead of you. . . . You will bring honor to the Church and you will be generously blessed because of that training.

There can be no doubt, none whatever, that education pays. Do not short-circuit your lives. If you do so, you will pay for it over and over and over again.[6]

It is not enough just to live, just to survive. It is incumbent on each of us to equip ourselves to do something worthwhile in society—to acquire more and more light, so that our personal light

"Begin early in exposing children to books."

can help illuminate a darkened world. And this is made possible through learning, through educating ourselves, through progressing and growing in both mind and spirit.[7]

 **2**

With planning and self-discipline, parents can create an atmosphere of learning in their homes.

What a marvelously interesting thing it is to watch young minds stretch and strengthen. I am one who greatly appreciates the vast potential of television for good. But I also am one who decries the terrible waste of time and opportunity as children in some homes watch, hour upon hour, that which neither enlightens nor strengthens.

When I was a boy we lived in a large old house. One room was called the library. It had a solid table and a good lamp, three or four comfortable chairs with good light, and books in cases that lined the walls. There were many volumes—the acquisitions of my father and mother over a period of many years.

We were never forced to read them, but they were placed where they were handy and where we could get at them whenever we wished.

There was quiet in that room. It was understood that it was a place to study.

There were also magazines—the Church magazines and two or three other good magazines. There were books of history and literature, books on technical subjects, dictionaries, a set of encyclopedias, and an atlas of the world. There was no television, of course, at that time. Radio came along while I was growing up. But there was an environment, an environment of learning. I would not have you believe that we were great scholars. But we were exposed to great literature, great ideas from great thinkers, and the language of men and women who thought deeply and wrote beautifully.

In so many of our homes today there is not the possibility of such a library. Most families are cramped for space. But with planning there can be a corner, there can be an area that becomes something of a hideaway from the noises about us where one can sit and read and think. It is a wonderful thing to have a desk or a table, be it ever so simple, on which are found the standard works of the Church, a few good books, the magazines issued by the Church, and other things worthy of our reading.

Begin early in exposing children to books. The mother who fails to read to her small children does a disservice to them and a disservice to herself. It takes time, yes, much of it. It takes self-discipline. It takes organizing and budgeting the minutes and hours of the day. But it will never be a bore as you watch young minds come to know characters, expressions, and ideas. Good reading can become a love affair, far more fruitful in long term effects than many other activities in which children use their time. . . .

Parents, . . . let your children be exposed to great minds, great ideas, everlasting truth, and those things which will build and motivate for good. . . . Try to create within your home an atmosphere of learning and the growth which will come of it.[8]

3

Education unlocks the door of opportunity for youth and young adults.

This is the great day of opportunity for you young people, this marvelous time to be upon the earth. You stand at the summit of all of the past ages. You are exposed to all of the learning of all who have walked the earth, that learning being distilled down into courses where you can acquire knowledge in a relatively short time, that knowledge which men stumbled over in learning through all of the centuries past. Do not sell yourselves short. Do not miss your great opportunity. Get at it, work at it, study hard.[9]

It is so important that you young men and you young women get all of the education that you can. . . . Education is the key which will unlock the door of opportunity for you. It is worth sacrificing for. It is worth working at, and if you educate your mind and your hands, you will be able to make a great contribution to the society of which you are a part, and you will be able to reflect honorably on the Church of which you are a member. My dear young brothers and sisters, take advantage of every educational opportunity that you can possibly afford, and you fathers and mothers, encourage your sons and daughters to gain an education which will bless their lives.[10]

Perhaps you do not have the funds to get all the schooling you would desire. Make your money go as far as you can, and take advantage of scholarships, grants, and loans within your capacity to repay.[11]

I do not care what you want to be as long as it is honorable. A car mechanic, a brick layer, a plumber, an electrician, a doctor, a lawyer, a merchant, but not a thief. But whatever you are, take the opportunity to train for it and make the best of that opportunity. Society will reward you according to your worth as it perceives that worth. Now is the great day of preparation for each of you. If it means sacrifice, then sacrifice. That sacrifice will become the best investment you have ever made, for you will reap returns from it all the days of your lives.[12]

I urge each of you young women to get all of the schooling you can get. You will need it for the world into which you will move. Life is becoming so exceedingly competitive. . . . The world is changing, and it is so very important that we equip ourselves to move with that change. But there is a bright side to all of this. No other generation in all of history has offered women so many opportunities. Your first objective should be a happy marriage, sealed in the temple of the

Lord, and followed by the rearing of a good family. Education can better equip you for the realization of those ideals.[13]

There are tremendous responsibilities for women in the Church as well as in the community consistent with and in total harmony with marriage, motherhood, and the rearing of good and able children.[14]

The whole gamut of human endeavor is now open to women. There is not anything that you cannot do if you will set your mind to it. You can include in your dream of the woman you would like to be a picture of one qualified to serve society and make a significant contribution to the world of which she will be a part.[15]

I am grateful that women today are afforded the same opportunity [as men] to study for science, for the professions, and for every other facet of human knowledge. You are as entitled as are men to the Spirit of Christ, which enlightens every man and woman who comes into the world. (See D&C 84:46.) Set your priorities in terms of marriage and family, but also pursue educational programs which will lead to satisfying work and productive employment in case you do not marry, or to a sense of security and fulfillment in the event you do marry.[16]

You [young men] face great challenges that lie ahead. You are moving into a world of fierce competition. You must get all of the education you can. The Lord has instructed us concerning the importance of education. It will qualify you for greater opportunities. It will equip you to do something worthwhile in the great world of opportunity that lies ahead. If you can go to college and that is your wish, then do it. If you have no desire to attend college, then go to a vocational or business school to sharpen your skills and increase your capacity.[17]

I hope you [young people] will look upon the educational opportunity that you have as a great blessing. I know it is a grind. I know it is difficult. I know you get discouraged at times. I know you wonder why you are doing it at times. But keep on, keep hammering away, and keep learning. You will never regret it as long as you live but will count it as a great blessing.[18]

The schooling of the spirit is as important, if not more so, than the schooling of the mind.

I am awed by the great forces of knowledge represented in our time. Never before have so many been educated in the learning of the world. What a powerful thing it is—the intensive schooling of a large percentage of the youth of the world, who meet daily at the feet of instructors to garner knowledge from all the ages of man.

The extent of that knowledge is staggering. It encompasses the stars of the universe, the geology of the earth, the history of nations, the culture and language of peoples, the operation of governments, the laws of commerce, the behavior of the atom, the functions of the body, and the wonders of the mind.

With so much knowledge available, one would think that the world might well be near a state of perfection. Yet we are constantly made aware of the other side of the coin—of the sickness of society, of the contentions and troubles that bring misery into the lives of millions.

Each day we are made increasingly aware of the fact that life is more than science and mathematics, more than history and literature. There is need for another education, without which the substance of secular learning may lead only to destruction. I refer to the education of the heart, of the conscience, of the character, of the spirit—these indefinable aspects of our personalities which determine so certainly what we are and what we do in our relationships one with another.

. . . While serving in England as a missionary, I went to the London Central YMCA. I suppose that old building has long since gone, but I can never forget the words that faced visitors in the foyer each time they entered. They were the words of Solomon: "With all thy getting get understanding." (Prov. 4:7.)

Understanding of what? Understanding of ourselves, of the purposes of life, of our relationship to God, who is our Father, of the great divinely given principles that for centuries have provided the sinew of man's real progress! . . .

"With all of our study, we need to seek knowledge of the Master."

As we pursue our secular studies, let us also add to our lives the cultivation of the Spirit. If we do so, God will bless us with that peace and those blessings which come from Him alone.[19]

Jesus said: "Learn of me. . . . For my yoke is easy, and my burden is light." (Matt. 11:29–30.)

I should like to suggest that we follow that injunction given by the Son of God. With all of our learning, let us also learn of him. With all of our study, we need to seek knowledge of the Master. That knowledge will complement in a wonderful way our secular training and will give us character and a fulness to life that can come in no other way.[20]

I challenge you to never forget that the schooling of the spirit is as important, if not more so, than the schooling of the mind.[21]

Our great program of Church education moves forward. The work of training students through the seminary and institute program is constantly being enlarged. . . . You who have been the recipients of this program know of its tremendous value. We urge all for whom it is available to take advantage of it. We do not hesitate to promise that your knowledge of the gospel will be increased, your faith will be strengthened, and you will develop wonderful associations.[22]

Let us take upon ourselves the name of the Lord and then with faith go forth to share with relevance that which will affect the lives of mankind and bring peace and joy to the world. The world needs a generation of men and women of learning and influence who can and will stand up and in sincerity and without equivocation declare that God lives and that Jesus is the Christ.[23]

5

No matter how old we grow, we can acquire knowledge, gather wisdom, and keep on growing.

What a remarkable thing is learning, the process whereby the accumulated knowledge of the centuries has been summarized and filtered so that in a brief period we can learn what was first learned only through long exercises of research and trial and error.

Education is the great conversion process under which abstract knowledge becomes useful and productive activity. It is something that need never stop. No matter how old we grow, we can acquire knowledge and use it. We can gather wisdom and profit from it. We can be entertained through the miracle of reading and exposure to the arts and add to the blessing and fulfillment of living. The older I grow, the more I enjoy the words of thoughtful writers, ancient and modern, and the savoring of that which they have written.[24]

None of us . . . knows enough. The learning process is an endless process. We must read, we must observe, we must assimilate, and we must ponder that to which we expose our minds. . . . I believe in improvement. I believe in growth. . . .

Keep on growing, my brothers and sisters, whether you are thirty or whether you are seventy. Your industry in so doing will cause the years to pass faster than you might wish, but they will be filled with a sweet and wonderful zest that will add flavor to your life and power to your teaching.[25]

Immediately to the east of [Brigham Young University in Provo, Utah] is a mountain. [Many], I am confident, have looked up at that mountain and thought, "If I could just climb to the top it would be interesting to see the valley on the other side." But those of you who have made that climb have discovered that the valley is only a small and rather shallow depression, and that beyond are many other higher mountains to be climbed.

So I hope it will be with you. . . . You will recognize that while your learning experience [may have] been great, there are even greater opportunities and challenges ahead. Add to your store of information, increase your knowledge, continue the great process of learning.[26]

Suggestions for Study and Teaching

Questions

- Why is it important to "acquire more and more light" through education? (See section 1.) How can learning help us progress individually? How can learning help us "illuminate a darkened world"?

- Review President Hinckley's account of how his parents created an atmosphere of learning in their home (see section 2). How can we help children develop a love for learning? How can we help children desire to seek learning from sources that enlighten and motivate for good?

- How does education "unlock the door of opportunity" for youth and young adults? (See section 3.) How can youth and young adults be resourceful in taking advantage of opportunities for education?

- How would you explain the meaning of the phrase "the schooling of the spirit"? (See section 4.) How can we educate the heart, character, and spirit? In your life, how have spiritual learning and secular learning complemented one another?

- Why should we continue to learn throughout our lives? (See section 5.) How can we maintain a lifelong love for learning? What have you learned recently that has been especially valuable to you?

Related Scriptures

Proverbs 1:5; 2 Peter 1:1–8; 2 Nephi 9:28–29; 28:29–30; D&C 6:7; 90:15; 131:6; 136:32–33

Teaching Help

One idea to encourage discussion about President Hinckley's teachings is to ask participants to share what they have learned from their personal study of the chapter (see pages vi–vii in this book for additional ideas).

Notes

1. *Standing for Something: Ten Neglected Virtues That Will Heal Our Hearts and Homes* (2000), 59.

2. In Sheri L. Dew, *Go Forward with Faith: The Biography of Gordon B. Hinckley* (1996), 449–50.

3. *Discourses of President Gordon B. Hinckley, Volume 1: 1995–1999* (2005), 406–7.

4. "A Prophet's Counsel and Prayer for Youth," *Ensign,* Jan. 2001, 4–5.

5. "A Conversation with Single Adults," *Ensign,* Mar. 1997, 62.

6. "A Prophet's Counsel and Prayer for Youth," 7.

7. *Standing for Something,* 67.

8. "The Environment of Our Homes," *Ensign,* June 1985, 4–5.

9. *Teachings of Gordon B. Hinckley* (1997), 171–72.

10. "Inspirational Thoughts," *Ensign,* June 1999, 4.

11. "Stay on the High Road," *Ensign* or *Liahona,* May 2004, 113.

12. *Teachings of Gordon B. Hinckley,* 172–73.

13. "Stand True and Faithful," *Ensign,* May 1996, 92.

14. "Youth Is the Season," *New Era,* Sept. 1988, 47.

15. "How Can I Become the Woman of Whom I Dream?" *Ensign,* May 2001, 95.

16. "Ten Gifts from the Lord," *Ensign,* Nov. 1985, 89.

17. "Converts and Young Men," *Ensign,* May 1997, 49–50.

18. *Discourses of President Gordon B. Hinckley, Volume 1,* 370.

19. "With All Thy Getting Get Understanding," *Ensign,* Aug. 1988, 2, 5.

20. "With All Thy Getting Get Understanding," 5.

21. In "President Hinckley Visits New Zealand, Australia, and Mexico," *Ensign,* Aug. 1997, 77.

22. "The Miracle Made Possible by Faith," *Ensign,* May 1984, 47.

23. "With All Thy Getting Get Understanding," 5.

24. "I Believe," *Ensign,* Aug. 1992, 4.

25. *Teachings of Gordon B. Hinckley,* 298–99.

26. *Teachings of Gordon B. Hinckley,* 299.

President Gordon B. Hinckley counseled, "Let virtue be a cornerstone on which to build your lives."

Virtue—A Cornerstone on Which to Build Our Lives

"You are, each one of you, children of a divine Father in Heaven. You were created after His design in the image of your Creator. Your body is sacred. It is the temple of your spirit. Do not defile it with sin."

From the Life of Gordon B. Hinckley

Speaking to students at Brigham Young University in 2007, President Gordon B. Hinckley said:

"I observed a very interesting thing the other day. In Salt Lake City, early on a Saturday morning, the Key Bank building was brought down with a series of well-placed detonations. It all happened in three or four seconds, with a great cloud of dust that rolled to the northwest. The process is called an implosion, in contrast with an explosion.

"The building was constructed nearly 30 years ago. I suppose construction extended over a period of at least a year, maybe two. Now it was gone in seconds.

"That, my friends, is the story of so many lives. We nurture them ever so carefully over a period of years. Then we find ourselves in highly charged circumstances. Mistakes are made. Chastity is compromised. There is an implosion, and a ball of dust is all that is left.

"I was reminded of this when I recalled a young man and a young woman who came to my office. He was a handsome boy and she was a beautiful girl. They were university students. Their future looked bright and beautiful. But they gave in to temptation. . . .

"Tears filled their eyes as they talked with me. But there was no escape from the reality that faced them. Their lives had suffered an implosion, and a tower of dreams had come tumbling down.

"Do not let this happen to you. Do not sell yourself short by compromising your commitment to morality. You are, each one of you, children of a divine Father in Heaven. You were created after His design in the image of your Creator. Your body is sacred. It is the temple of your spirit. Do not defile it with sin.

"Now, hearkening back to the illustration of the tower that collapsed, I remind you that in its place will be constructed a new and beautiful building. Similarly, those who have transgressed can turn to their Redeemer, our Savior Jesus Christ, and, through the power of His Atonement, be made clean and new again."[1]

Teachings of Gordon B. Hinckley

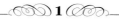

Virtuous living brings marvelous and wonderful blessings.

There is nothing in all this world as magnificent as virtue. It glows without tarnish. It is precious and beautiful. It is above price. It cannot be bought or sold. It is the fruit of self-mastery.

. . . The Lord has given a wonderful mandate. He has said, "Let virtue garnish thy thoughts unceasingly" (D&C 121:45). This becomes a commandment to be observed with diligence and discipline. And there is attached to it the promise of marvelous and wonderful blessings. He has said to those who live with virtue:

"Then shall thy confidence wax strong in the presence of God. . . .

"The Holy Ghost shall be thy constant companion, and thy scepter an unchanging scepter of righteousness and truth; and thy dominion shall be an everlasting dominion, and without compulsory means it shall flow unto thee forever and ever" (D&C 121:45–46).

Could there be a greater or more beautiful promise than this?[2]

Is there a valid case for virtue? It is the only way to freedom from regret. The peace of conscience which flows therefrom is the only personal peace that is not counterfeit.

And beyond all of this is the unfailing promise of God to those who walk in virtue. Declared Jesus of Nazareth, speaking on the mountain, "Blessed are the pure in heart: for they shall see God" (Matt. 5:8). That is a covenant, made by Him who has the power to fulfill.[3]

You should recognize, you *must* recognize, that both experience and divine wisdom dictate virtue and moral cleanliness as the way that leads to strength of character, peace in the heart, and happiness in life.[4]

Let virtue be a cornerstone on which to build your lives.[5]

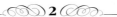

When we rise above the filth and immorality of the world, we enjoy greater happiness, security, and peace of mind.

As we look out over the world, it seems that morality has been cast aside. The violation of old standards has become common. Studies, one after another, show that there has been an abandonment of time-tested principles. Self-discipline has been forgotten, and promiscuous indulgence has become widespread.

But, my dear friends, we cannot accept that which has become common in the world. Yours, as members of this Church, is a higher standard and more demanding. It declares as a voice from Sinai that thou shalt not indulge. You must keep control of your desires.[6]

Paul's words to the Corinthian Saints are as applicable to us today as they were to those to whom he wrote. Said he:

"Know ye not that ye are the temple of God, and that the Spirit of God dwelleth in you?

"If any man defile the temple of God, him shall God destroy; for the temple of God is holy, which temple ye are" (1 Corinthians 3:16–17).[7]

Again Paul's counsel to Timothy, "Keep thyself pure" (1 Tim. 5:22).

Those are simple words. But they are ever so important. Paul is saying, in effect, stay away from those things which will tear you down and destroy you spiritually. Stay away from television shows

Chastity is "the way to happiness in living."

which lead to unclean thoughts and unclean language. Stay away from videos which will lead to evil thoughts. They won't help you. They will only hurt you. Stay away from books and magazines which are sleazy and filthy in what they say and portray. Keep thyself pure.[8]

Marriage is ordained of God, marriage between a man and a woman. It is the institution under which He designed that children should come into the world. Sexual relationships under any other circumstances become transgression and are totally at odds with the teachings of the gospel of Jesus Christ.[9]

We believe in chastity before marriage and total fidelity after marriage. That sums it up. That is the way to happiness in living. That is the way to satisfaction. It brings peace to the heart and peace to the home.[10]

No family can have peace, no life can be free from the storms of adversity unless that family and that home are built on foundations of morality, fidelity, and mutual respect. There cannot be peace where there is not trust; there cannot be freedom where there is not loyalty. The warm sunlight of love will not rise out of a swamp of immorality.[11]

I believe that it should be the blessing of every child to be born into a home where that child is welcomed, nurtured, loved, and blessed with parents, a father and a mother, who live with loyalty to one another and to their children. . . . Stand strong against the wiles of the world. The creators of our entertainment, the purveyors of much of our literature, would have you believe otherwise. The accumulated wisdom of centuries declares with clarity and certainty that the greater happiness, the greater security, the greater peace of mind, the deeper reservoirs of love are experienced only by those who walk according to time-tested standards of virtue before marriage and total fidelity within marriage.[12]

We live in a world of filth and immorality and trouble. Rise above it, stand taller, leave the world behind you, and walk as the Lord would have you walk.[13]

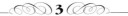 **3**

Pornography is addictive and destructive, but we can rise above it.

I rather reluctantly speak to a theme that I have dealt with before. I do it in the spirit of the words of Alma, who said: "This is my glory, that perhaps I may be an instrument in the hands of God to bring some soul to repentance" (Alma 29:9).

. . . I speak of pornography in all of its manifestations. . . . It is devilish. It is totally inconsistent with the spirit of the gospel, with personal testimony of the things of God. . . .

. . . All who are involved become victims. Children are exploited, and their lives are severely damaged. The minds of youth become warped with false concepts. Continued exposure leads to addiction that is almost impossible to break. . . . So very many . . . find they cannot leave it alone. Their energies and their interests are consumed in their dead-end pursuit of this raw and sleazy fare.

The excuse is given that it is hard to avoid, that it is right at our fingertips and there is no escape.

Suppose a storm is raging and the winds howl and the snow swirls about you. You find yourself unable to stop it. But you can dress properly and seek shelter, and the storm will have no effect upon you.

Likewise, even though the Internet is saturated with sleazy material, you do not have to watch it. You can retreat to the shelter of the gospel and its teaching of cleanliness and virtue and purity of life.

I know that I am speaking directly and plainly. I do so because the Internet has made pornography more widely accessible, adding to what is available on DVDs and videos, on television and magazine stands. It leads to fantasies that are destructive of self-respect. It leads to illicit relationships, often to disease, and to abusive criminal activity.[14]

You live in a world of terrible temptations. Pornography, with its sleazy filth, sweeps over the earth like a horrible, engulfing tide. It is poison. Do not watch it or read it. It will destroy you if you do. It will take from you your self-respect. It will rob you of a sense of the beauties of life. It will tear you down and pull you into a slough of evil thoughts and possibly of evil actions. Stay away from it. Shun it as you would a foul disease, for it is just as deadly. Be virtuous in thought and in deed.[15]

There is so much of filth and lust and pornography in this world. We as Latter-day Saints must rise above it and stand tall against it. You can't afford to indulge in it. You just cannot afford to indulge in it. You have to keep it out of your heart. Like tobacco it's addictive, and it will destroy those who tamper with it. "Let virtue garnish thy thoughts unceasingly" [D&C 121:45].[16]

With discipline and effort, we can control our thoughts and actions.

Be clean in mind, and then you will have greater control over your bodies. It was said of old, "As [a man] thinketh in his heart, so is he" (Prov. 23:7). Unclean thoughts lead to unclean acts.[17]

When tempted we can substitute for thoughts of evil thoughts of [our Savior] and His teachings. He has said: "And if your eye be single to my glory, your whole bodies shall be filled with light, and there shall be no darkness in you; and that body which is filled with light comprehendeth all things.

"Therefore, sanctify yourselves that your minds become single to God, and the days will come that you shall see him; for he will unveil his face unto you" (D&C 88:67–68).[18]

Jesus gave a commandment to control our thoughts as well as our deeds. He said, "Whosoever looketh on a woman to lust after her hath committed adultery with her already in his heart" (Matthew 5:28). . . .

Mental control must be stronger than physical appetites or desires of the flesh. As thoughts are brought into complete harmony with revealed truth, actions will then become appropriate. . . . Each of us, with discipline and effort, has the capacity to control our thoughts and our actions. This is part of the process of developing spiritual, physical, and emotional maturity. . . .

We plead with people everywhere to live in accordance with the teachings of our Creator and rise above carnal attractions that often result in the tragedies that follow moral transgression.[19]

Those who have been involved in immoral behavior can be forgiven and can rise above the past.

I do not wish to be negative. I am by nature optimistic. But in such matters as this [pornography and immorality] I am a realist. If we are involved in such behavior, now is the time to change. Let this be our hour of resolution. Let us turn about to a better way.[20]

If you find yourself slipping under the pressure of circumstances, discipline yourselves. Stop before it is too late. You will be forever grateful that you did.

Be true to yourselves and the best you have within you.[21]

Let me . . . assure you that if you have made a mistake, if you have become involved in any immoral behavior, all is not lost. Memory of that mistake will likely linger, but the deed can be forgiven, and you can rise above the past to live a life fully acceptable unto the Lord where there has been repentance. He has promised that

He will forgive your sins and remember them no more against you (see D&C 58:42).

. . . Church leaders [can] assist you in your difficulty. You can put behind you any evil with which you have been involved. You can go forward with a renewal of hope and acceptability to a far better way of life.[22]

Suggestions for Study and Teaching

Questions

- President Hinckley taught that there is "a valid case for virtue" (section 1). How might you respond to someone who argues that there is *not* a valid case for virtue?

- Why is chastity "the way to happiness in living"? Why does chastity bring "peace to the heart and peace to the home"? (See sections 1 and 2.)

- President Hinckley said, "We as Latter-day Saints must rise above [pornography] and stand tall against it" (section 3). What can we do to rise above it? How can we help others rise above it? What do you think it means to stand tall against it?

- As you read President Hinckley's counsel in section 4, what do you learn about controlling your thoughts? What are some practical things we can do to keep our thoughts clean?

Related Scriptures

Psalm 24:3–4; Matthew 5:27–28; Philippians 4:6–8; Jacob 3:2; D&C 46:31–33; 59:6; Articles of Faith 1:13

Study Help

As you read, "underline and mark words or phrases so that you distinguish between ideas in a single [passage]. . . . In the margins write scripture references that clarify the passages you are studying" (*Preach My Gospel* [2004], 23).

Notes

1. "True to the Faith" (Brigham Young University devotional, Sept. 18, 2007), 2–3, speeches.byu.edu.

2. "How Can I Become the Woman of Whom I Dream?" *Ensign,* May 2001, 95.

3. "Words of the Prophet: Blessed Are the Pure in Heart," *New Era,* July 1999, 4.

4. "Reverence and Morality," *Ensign,* May 1987, 48.

5. In Conference Report, Oct. 1964, 118.

6. "Stay on the High Road," *Ensign* or *Liahona,* May 2004, 114.

7. "In These Three I Believe," *Ensign,* July 2006, 4.

8. "Converts and Young Men," *Ensign,* May 1997, 49.

9. "True to the Faith," *Ensign,* June 1996, 5.

10. "This Thing Was Not Done in a Corner," *Ensign,* Nov. 1996, 49.

11. "In Search of Peace and Freedom," *Ensign,* Aug. 1989, 5.

12. "Stand Strong against the Wiles of the World," *Ensign,* Nov. 1995, 99.

13. "Inspirational Thoughts," *Ensign,* Feb. 2007, 7.

14. "A Tragic Evil among Us," *Ensign* or *Liahona,* Nov. 2004, 59–62.

15. "Some Thoughts on Temples, Retention of Converts, and Missionary Service," *Ensign,* Nov. 1997, 51.

16. "Inspirational Thoughts," *Ensign,* Aug. 1997, 6–7.

17. "Be Ye Clean," *Ensign,* May 1996, 48.

18. "A Tragic Evil among Us," 62.

19. "Reverence and Morality," 47.

20. "A Tragic Evil among Us," 62.

21. "Stand True and Faithful," *Ensign,* May 1996, 92.

22. "How Can I Become the Woman of Whom I Dream?" 95.

The First Presidency, 1995. President Gordon B. Hinckley (center);
President Thomas S. Monson, First Counselor (left); *and*
President James E. Faust, Second Counselor (right).

258

Priesthood Leadership in the Church of Jesus Christ

"The Lord is watching over this work. This is His kingdom. We are not as sheep without a shepherd. We are not as an army without a leader."

From the Life of Gordon B. Hinckley

President Gordon B. Hinckley recalled: "My first responsibility in the Church, the first office I ever held, was counselor to the boy who presided over our deacons quorum. Our good bishop called me in and talked with me about this calling. I was tremendously impressed. I was worried and concerned. I was by nature, believe it or not, a rather shy and backward boy, and I think this call to serve as a counselor in a deacons quorum was of as much concern to me, in terms of my age and experience, as is my present responsibility in terms of my age and experience."[1]

President Hinckley had similar feelings in 1961, when he was called to serve as a member of the Quorum of the Twelve Apostles. In his first general conference talk as an Apostle, he said:

"I think I feel some sense of the burden of this responsibility to stand as a witness of the Lord Jesus Christ before a world that is reluctant to accept him. 'I stand all amazed at the love Jesus offers me.' I am subdued by the confidence of the Lord's Prophet in me, and by the expressed love of these, my brethren. . . . I pray for strength; I pray for help; and I pray for the faith and the will to be obedient."[2]

On April 1, 1995, President Hinckley spoke in the priesthood session of general conference after Church members had sustained him for the first time as their prophet and President. For the previous 14 years, he had served as a counselor to three other Presidents of the Church. He had repeatedly testified of their divine callings and urged the Latter-day Saints to follow their counsel. Now, finding himself in that position, his feelings of dependence on the Lord were not diminished from the time he was a deacon or a newly called Apostle. Rather, he had become even more aware of his need for the Lord's sustaining strength. He said:

"Your uplifted hands in the solemn assembly this morning became an expression of your willingness and desire to uphold us, your brethren and your servants, with your confidence, faith, and prayer. I am deeply grateful for that expression. I thank you, each of you. I assure you, as you already know, that in the processes of the Lord, there is no aspiring for office. As the Lord said to His disciples, 'Ye have not chosen me, but I have chosen you, and ordained you' (John 15:16). This office is not one to be sought after. The right to select rests with the Lord. He is the master of life and death. His is the power to call. His is the power to take away. His is the power to retain. It is all in His hands.

"I do not know why in His grand scheme one such as I would find a place. But having this mantle come upon me, I now rededicate whatever I have of strength or time or talent or life to the work of my Master in the service of my brethren and sisters. Again, I thank you . . . for your actions this day. The burden of my prayer is that I will be worthy. I hope that I may be remembered in your prayers."[3]

Teachings of Gordon B. Hinckley

 **1**

The Lord calls each President of the Church after testing, refining, and polishing him.

I have worked with the Presidents of the Church from President Heber J. Grant onward. . . . I have known the counselors of all of these men, and I have known the Council of the Twelve during the years of the administrations of these Presidents. All of these men have been human. They have had human traits and perhaps some human weaknesses. But over and above all of that, there has been in the life of every one of them an overpowering manifestation of the inspiration of God. Those who have been Presidents have been prophets in a very real way. I have intimately witnessed the spirit of revelation upon them. Each man came to the Presidency after many years of experience as a member of the Council of the Twelve and in other capacities. The Lord refined and polished each one, let him know discouragement and failure, let him experience illness and in some cases deep sorrow. All of this became part of a great refining process, and the effect of that process became beautifully evident in their lives.

My dear friends in the gospel, this is God's work. This is his Church and the Church of his Beloved Son whose name it carries. God will never permit an imposter to stand at its head. He will name his prophets, and he will inspire and direct them.[4]

Some express concern that the President of the Church is likely always to be a rather elderly man, to which my response is, "What a blessing!" . . . He does not need to be youthful. He has and will continue to have younger men to travel over the earth in the work of the ministry. He is the presiding high priest, the repository of all of the keys of the holy priesthood, and the voice of revelation from God to his people. . . .

To my mind there is something tremendously reassuring in knowing that . . . we shall have a President who has been disciplined and schooled, tried and tested, whose fidelity to the work and whose integrity in the cause have been tempered in the forge of service, whose faith has matured, and whose nearness to God has been cultivated over a period of many years.[5]

I speak . . . in gratitude for a prophet to guide us in these latter days. I plead for loyalty to him whom the Lord has called and anointed. I plead for steadfastness in upholding him and giving attention to his teachings. I have said . . . that if we have a prophet, we have everything. If we do not have a prophet, we have nothing. We do have a prophet. We have had prophets since the founding of this Church. We shall never be without a prophet if we live worthy of a prophet.

The Lord is watching over this work. This is His kingdom. We are not as sheep without a shepherd. We are not as an army without a leader.[6]

2

When a President of the Church dies, the senior Apostle becomes the next President.

Transition of authority [to a new President of the Church], in which I have participated a number of times, is beautiful in its simplicity. It is indicative of the way the Lord does things. Under His procedure a man is selected by the prophet to become a member of the Council of the Twelve Apostles. He does not choose this as a career. He is called, as were the Apostles in Jesus' time, to whom the Lord said, "Ye have not chosen me, but I have chosen you, and ordained you." (John 15:16.) The years pass. He is schooled and disciplined in the duties of his office. He travels over the earth in fulfilling his apostolic calling. It is a long course of preparation, in which he comes to know the Latter-day Saints wherever they may be, and they come to know him. The Lord tests his heart and his substance. In the natural course of events, vacancies occur in that council and new appointments are made. Under this process a particular man becomes the senior Apostle. Residing latent in him, and in his associate Brethren, given to each at the time of ordination, are all of the keys of the priesthood. But authority to exercise those keys is restricted to the President of the Church. At [the prophet's] passing, that authority becomes operative in the senior Apostle, who is then named, set apart, and ordained a prophet and President by his associates of the Council of the Twelve.

There is no electioneering. There is no campaigning. There is only the quiet and simple operation of a divine plan which provides inspired and tested leadership.

I have been a witness, a personal witness, to this wondrous process. I give you my testimony that it is the Lord who [selects the prophet].[7]

With President [Howard W.] Hunter's passing, the First Presidency was dissolved. Brother Monson and I, who had served as his counselors, took our places in the Quorum of the Twelve, which became the presiding authority of the Church.

. . . All of the living ordained Apostles gathered in a spirit of fasting and prayer in the upper room of the temple. Here we sang a sacred hymn and prayed together. We partook of the sacrament of the Lord's supper, renewing in that sacred, symbolic testament our covenants and our relationship with Him who is our divine Redeemer.

The presidency was then reorganized, following a precedent well established through generations of the past.

There was no campaigning, no contest, no ambition for office. It was quiet, peaceful, simple, and sacred. It was done after the pattern which the Lord Himself had put in place.[8]

3

The Lord has provided principles and procedures for governing His Church if the President is not able to function fully.

President Hinckley made the following statement in 1992, when he was serving as First Counselor in the First Presidency: The head of the Church is the Lord Jesus Christ. It is His Church. But the earthly head is our prophet. Prophets are men who are endowed with a divine calling. Notwithstanding the divinity of that calling, they are human. They are subject to the problems of mortality.

We love and respect and honor and look to the prophet of this day, President Ezra Taft Benson. He has been a great and gifted leader, a man whose voice has rung out in testimony of this work across the world. He holds all the keys of the priesthood on the earth in this day. But he has reached an age where he cannot do many of the things he once did. This does not detract from his calling as a prophet. But it places limitations upon his physical activities.[9]

President Hinckley made the following statement in 1994, when he was serving as First Counselor in the First Presidency: People throughout the Church are naturally anxious to know of the President's condition. President Benson is now in his ninety-fifth year. . . . He suffers seriously from the effects of age and illness and has been unable to fulfill important duties of his sacred office. This is not a situation without precedent. Other Presidents of the Church have also been ill or unable to function fully in the closing months or years of their lives. It is possible that this will happen again in the future.

The Quorum of the Twelve Apostles, 1965. Seated left to right: *Ezra Taft Benson, Mark E. Petersen (on arm of chair), Joseph Fielding Smith (quorum president), and LeGrand Richards.* Standing left to right: *Gordon B. Hinckley, Delbert L. Stapley, Thomas S. Monson, Spencer W. Kimball, Harold B. Lee, Marion G. Romney, Richard L. Evans, and Howard W. Hunter.*

The principles and procedures which the Lord has put in place for the governance of His church make provision for any such circumstance. It is important . . . that there be no doubts or concerns about the governance of the Church and the exercise of the prophetic gifts, including the right to inspiration and revelation in administering the affairs and programs of the Church, when the President may be ill or is not able to function fully.

The First Presidency and the Council of the Twelve Apostles, called and ordained to hold the keys of the priesthood, have the authority and responsibility to govern the Church, to administer its ordinances, to expound its doctrine, and to establish and maintain its practices. Each man who is ordained an Apostle and sustained a member of the Council of the Twelve is sustained as a prophet, seer, and revelator. Like those before him, President Benson was the senior Apostle at the time he was called as President of the Church. His Counselors were drawn from the Council of the Twelve. Therefore, all incumbent members of the Quorum of the First Presidency and of the Council of the Twelve have been the recipients of the keys, rights, and authority pertaining to the holy apostleship.

I quote from the Doctrine and Covenants:

"Of the Melchizedek Priesthood, three Presiding High Priests, chosen by the body, appointed and ordained to that office, and upheld by the confidence, faith, and prayer of the church, form a quorum of the Presidency of the Church" (D&C 107:22).

When the President is ill or not able to function fully in all of the duties of his office, his two Counselors together comprise a Quorum of the First Presidency. They carry on with the day-to-day work of the Presidency. In exceptional circumstances, when only one may be able to function, he may act in the authority of the office of the Presidency as set forth in the Doctrine and Covenants, section 102, verses 10–11. . . .

. . . The Counselors in the First Presidency carry on with the regular work of this office. But any major questions of policy, procedures, programs, or doctrine are considered deliberately and prayerfully by the First Presidency and the Twelve together. These two quorums, the Quorum of the First Presidency and the Quorum of the Twelve, meeting together, with every man having total freedom to express himself, consider every major question.

And now I quote again from the word of the Lord: "And every decision made by either of these quorums must be by the unanimous voice of the same; that is, every member in each quorum must be agreed to its decisions, in order to make their decisions of the same power or validity one with the other" (D&C 107:27). . . .

. . . Let it be understood by all that Jesus Christ stands at the head of this church which bears His sacred name. He is watching over it. He is guiding it. Standing at the right hand of His Father, He directs this work. His is the prerogative, the power, the option to call men in His way to high and sacred offices and to release them according to His will by calling them home. He is the Master of life and death. I do not worry about the circumstances in which we find ourselves. I accept these circumstances as an expression of His will. I likewise accept the responsibility, acting with my Brethren, to do all we can to move forward this holy work in a spirit of consecration, love, humility, duty, and loyalty.[10]

Apostles are special witnesses of the name of Christ in all the world.

After [being] ordained to the holy apostleship and . . . set apart as members of the Council of the Twelve, [Apostles are] expected to devote themselves primarily to the work of the ministry. They . . . place first in their lives, above all other considerations, the responsibility to stand as special witnesses of the name of Christ in all the world. . . .

As with all of us, they are men who are human. They have their strengths and their weaknesses. But henceforth, for the remainder of their lives, as long as they remain faithful, their one chief concern must be the advancement of the work of God on the earth. They must be concerned with the welfare of our Father's children, both those within the Church and those out of the Church. They must do all that they can to give comfort to those who mourn, to give strength to those who are weak, to give encouragement to those who falter, to befriend the friendless, to nurture the destitute, to bless the sick, to bear witness, not out of belief but out of a certain knowledge of the Son of God, their Friend and Master, whose servants they are. . . .

. . . I give witness to their brotherhood, to their devotion, their faith, their industry, and their tremendous service in advancing the kingdom of God.[11]

The First Presidency and the Twelve seek revelation and total harmony before they reach decisions.

No decision emanates from the deliberations of the First Presidency and the Twelve without total unanimity among all concerned. At the outset in considering matters, there may be differences of opinion. These are to be expected. These men come from different backgrounds. They are men who think for themselves. But before a final decision is reached, there comes a unanimity of mind and voice.

This is to be expected if the revealed word of the Lord is followed [see D&C 107:27, 30–31]. . . .

. . . [When] I served as a member of the Council of the Twelve and [when] I have served in the First Presidency, there has never been a major action taken where this was not observed. . . . Out of this very process of men speaking their minds has come a sifting and winnowing of ideas and concepts. But I have never observed serious discord or personal enmity among my Brethren. I have, rather, observed a beautiful and remarkable thing—the coming together, under the directing influence of the Holy Spirit and under the power of revelation, of divergent views until there is total harmony and full agreement. . . .

I know of no other governing body of any kind of which this might be said.[12]

A stake president is called by inspiration to serve as an adviser to bishops and a leader for the people.

The president of the stake is the officer called under revelation to stand between the bishops of wards and the General Authorities of the Church. It is a most important responsibility. He is trained by the General Authorities, and in turn he trains the bishops. . . .

The stake president serves as an adviser to the bishops. Every bishop knows that when he has to deal with a difficult problem there is one readily available to whom he may go to share his burden and receive counsel.

He provides a secondary measure of safety in determining those worthy to go to the house of the Lord. . . . The president likewise becomes a second screen in determining the worthiness of those who go out to represent the Church in the mission field. He too interviews the candidate, and only when he is satisfied of his or her worthiness does he endorse the recommendation. He likewise has been given authority to set apart those called on missions and to extend releases when they have completed their service.

Most importantly, he is the principal disciplinary officer of the stake. . . . He carries the very heavy responsibility of seeing that the doctrine taught in the stake is kept pure and unsullied. It is his duty to see that there is no false doctrine that is taught nor false practice that occurs. If there be any Melchizedek Priesthood holder out of line, or any other person for that matter, under some circumstances, he is to counsel with them, and if the individual persists in his or her practice, then the president is obliged to take action. He will summon the offender to appear before a disciplinary council, where action may be taken to assign a probationary period or to disfellowship or excommunicate him or her from the Church.

This is a most onerous and unwelcome task, but the president must face up to it without fear or favor. All of this is done in harmony with the direction of the Spirit and as set forth in section 102 of the Doctrine and Covenants.

Then subsequently he must do all he can to labor with and bring back in due time the one who was disciplined.

All of this and much more comprise his responsibilities. It follows, therefore, that his own life must be exemplary before his people. . . .

. . . Because we have such confidence in [stake presidents], we urge local members that they not seek out General Authorities to counsel with and bless them. Their stake presidents have been called under the same inspiration under which the General Authorities were called.[13]

Bishops are shepherds of the flock.

The [Church] can grow and multiply in numbers, as it surely will. This gospel must be carried to every nation, kindred, tongue, and people. There can never be in the foreseeable future a standing still or a failure to reach out, to move forward, to build, to enlarge Zion across the world. But with all of this there must continue to be an intimate pastoral relationship of every member with a wise and caring bishop or branch president. These are the shepherds of the flock whose responsibility it is to look after the people in relatively small numbers so that none is forgotten, overlooked, or neglected. Jesus was the true shepherd who reached out to those in distress, one at a time, bestowing an individual blessing upon them.[14]

The bishops of the Church . . . are in a very real sense the shepherds of Israel. Everyone [in the Church] is accountable to a bishop or a branch president. Tremendous are the burdens which they carry, and I invite every member of the Church to do all that he or she can to lift the burden under which our bishops and branch presidents labor.

We must pray for them. They need help as they carry their heavy loads. We can be more supportive and less dependent upon them. We can assist them in every way possible. We can thank them for all that they do for us. We are wearing them out in a short time by the burdens which we impose upon them.

. . . Every [bishop] is a man who has been called by the spirit of prophecy and revelation and set apart and ordained by the laying on of hands. Every one of them holds the keys of the presidency of his ward. Each is a high priest, the presiding high priest of his ward. Each carries tremendous responsibilities of stewardship. Each stands as a father to his people.

None receives money for his service. No ward bishop is compensated by the Church for his work as a bishop.

The requirements of a bishop today are as they were in the days of Paul, who wrote to Timothy [see 1 Timothy 3:2–6]. . . .

In his letter to Titus, Paul adds that "a bishop must be blameless, as the steward of God; . . .

"Holding fast the faithful word as he hath been taught, that he may be able by sound doctrine both to exhort and to convince the gainsayers" (Titus 1:7, 9).

Those words aptly describe a bishop today in The Church of Jesus Christ of Latter-day Saints.[15]

I urge the people of the Church, wherever you may be, when you are faced with problems, first to try to solve those problems yourselves. Think about them, study alternatives available to you, pray about them, and look to the Lord for direction. If you are unable to settle them yourselves, then talk with your bishop or branch president. He is a man of God, called under the authority of the holy priesthood as the shepherd of the flock.[16]

Suggestions for Study and Teaching

Questions
- Why do we need living prophets? What impresses you about the Lord's "refining process" for preparing and calling a President of the Church? (See section 1.)

- What are your impressions as you review President Hinckley's description of the way a new President of the Church is chosen? (See section 2.) Why is it important to know that the President is chosen according to "a divine plan which provides inspired and tested leadership"?

- What principles and procedures has the Lord established for governing the Church if the President is not able to function fully in all his duties? (See section 3.)

- How do latter-day Apostles show concern for all of God's children, "both those within the Church and those out of the Church"? (See section 4.) How do recent conference addresses reflect this concern? How have you benefited from the teachings of living prophets and apostles?

- Study President Hinckley's teachings about how the First Presidency and Quorum of the Twelve reach decisions (see section 5). What can we learn from the way they reach decisions? How can we apply these principles in our families and in the Church?

- As you review sections 6 and 7, what do you learn about the callings of stake president and bishop? How can we better sustain our Church leaders?

Related Scriptures
Ephesians 2:19–20; 4:11–14; D&C 1:38; 21:1–6; Abraham 3:22–23; Articles of Faith 1:5–6

Teaching Help

"Testify whenever the Spirit prompts you to do so, not just at the end of each lesson. Provide opportunities for those you teach to bear their testimonies" (*Teaching, No Greater Call* [1999], 45).

Notes

1. "In . . . Counsellors There Is Safety," *Ensign,* Nov. 1990, 49.

2. In Conference Report, Oct. 1961, 115–16; quoting "I Stand All Amazed," *Hymns,* no. 193.

3. "This Work Is Concerned with People," *Ensign,* May 1995, 51.

4. "Strengthening Each Other," *Ensign,* Feb. 1985, 5.

5. "He Slumbers Not, nor Sleeps," *Ensign,* May 1983, 6–7.

6. "Believe His Prophets," *Ensign,* May 1992, 53.

7. "Come and Partake," *Ensign,* May 1986, 46–47.

8. "This Is the Work of the Master," *Ensign,* May 1995, 69.

9. "The Church Is on Course," *Ensign,* Nov. 1992, 53–54.

10. "God Is at the Helm," *Ensign,* May 1994, 54, 59.

11. "Special Witnesses for Christ," *Ensign,* May 1984, 49–51.

12. "God Is at the Helm," 54, 59.

13. "The Stake President," *Ensign,* May 2000, 50–51.

14. "This Work Is Concerned with People," 52–53.

15. "The Shepherds of Israel," *Ensign* or *Liahona,* Nov. 2003, 60.

16. "Live the Gospel," *Ensign,* Nov. 1984, 86.

President Hinckley encouraged us to join with those
not of our faith "in good community causes."

Fellowship with Those Who Are Not of Our Faith

"Let us reach out to help men and women of goodwill, whatever their religious persuasion and wherever they live."

From the Life of Gordon B. Hinckley

Speaking at a conference of religious leaders in November 1994, President Gordon B. Hinckley said:

"We are of various doctrinal persuasions. While recognizing our theological differences, I think we are of one mind in our awareness of the evils and problems of the world and the society in which we live, and of our great responsibility and opportunity to stand united for those qualities in public and private life which speak of virtue and morality, of respect for all men and women as children of God, of the need for civility and courtesy in our relationships, and of preservation of the family as the divinely ordained basic unit of society.

". . . All of us carry in our hearts a desire to assist the poor, to lift the distressed, to give comfort, hope, and help to all who are in trouble and pain from whatever cause.

"We recognize the need to heal the wounds of society and replace with optimism and faith the pessimism of our times. We must recognize that there is no need for recrimination or criticism against one another. We must use our influence to still the voices of angry and vindictive argument.

". . . Our strength lies in our freedom to choose. There is strength even in our very diversity. But there is greater strength in the God-given mandate to each of us to work for the uplift and blessing of all His sons and daughters, regardless of their ethnic or national origin or other differences. . . .

"May the Lord bless us to work unitedly to remove from our hearts and drive from our society all elements of hatred, bigotry, racism, and other divisive words and actions. The snide remark, the racial slur, hateful epithets, malicious gossip, and mean and vicious rumor-mongering should have no place among us.

"May God bless us all with the peace that comes from Him. May He bless us with thankful hearts and with the will to mingle together with respect one for another, uniting our efforts to the blessing of the communities where we are fortunate to live."[1]

A year after delivering this message, President Hinckley spoke to a group of secular leaders. It was a small group—only about 30 people—but it was a group with far-reaching influence: presidents, editors-in-chief, producers, and reporters representing the major news outlets in the United States. In a "congenial and sometimes humorous interchange," he gave "an overview of the international scope of the Church, commented on its missionary, humanitarian, and educational pursuits, and then offered to answer questions. . . . He answered each question candidly and without hesitation or any hint of awkwardness." Attendees expressed some surprise at his openness, to which he replied that the only thing he would not discuss was the details of sacred temple ordinances. "The door is wide open on everything else," he said.

At one point in the question-and-answer session, Mike Wallace, a senior reporter with the television show *60 Minutes,* said that he wanted to do a special report on President Hinckley. President Hinckley paused and then responded, "Thank you. I'll take a chance."[2]

President Hinckley later admitted that he had some apprehension about being interviewed by Mike Wallace, who had a reputation as a tough reporter. He explained why he agreed to the interview despite this apprehension:

"I felt that it offered the opportunity to present some affirmative aspects of our culture and message to many millions of people.

I concluded that it was better to lean into the stiff wind of opportunity than to simply hunker down and do nothing."[3]

The wide-ranging interview included the following exchange:

Mr. Wallace: "How do you view non-Mormons?"

President Hinckley: "With love and respect. I have many non-Mormon friends. I respect them. I have the greatest of admiration for them."

Mr. Wallace: "Despite the fact that they haven't really seen the light yet?"

President Hinckley: "Yes. To anybody who is not of this Church, I say we recognize all of the virtues and the good that you have. Bring it with you and see if we might add to it."[4]

By the time the interview process was over, President Hinckley and Mike Wallace were friends. Mr. Wallace spoke of President Hinckley as a "warm and thoughtful and decent and optimistic leader" who "fully deserves the almost universal admiration that he gets."[5]

Teachings of Gordon B. Hinckley

When we remember that all people are children of God, we reach out more to lift and help those among us.

We must never forget that we live in a world of great diversity. The people of the earth are all our Father's children and are of many and varied religious persuasions. We must cultivate tolerance and appreciation and respect one another.[6]

There is no need in any land for conflict between diverse groups of any kind. Let there be taught in the homes of people that we are all children of God, our Eternal Father, and that as surely as there is fatherhood, there can and must be brotherhood.[7]

If we would hold before us that image of divine inheritance constantly, of the fatherhood of God and the brotherhood of man as realities, we would be a little more tolerant, a little more kind, a little more outreaching to lift and help and sustain those among us. We would be less prone to stoop to those things which clearly are unbecoming us. We are children of God and we love Him. Act that way a little more.[8]

 **2**

We should live with respect, appreciation, and friendship toward people who are not of our faith.

"We claim the privilege of worshiping Almighty God according to the dictates of our own conscience, and allow all men the same privilege, let them worship how, where, or what they may" (Articles of Faith 1:11).

How very important that is—that while we believe in worshipping God according to our doctrine, we do not become arrogant or self-righteous or prideful but that we extend to others the privilege of worshipping according to their desires. Much of the trouble in the world comes from conflict between religions. I am happy to be able to say that I can sit down with my Catholic friends and talk with them, that I can sit down with my Protestant friends and talk with them. I would stand in their defense, as this Church has done and will continue to do, in defending them in this world.[9]

I plead with our people everywhere to live with respect and appreciation for those not of our faith. There is so great a need for civility and mutual respect among those of differing beliefs and philosophies. We must not be partisans of any doctrine of ethnic superiority. We live in a world of diversity. We can and must be respectful toward those with whose teachings we may not agree. We must be willing to defend the rights of others who may become the victims of bigotry.

I call attention to these striking words of Joseph Smith spoken in 1843:

"If it has been demonstrated that I have been willing to die for a 'Mormon,' I am bold to declare before Heaven that I am just as ready to die in defending the rights of a Presbyterian, a Baptist, or a good man of any other denomination; for the same principle which would trample upon the rights of the Latter-day Saints would trample upon the rights of the Roman Catholics, or of any other denomination" (*History of the Church,* 5:498).[10]

We must not be clannish. We must never adopt a holier-than-thou attitude. We must not be self-righteous. We must be magnanimous and open and friendly. We can keep our faith. We can practice our religion. We can cherish our method of worship without being offensive to others. I take this occasion to plead for a spirit of tolerance and neighborliness, of friendship and love toward those of other faiths.[11]

We must not become disagreeable as we talk of doctrinal differences. There is no place for acrimony. But we can never surrender or compromise that knowledge which has come to us through revelation and the direct bestowal of keys and authority under the hands of those who held them anciently. Let us never forget that this is a restoration of that which was instituted by the Savior of the world. . . .

We can respect other religions, and must do so. We must recognize the great good they accomplish. We must teach our children to be tolerant and friendly toward those not of our faith.[12]

We are not out to injure other churches. We are not out to hurt other churches. We do not argue with other churches. We do not debate with other churches. We simply say to those who may be of other faiths or of no faith, "You bring with you such truth as you have and let us see if we can add to it."[13]

Without compromising our doctrine, we can work with others in good causes.

We can and do work with those of other religions in various undertakings in the everlasting fight against social evils which threaten the treasured values which are so important to all of us. These people are not of our faith, but they are our friends, neighbors, and co-workers in a variety of causes. We are pleased to lend our strength to their efforts.

But in all of this there is no doctrinal compromise. There need not be and must not be on our part. But there is a degree of fellowship as we labor together.[14]

*"Our kindness may be the most persuasive
argument for that which we believe."*

Let us not forget that we believe in being benevolent and in doing good to all men. I am convinced that we can teach our children
effectively enough that we need not fear that they will lose their
faith while being friendly and considerate with those who do not
subscribe to the doctrine of this Church. . . . Let us be involved
in good community causes. There may be situations where, with
serious moral issues involved, we cannot bend on matters of principle. But in such instances we can politely disagree without being
disagreeable. We can acknowledge the sincerity of those whose
positions we cannot accept. We can speak of principles rather than
personalities.

In those causes which enhance the environment of the community, and which are designed for the blessing of all of its citizens,
let us step forward and be helpful. . . .

. . . Teach those for whom you are responsible the importance of
good civic manners. Encourage them to become involved, remembering in public deliberations that the quiet voice of substantive
reasoning is more persuasive than the noisy, screaming voice of

protest. In accepting such responsibilities our people will bless their communities, their families, and the Church.[15]

We must never surrender to the forces of evil. We can and must maintain the standards for which this Church has stood since it was organized. There is a better way than the way of the world. If it means standing alone, we must do it.

But we shall not be alone. I am confident that there are millions of people throughout the world who grieve over the evil they see about them. They love the virtuous, the good, and the uplifting. They too will raise their voices and give of their strength to the preservation of those values which are worthy of maintenance and cultivation.[16]

Let us pray for the forces of good. Let us reach out to help men and women of goodwill, whatever their religious persuasion and wherever they live. Let us stand firm against evil, both at home and abroad. . . . We can be an influence for good in this world, every one of us.[17]

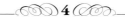

When we treat others with love, respect, and kindness, we show that we are true disciples of Jesus Christ.

As we carry forward our distinctive mission, we work under a mandate given us by the risen Lord, who has spoken in this last and final dispensation. This is His unique and wonderful cause. We bear testimony and witness of Him. But we need not do so with arrogance or self-righteousness.

As Peter expressed it, we are "a chosen generation, a royal priesthood, an holy nation, a peculiar people." Why? That we might "shew forth the praises of him who hath called [us] out of darkness into his marvellous light" (1 Pet. 2:9). . . .

. . . Let us be true disciples of the Christ, observing the Golden Rule, doing unto others as we would have them do unto us. Let us strengthen our own faith and that of our children while being gracious to those who are not of our faith. Love and respect will overcome every element of animosity. Our kindness may be the most persuasive argument for that which we believe.[18]

I want to suggest that we develop an outreaching attitude to help those who are not of us, to encourage them, to lead them in a gracious and kindly way toward those associations which could expose them to the wonderful programs of the Church.

I think of Edwin Markham's poem:

He drew a circle that shut me out—
Heretic, rebel, a thing to flout.
But Love and I had the wit to win:
We drew a circle that took him in![19]

We certainly do not need to be boastful about [our religion] or to be arrogant in any way. Such becomes a negation of the Spirit of the Christ whom we ought to try to emulate. That Spirit finds expression in the heart and the soul, in the quiet and unboastful manner of our lives.

All of us have seen those we almost envy because they have cultivated a manner that, without even mentioning it, speaks of the beauty of the gospel they have incorporated in their behavior.

We can lower our voices a few decibels. We can return good for evil. We can smile when anger might be so much easier. We can exercise self-control and self-discipline and dismiss any affront levied against us.[20]

Do we really comprehend, do we understand the tremendous significance of that which we have? This is the summation of the generations of man, the concluding chapter in the entire panorama of the human experience.

But this does not put us in a position of superiority. Rather, it should humble us. It places upon us an unforgiving responsibility to reach out with concern for all others in the Spirit of the Master, who taught, "Thou shalt love thy neighbour as thyself" (Matthew 19:19). We must cast out self-righteousness and rise above petty self-interest. . . .

We of this generation are the end harvest of all that has gone before. It is not enough to simply be known as a member of this Church. A solemn obligation rests upon us. Let us face it and work at it.

We must live as true followers of the Christ, with charity toward all, returning good for evil, teaching by example the ways of the Lord, and accomplishing the vast service He has outlined for us.[21]

From the dedicatory prayer for the Conference Center in Salt Lake City, Utah: May we of Thy Church be hospitable and gracious. May we maintain the standards and practices for which we are known and accord to others the privilege of worshiping who, "where, or what they may" [Articles of Faith 1:11]. Bless us to reach out as good neighbors and be helpful to all. May we lift up the hands and strengthen the faltering knees of any in distress [see D&C 81:5]. May we all live together in peace with appreciation and respect one for another.[22]

Suggestions for Study and Teaching

Questions
- In our relationships with others, why is it helpful to remember that we are all children of God? (See section 1.) How can we cultivate greater appreciation and respect for others? How can adults teach children to appreciate and respect others?

- Review President Hinckley's counsel about our relationships with people who are not of our faith (see section 2). How can we recognize if we are manifesting arrogance or self-righteousness in these relationships? How can we show greater friendship and love toward those who have different beliefs?

- Why is it important that Church members work together with other people in good causes? (See section 3.) What are some examples of such efforts? How can we become a greater influence for good in our community?

- What can we learn about discipleship from President Hinckley's teachings in section 4? How have you seen love and respect overcome feelings of animosity? Why is our behavior toward others "the most persuasive argument for that which we believe"? Consider specific ways you can reach out to others.

Related Scriptures
Matthew 7:12; Luke 9:49–50; John 13:34–35; 1 John 4:7–8; D&C 1:30; 123:12–14; Articles of Faith 1:13

Study Help

"As you feel the joy that comes from understanding the gospel, you will want to apply what you learn. Strive to live in harmony with your understanding. Doing so will strengthen your faith, knowledge, and testimony" (*Preach My Gospel* [2004], 19).

Notes

1. *Teachings of Gordon B. Hinckley* (1997), 663–64.

2. In Sheri L. Dew, *Go Forward with Faith: The Biography of Gordon B. Hinckley* (1996), 537–38.

3. "Remember . . . Thy Church, O Lord," *Ensign,* May 1996, 83.

4. "This Thing Was Not Done in a Corner," *Ensign,* Nov. 1996, 51.

5. Mike Wallace, in Gordon B. Hinckley, *Standing for Something: Ten Neglected Virtues That Will Heal Our Hearts and Homes* (2000), viii.

6. "The Work Moves Forward," *Ensign,* May 1999, 5.

7. "Four Simple Things to Help Our Families and Our Nations," *Ensign,* Sept. 1996, 7.

8. "Messages of Inspiration from President Hinckley," *Church News,* Oct. 5, 1996, 2.

9. *Discourses of President Gordon B. Hinckley, Volume 2: 2000–2004* (2005), 417.

10. "This Is the Work of the Master," *Ensign,* May 1995, 71; see also *Teachings of Presidents of the Church: Joseph Smith* (2007), 345.

11. "Remarks at Pioneer Day Commemoration Concert," *Ensign,* Oct. 2001, 70.

12. "We Bear Witness of Him," *Ensign,* May 1998, 4.

13. *Discourses of President Gordon B. Hinckley, Volume 2,* 350.

14. "We Bear Witness of Him," 4–5.

15. *Teachings of Gordon B. Hinckley,* 131.

16. "Standing Strong and Immovable," *Worldwide Leadership Training Meeting,* Jan. 10, 2004, 20.

17. "The Times in Which We Live," *Ensign,* Nov. 2001, 74.

18. "We Bear Witness of Him," 5.

19. "Four B's for Boys," *Ensign,* Nov. 1981, 41; quoting Edwin Markham, "Outwitted," in *The Best Loved Poems of the American People,* sel. Hazel Felleman (1936), 67.

20. "Each a Better Person," *Ensign* or *Liahona,* Nov. 2002, 100.

21. "The Dawning of a Brighter Day," *Ensign* or *Liahona,* May 2004, 83–84.

22. Dedicatory prayer for the Conference Center, in "This Great Millennial Year," *Ensign,* Nov. 2000, 71.

The Latter-Day Miracle
of Missionary Work

*"I invite you to become a vast army with enthusiasm for
this work and a great overarching desire to assist the
missionaries in the tremendous responsibility they have."*

From the Life of Gordon B. Hinckley

As a young man, Gordon B. Hinckley was a faithful priesthood
holder, but he did not expect to be called to serve a full-time mission. "It was the time of the worst economic depression in the history of the world," he later explained. "Unemployment in [Salt Lake
City] was about 35 percent, and most of the unemployed were husbands and fathers, since relatively few women worked in the labor
force. Very few missionaries were going into the field at that time.
. . . I received my bachelor's degree and planned on somehow attending graduate school. Then the bishop came with what seemed
to me a shocking suggestion. He spoke of a mission."[1]

Gordon accepted his bishop's "shocking suggestion," and in 1933
he was called to serve in England—one of only 525 missionaries
who were called that year.[2] He faced many trials during his mission,
but his service anchored his faith:

"The work in the field was not easy. It was difficult and discouraging. But what a wonderful experience it was. In retrospect, I recognize that I was probably a selfish young man when I arrived in
Britain. What a blessing it became to set aside my own selfish interests to the greater interests of the work of the Lord. . . .

"How profoundly grateful I am for the experience of that mission.
I touched the lives of a few who have, over the years, expressed appreciation. That has been important. But I have never been greatly

*"Let us reach out to the world in our missionary service, teaching
all who will listen concerning the restoration of the gospel."*

concerned over the number of baptisms that I had or that other missionaries had. My satisfaction has come from the assurance that I did what the Lord wanted me to do and that I was an instrument in His hands for the accomplishment of His purposes. In the course of that experience, there became riveted into my very being a conviction and knowledge that this is in very deed the true and living work of God, restored through a prophet for the blessing of all who will accept it and live its principles."[3]

President Hinckley's mission set the course for a lifetime dedicated to the Lord's work. During his service as President of the Church, he traveled more than a million miles (1.6 million kilometers) to more than 70 countries to bear testimony of Jesus Christ and His restored gospel.[4]

President Hinckley frequently sounded a call for Church members to join with him in sharing the gospel. More than 400,000 full-time missionaries answered that call during his time as President. Assisted by their service and the work of member missionaries, more than 3,500,000 converts were baptized during that time.[5]

Ever optimistic, President Hinckley shared an expansive vision of how the Lord's work would continue to grow:

"If we will go forward, never losing sight of our goal, speaking ill of no one, living the great principles we know to be true, this cause will roll on in majesty and power to fill the earth. Doors now closed to the preaching of the gospel will be opened."[6]

"Our hope concerning the future is great and our faith is strong. We know that we have scarcely scratched the surface of that which will come to pass in the years that lie ahead. . . . Our burden in going forward is tremendous. But our opportunity is glorious."[7]

Teachings of Gordon B. Hinckley

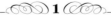

We are to reach out to the world in missionary service, teaching all who will listen.

We have a divine mandate to carry the gospel to every nation, kindred, tongue, and people. We have a charge to teach and baptize in the name of the Lord Jesus Christ. Said the resurrected Savior,

"Go ye into all the world, and preach the gospel to every creature" [Mark 16:15]. We are engaged in a great and consuming crusade for truth and goodness.[8]

Before the Church was organized, there was missionary work. It has continued ever since, notwithstanding the difficulties of many of the seasons through which our people have passed. Let us, every one, resolve within ourselves to arise to a new opportunity, a new sense of responsibility, a new shouldering of obligation to assist our Father in Heaven in His glorious work of bringing to pass the immortality and eternal life of His sons and daughters throughout the earth.[9]

Let us as Latter-day Saints reach out to others not of our faith. Let us never act in a spirit of arrogance or with a holier-than-thou attitude. Rather, may we show love and respect and helpfulness toward them. We are greatly misunderstood, and I fear that much of it is of our own making. We can be more tolerant, more neighborly, more friendly, more of an example than we have been in the past. Let us teach our children to treat others with friendship, respect, love, and admiration. That will yield a far better result than will an attitude of egotism. . . .

Let us reach out to the world in our missionary service, teaching all who will listen concerning the restoration of the gospel, speaking without fear but also without self-righteousness, of the First Vision, testifying of the Book of Mormon and of the restoration of the priesthood. Let us, my brothers and sisters, get on our knees and pray for the opportunity to bring others into the joy of the gospel.[10]

It is a marvelous and wonderful thing that thousands are touched by the miracle of the Holy Spirit, that they believe and accept and become members. They are baptized. Their lives are forever touched for good. Miracles occur. A seed of faith comes into their hearts. It enlarges as they learn. And they accept principle upon principle, until they have every one of the marvelous blessings that come to those who walk with faith in this, The Church of Jesus Christ of Latter-day Saints.[11]

We are to help the full-time missionaries bring others to a knowledge of the truth.

I met a woman in South America who had just joined the Church. Fired by a great love for that which she had found, she had gone about enthusiastically telling others. During a period of only seven months since her baptism, she had referred three hundred acquaintances to the missionaries so that they might explain the gospel to them. At one point, sixty had come into the Church. More likely came in. In São Paulo, Brazil, I met the young missionary who first had taught her the gospel. He too had been a convert, had gone on a mission to represent the Church at considerable financial sacrifice. The woman of whom I speak was one of forty-three he had assisted in bringing into the Church to that point. This young man of Brazil had expanded himself more than one hundred times—forty-three converts of his own and sixty through one of those he converted, with more from others of his converts to come.[12]

So many of us look upon missionary work as simply tracting. Everyone who is familiar with this work knows there is a better way. That way is through the members of the Church. Whenever there is a member who introduces an investigator, there is an immediate support system. The member bears testimony of the truth of the work. He is anxious for the happiness of his investigator friend. He becomes excited as that friend makes progress in learning the gospel.

The full-time missionaries may do the actual teaching, but the member, wherever possible, will back up that teaching with the offering of his home to carry on this missionary service. He will bear sincere testimony of the divinity of the work. He will be there to answer questions when the missionaries are not around. He will be a friend to the convert who is making a big and often difficult change.

The gospel is nothing to be ashamed of. It is something to be proud of. "Be not thou therefore ashamed of the testimony of our Lord," wrote Paul to Timothy (2 Tim. 1:8). Opportunities for sharing the gospel are everywhere. . . .

"Opportunities for sharing the gospel are everywhere."

The process of bringing new people into the Church is not the responsibility alone of the missionaries. They succeed best when members become the source from which new investigators are found. . . .

Let there be cultivated an awareness in every member's heart of his own potential for bringing others to a knowledge of the truth. Let him work at it. Let him pray with great earnestness about it. . . .

. . . My brethren and sisters, we can let the missionaries try to do it alone, or we can help them. If they do it alone, they will knock on doors day after day and the harvest will be meager. Or as members we can assist them in finding and teaching investigators. . . .

Let there develop in every stake an awareness of the opportunity to find those who will listen to the gospel message. In this process we need not be offensive. We need not be arrogant. The most effective tract we will carry will be the goodness of our own lives and example. And as we engage in this service, our lives will improve, for we shall be alert to see that we do not do or say anything which might impede the progress of those we are trying to lead toward the truth. . . .

There needs to be an infusion of enthusiasm at every level in the Church. Let this subject [of missionary work] be dealt with occasionally in sacrament meeting. Let it be discussed by the priesthood and the Relief Society in their weekly meetings. Let the Young Men and the Young Women talk about and plan ways to help in this most important undertaking. Let even the Primary children think of ways to assist. Many a parent has come into the Church because of a child who was invited to Primary. . . .

Brothers and sisters, all of you out in the wards and stakes and in the districts and branches, I invite you to become a vast army with enthusiasm for this work and a great overarching desire to assist the missionaries in the tremendous responsibility they have to carry the gospel to every nation, kindred, tongue, and people. "The field is white [and ready] to harvest" (D&C 4:4). The Lord has repeatedly declared this. Shall we not take Him at His word?[13]

In behalf of the missionaries . . . I want to plead with the Saints to do all that you possibly can to provide referrals [of people] whom they might teach. You will be happy if you do so. Everyone that you see come into the Church because of your effort will bring happiness into your lives. I make that as a promise to each of you.[14]

Full-time missionary work brings lasting happiness to those who serve.

We must raise the bar on the worthiness and qualifications of those who go into the world as ambassadors of the Lord Jesus Christ.[15]

The world today needs the power of pure testimony. It needs the gospel of Jesus Christ, and if the world is to hear that gospel, there must be messengers to teach it.

We ask that parents begin early to train their children [for missionary service]. Where there is family prayer, where there are family home evenings, where there is scripture reading, where the father and mother are active in the Church and speak with enthusiasm concerning the Church and the gospel, the children in such homes become imbued in a natural way with a desire to teach the gospel to others. There is usually a tradition of missionary work in such homes. Savings accounts are set up while children are small. Boys grow up with a natural expectation that they will be called to serve as missionaries for the Church. A mission becomes as much a part of a boy's program for life as is an education.[16]

Missionary work is essentially a priesthood responsibility. As such, our young men must carry the major burden. This is their responsibility and their obligation.[17]

Young [men], I hope all of you are pointed in the direction of missionary service. I cannot promise you fun. I cannot promise you ease and comfort. I cannot promise you freedom from discouragement, from fear, from downright misery at times. But I can promise you that you will grow as you have never grown in a similar period during your entire lives. I can promise you a happiness that will be unique and wonderful and lasting. I can promise you that you will reevaluate your lives, that you will establish new priorities, that you will live closer to the Lord, that prayer will become a real and wonderful experience, that you will walk with faith in the outcome of the good things you do.[18]

We need some young women [to serve missions]. They perform a remarkable work. They can get in homes where the elders cannot. . . .

[However], . . . young women should not feel that they have a duty comparable to that of young men. Some of them will very much wish to go. If so, they should counsel with their bishop as well as their parents. . . . To the sisters I say that you will be as highly respected, you will be considered as being as much in the line of duty, your efforts will be as acceptable to the Lord and to the Church whether you go on a mission or do not go on a mission.[19]

Along with the need for young elders and sisters, there is a growing need for couples in the mission field. Older married couples are doing a wonderful work in the missions. Many more are needed. Particularly we need those with foreign language abilities. They can serve in many responsibilities under the direction of sensitive and considerate mission presidents.

*"The world today . . . needs the gospel of Jesus Christ, and if the world
is to hear that gospel, there must be messengers to teach it."*

With an increasing number of people retiring while they are still possessed of health and vitality, there are many who can fill a tremendous need in the work of the Lord.[20]

We [have] retired men and women serving in a meaningful missionary capacity for this Church throughout the world. The number is growing. They go where they are called. They serve where they are needed. Friendships are established; skills are shared; opportunities are opened for those who will never forget the men and women who have come among them in a spirit of entire unselfishness to teach and do good. They receive no money. They go at their own expense. The measure of their devotion is unlimited. The fruits of their efforts are beyond calculation.[21]

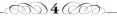

**As we introduce others to the gospel, the Spirit of
the Lord helps overcome differences between us.**

Because we have all come of the same parentage [as children of God], we respond to the same truth. The fact that one's skin may be of a slightly different color, that one's eyes may have a slightly different set, that one may wear a different type of clothing does not in any sense make of him or her a different kind of individual. Men and women the world over respond to the same stimuli in essentially the same way. They seek warmth when they are cold; they know the same kinds of pain; they experience sadness, and they know joy. . . .

When differences—either with our neighbors or in other cultures—seem to stand as hurdles as we seek to share the gospel, quiet courtesy usually removes these hurdles. As we keep the Lord's commandment to introduce others to the gospel, I testify that the Spirit of the Lord helps overcome the differences between him who is teaching and him who is being taught. The Lord made the process clear when he said, "Wherefore, he that preacheth [by the Spirit] and he that receiveth [by the Spirit], understand one another, and both are edified and rejoice together." (D&C 50:22.)

I am satisfied that the most effective means each of us has in our calling to share the gospel is the Spirit of the Lord. We have all seen it in others. As we do the Lord's work, we have also sensed it in ourselves. On such occasions, superficial differences between us and those we teach seem to fall like scales from our eyes. (See 2 Nephi 30:6.) A warmth of kinship and understanding emerges which is marvelous to behold. We literally understand one another, and we literally are edified and rejoice together.[22]

As we go forward in faith, the Lord will bless our efforts to introduce others to the gospel.

Truly we are engaged in a marvelous work and a wonder. . . . The God of heaven has brought to pass this latter-day miracle, and what we have seen is but a foretaste of greater things yet to come. The work will be accomplished by humble men and women, young and old.[23]

The work will succeed because it is the Lord who has promised:

"And whoso receiveth you, there I will be also, for I will go before your face. I will be on your right hand and on your left, and my Spirit shall be in your hearts, and mine angels round about you, to bear you up." (D&C 84:88.)

With our charge divinely given, with blessings divinely promised, let us go forward in faith. As we do so, the Lord will bless our efforts. Let us do our part in sharing the gospel with those around us, by example first and then by inspired precept.

The stone cut out of the mountains without hands will continue to roll forth until it has filled the whole earth. (See Dan. 2.) I give you my witness of this truth and of the truth that each of us can help in ways that are appropriate to our circumstances if we will seek our Father in Heaven's guidance and inspiration. This is God's work that we do, and with his blessing we shall not fail.[24]

Suggestions for Study and Teaching

Questions

- Why are we sometimes afraid to share the gospel? What are some ways we can overcome that fear and reach out to others? (See section 1.) What are some miracles of missionary work that you have witnessed?

- Why do missionaries "succeed best when members become the source from which new investigators are found"? (See section 2.) What are some other ways that members can assist the full-time missionaries?

- Why are full-time missions so influential in the lives of those who serve? How can parents help their children prepare to serve full-time missions? (See section 3.) How can families help older couples prepare to serve?

- Review section 4. What are some of the common characteristics of all people? How can we overcome differences that seem to be hurdles to sharing the gospel? How have you seen the Spirit of the Lord help people overcome differences?

- President Hinckley emphasized that the Lord will bless our efforts to share the gospel if we "go forward in faith" (section 5). How can you increase your desire and faith to share the gospel?

Related Scriptures

Isaiah 52:7; Matthew 28:19–20; Alma 26:1–5; D&C 1:20–23; 4; 18:15–16; 38:40–41

Teaching Help

"Do not be afraid of silence. People often need time to think about and reply to questions or to express what they are feeling. You might pause after you have asked a question, after a spiritual experience has been shared, or when a person is having difficulty expressing himself or herself" (*Teaching, No Greater Call* [1999], 67).

Notes

1. "The Question of a Mission," *Ensign,* May 1986, 40.

2. See Sheri L. Dew, *Go Forward with Faith: The Biography of Gordon B. Hinckley* (1996), 58.

3. "The Question of a Mission," 40.

4. See "Opening Remarks," *Ensign* or *Liahona,* May 2005, 5.

5. See "I Am Clean," *Ensign* or *Liahona,* May 2007, 60.

6. "Look to the Future," *Ensign,* Nov. 1997, 68.

7. "Opening Remarks," 6.

8. "True to the Faith," *Ensign,* May 1997, 67.

9. "Find the Lambs, Feed the Sheep," *Ensign,* May 1999, 110.

10. "A Time of New Beginnings," *Ensign,* May 2000, 87.

11. "The Miracle of Faith," *Ensign,* May 2001, 68.

12. "Be Not Afraid, Only Believe," *Ensign,* Feb. 1996, 5.

13. "Find the Lambs, Feed the Sheep," 105–7, 110.

14. *Teachings of Gordon B. Hinckley* (1997), 374.

15. "To Men of the Priesthood," *Ensign* or *Liahona,* Nov. 2002, 57.

16. "There Must Be Messengers," *Ensign,* Oct. 1987, 2.

17. "Some Thoughts on Temples, Retention of Converts, and Missionary Service," *Ensign,* Nov. 1997, 52.

18. "To the Boys and to the Men," *Ensign,* Nov. 1998, 52.

19. "Some Thoughts on Temples, Retention of Converts, and Missionary Service," 52.

20. "There Must Be Messengers," 4.

21. *Discourses of President Gordon B. Hinckley, Volume 2: 2000–2004* (2005), 517–18.

22. "We Have a Work to Do," *Ensign,* Feb. 1988, 5–6.

23. "We Have a Work to Do," 6.

24. "We Have a Work to Do," 6.

Reaching Out with Love to New Converts and Less-Active Members

"We must constantly [be] aware of the tremendous obligation to fellowship . . . those who come into the Church as converts, and to reach out with love to those who . . . step into the shadows of inactivity."

From the Life of Gordon B. Hinckley

One theme that President Hinckley emphasized throughout his service as President of the Church was the importance of reaching out to new converts and to those who are not active in the Church. He shared many examples of his personal efforts in this regard, one of which he poignantly described as "one of my failures." He explained:

"While serving as a missionary in the British Isles, my companion and I taught, and it was my pleasure to baptize, a young man. He was well educated. He was refined. He was studious. I was so proud of this gifted young man who had come into the Church. I felt he had all of the qualifications someday to become a leader among our people.

"He was in the course of making the big adjustment from convert to member. For a short period before I was released, mine was the opportunity to be his friend. Then I was released to return home. He was given a small responsibility in the branch in London. He knew nothing of what was expected of him. He made a mistake. The head of the organization where he served was a man I can best describe as being short on love and strong on criticism. In a

"The Lord left the ninety and nine to find the lost sheep."

rather unmerciful way, he went after my friend who had made the simple mistake.

"The young man left our rented hall that night smarting and hurt. . . . He said to himself, 'If that is the kind of people they are, then I am not going back.'

"He drifted into inactivity. The years passed. . . . When I was in England [again], I tried desperately to find him. . . . I came home and finally, after a long search, was able to track him down.

"I wrote to him. He responded but with no mention of the gospel.

"When next I was in London, I again searched for him. The day I was to leave, I found him. I called him, and we met in the underground station. He threw his arms around me as I did around him. I had very little time before I had to catch my plane, but we talked briefly and with what I think was a true regard for one another. He gave me another embrace before I left. I determined that I would never lose track of him again. . . .

"The years passed. I grew older as did he. He retired from his work and moved to Switzerland. On one occasion when I was in Switzerland, I went out of my way to find the village where he lived. We spent the better part of the day together—he, his wife, my wife, and myself. We had a wonderful time, but it was evident that the fire of faith had long since died. I tried every way I knew, but I could not find a way to rekindle it. I continued my correspondence. I sent him books, magazines, recordings of the Tabernacle Choir, and other things for which he expressed appreciation.

"He died a few months ago. His wife wrote me to inform me of this. She said, 'You were the best friend he ever had.'

"Tears coursed my cheeks when I read that letter. I knew I had failed. Perhaps if I had been there to pick him up when he was first knocked down, he might have made a different thing of his life. I think I could have helped him then. I think I could have dressed the wound from which he suffered. I have only one comfort: I tried. I have only one sorrow: I failed.

"The challenge now is greater than it has ever been because the number of converts is greater than we have ever before known.

. . . Every convert is precious. Every convert is a son or daughter of God. Every convert is a great and serious responsibility."[1]

President Hinckley's concern for new converts and less-active members was a result of his experience in seeing how the gospel blesses lives. A news reporter once asked him, "What brings you the greatest satisfaction as you see the work of the Church today?" President Hinckley replied:

"The most satisfying experience I have is to see what this gospel does for people. It gives them a new outlook on life. It gives them a perspective that they have never felt before. It raises their sights to things noble and divine. Something happens to them that is miraculous to behold. They look to Christ and come alive."[2]

Teachings of Gordon B. Hinckley

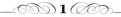 1

We have a great responsibility to minister to the individual.

We must look after the individual. Christ always spoke of individuals. He healed the sick, individually. He spoke in His parables of individuals. This Church is concerned with individuals, notwithstanding our numbers. Whether they be 6 or 10 or 12 or 50 million, we must never lose sight of the fact that the individual is the important thing.[3]

We are becoming a great global society. But our interest and concern must always be with the individual. Every member of this church is an individual man or woman, boy or girl. Our great responsibility is to see that each is "remembered and nourished by the good word of God" (Moro. 6:4), that each has opportunity for growth and expression and training in the work and ways of the Lord, that none lacks the necessities of life, that the needs of the poor are met, that each member shall have encouragement, training, and opportunity to move forward on the road of immortality and eternal life. . . .

This work is concerned with people, each a son or daughter of God. In describing its achievements we speak in terms of numbers, but all of our efforts must be dedicated to the development of the individual.[4]

I want to emphasize that there is a very positive and wonderful net growth in the Church. . . . We have every reason to feel encouraged. But any convert whose faith grows cold is a tragedy. Any member who falls into inactivity is a matter for serious concern. The Lord left the ninety and nine to find the lost sheep. His concern for [the one] was so serious that He made it the theme of one of His great lessons [see Luke 15:1–7]. We cannot let down. We must constantly keep Church officers and the membership aware of the tremendous obligation to fellowship in a very real and warm and wonderful way those who come into the Church as converts, and to reach out with love to those who for one reason or another step into the shadows of inactivity. There is ample evidence that it can be done where there is a will to do it.[5]

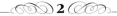

2

Every convert is precious and is a great and serious responsibility.

I have come to feel that the greatest tragedy in the Church is the loss of those who join the Church and then fall away. With very few exceptions it need not happen. I am convinced that almost universally those who are baptized by the missionaries have been taught sufficiently to have received knowledge and testimony enough to warrant their baptism. But it is not an easy thing to make the transition incident to joining this Church. It means cutting old ties. It means leaving friends. It may mean setting aside cherished beliefs. It may require a change of habits and a suppression of appetites. In so many cases it means loneliness and even fear of the unknown. There must be nurturing and strengthening during this difficult season of a convert's life. A tremendous price has been paid for his or her presence in the Church. The long efforts of the missionaries and the cost of their service, the separation from old relationships and the trauma associated with all of this make it imperative that these precious souls be welcomed, reassured, helped in their times of weakness, given responsibility under which they may grow strong, and encouraged and thanked for all they do.[6]

"I invite every member to reach out in friendship and love for those who come into the Church as converts."

There is absolutely no point in doing missionary work unless we hold on to the fruits of that effort. The two must be inseparable. These converts are precious. . . . Every convert is a great and serious responsibility. It is an absolute imperative that we look after those who have become a part of us. . . .

I received the other day a very interesting letter. It was written by a woman who joined the Church a year ago. She writes:

"My journey into the Church was unique and quite challenging. This past year has been the hardest year that I have ever lived in my life. It has also been the most rewarding. As a new member, I continue to be challenged every day." . . .

She states that "Church members don't know what it is like to be a new member of the Church. Therefore, it's almost impossible for them to know how to support us."

I challenge you, my brothers and sisters, that if you do not know what it is like, you try to imagine what it is like. It can be terribly lonely. It can be disappointing. It can be frightening. We of this Church are far more different from the world than we are prone to think we are. This woman goes on:

"When we as investigators become members of the Church, we are surprised to discover that we have entered into a completely foreign world, a world that has its own traditions, culture, and language. We discover that there is no one person or no one place of reference that we can turn to for guidance in our trip into this new world. At first the trip is exciting, our mistakes even amusing, then it becomes frustrating and eventually, the frustration turns into anger. And it's at these stages of frustration and anger that we leave. We go back to the world from which we came, where we knew who we were, where we contributed, and where we could speak the language."[7]

Some individuals have been baptized only, they have not been fellowshipped, and in two or three months they say goodbye. It is so important, my brethren and sisters, to see that [newly baptized members] are converted, that they have in their hearts a conviction concerning this great work. It is not a matter of the head only. It is a matter of the heart and its being touched by the Holy Spirit until they know that this work is true, that Joseph Smith was verily a prophet of God, that God lives and that Jesus Christ lives and that they appeared to the boy Joseph Smith, that the Book of Mormon is true, that the priesthood is here with all of its gifts and blessings. I just cannot emphasize this too strongly.[8]

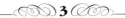

Every convert needs friendship, a responsibility, and nurturing with the word of God.

With the ever-increasing number of converts, we must make an increasingly substantial effort to assist them as they find their way. Every one of them needs three things: a friend, a responsibility, and nurturing with "the good word of God" (Moro. 6:4). It is our duty and opportunity to provide these things.[9]

Friendship

[Converts] come into the Church with enthusiasm for what they have found. We must immediately build on that enthusiasm. . . . Listen to them, guide them, answer their questions, and be there to help in all circumstances and in all conditions. . . . I invite every member to reach out in friendship and love for those who come into the Church as converts.[10]

We have such an obligation to those who are baptized into the Church. We cannot neglect them. We cannot leave them to stand alone. They need help as they become accustomed to the ways and culture of this Church. And it is our great blessing and opportunity to afford that help. . . . A warm smile, a friendly handshake, an encouraging word will do wonders.[11]

Let us reach out to these people! Let us befriend them! Let us be kind to them! Let us encourage them! Let us add to their faith and their knowledge of this, the work of the Lord.[12]

I plead with you . . . that you will put your arms around those who come into the Church and be friends to them and make them feel welcome and comfort them and we will see wonderful results. The Lord will bless you to aid in this great process of retention of converts.[13]

Responsibility

This Church expects something of people. It has high standards. It has strong doctrine. It expects great service from people. They don't just idly go along. We expect them to do things. People respond to that. They welcome the opportunity to be of service, and as they do so, they grow in their capacity, in their understanding, and in their qualifications to do things and do them well.[14]

Give [new members] something to do. They will not grow strong in the faith without exercise. Faith and testimony are like the muscles of my arm. If I use those muscles and nourish them, they grow stronger. If I put my arm in a sling and leave it there, it becomes weak and ineffective, and so it is with testimonies.

Now, some of you say they are not ready to assume responsibility. But none of us was ready when the call came. I can say that

*President Hinckley taught that new converts need to
receive opportunities to serve in the Church.*

of myself. Do you think I was ready for this great and sacred calling? I felt overwhelmed. I felt inadequate. I still feel overwhelmed. I still feel inadequate. But I am trying to go forward, seeking the blessing of the Lord and trying to do His will and hoping and praying that my service will be acceptable to Him. The first responsibility I had in this Church was a counselor to a deacons quorum president when I was twelve years of age. I didn't feel adequate. I felt overwhelmed. But I tried, just as you do, and after that came other responsibilities. Never a feeling of adequacy, but always a feeling of gratitude and a willingness to try.[15]

Every convert who comes into this Church should have an immediate responsibility. It may be ever so small, but it will spell the difference in his life.[16]

Of course the new convert will not know everything. He likely will make some mistakes. So what? We all make mistakes. The important thing is the growth that will come of activity.[17]

Nurturing with the good word of God

I believe . . . that these converts have a testimony of the gospel. I believe they have faith in the Lord Jesus Christ and know of His divine reality. I believe they have truly repented of their sins and have a determination to serve the Lord.

Moroni [says] concerning them after they are baptized: "And after they had been received unto baptism, and were wrought upon and cleansed by the power of the Holy Ghost, they were numbered among the people of the church of Christ; and their names were taken, that they might be remembered and nourished by the good word of God, to keep them in the right way, to keep them continually watchful unto prayer, relying alone upon the merits of Christ, who was the author and the finisher of their faith" (Moro. 6:4).

In these days as in those days, converts are "numbered among the people of the church . . . [to] be remembered and nourished by the good word of God, to keep them in the right way, to keep them continually watchful unto prayer." . . . Let us help them as they take their first steps as members.[18]

It is imperative that [every new convert] become affiliated with a priesthood quorum or the Relief Society, the Young Women, the Young Men, the Sunday School, or the Primary. He or she must be encouraged to come to sacrament meeting to partake of the sacrament, to renew the covenants made at the time of baptism.[19]

4

There is everything to gain and nothing to lose by coming back to Church activity.

There are thousands across the world . . . who are members of the Church in name, but who have left, and who now in their hearts long to return, but do not know how and are too timid to try. . . .

To you, my brethren and sisters, who have taken your spiritual inheritance and left, and now find an emptiness in your lives, the way is open for your return. . . . If you will take the first timid step to return, you will find open arms to greet you and warm friends to make you welcome.

I think I know why some of you left. You were offended by a thoughtless individual who injured you, and you mistook his actions as representative of the Church. Or you may have moved from an area where you were known to an area where you were largely alone, and there grew up with only little knowledge of the Church.

Or you may have been drawn to other company or habits which you felt were incompatible with association in the Church. Or you may have felt yourself wiser in the wisdom of the world than those of your Church associates, and with some air of disdain, withdrawn yourself from their company.

I am not here to dwell on the reasons. I hope you will not. Put the past behind you. . . . There is everything to gain and nothing to lose. Come back, my friends. There is more of peace to be found in the Church than you have known in a long while. There are many whose friendship you will come to enjoy.[20]

My beloved brethren and sisters who may . . . have drifted, the Church needs you, and you need the Church. You will find many ears that will listen with understanding. There will be many hands to help you find your way back. There will be hearts to warm your own. There will be tears, not of bitterness but of rejoicing.[21]

 **5**

For Latter-day Saints who return to Church activity, it will feel good to be home again.

One Sunday I found myself in a California city for a stake conference. My name and picture had been in the local newspaper. The phone rang at the stake center as the stake president and I entered the building that morning. The call was for me, and the caller identified himself. He wanted to see me. I excused myself from the meeting I was to have held early that morning and asked the stake president to carry on with it. I had something more important to do.

He came, this friend of mine, timidly and somewhat fearfully. He had been away for a long time. We embraced as brothers long separated. At first the conversation was awkward, but it soon warmed as we discussed together days spent in England many years ago. There were tears in the eyes of this strong man as he spoke of the Church of which he had once been so effective a part, and then told of the long, empty years that had followed. He dwelt upon them as a man speaks of nightmares. When he had described those wasted years, we talked of his returning. He thought it would be difficult, that it would be embarrassing, but he agreed to try.

I [received] a letter from him not long ago. He said, "I'm back. I'm back, and how wonderful it feels to be home again."

And so to you, my friends, who, like him, long to return but are reluctant to take the first step, try. Let us meet you where you now stand, and take you by the hand and help you. I promise you it will feel good to be home again.[22]

Suggestions for Study and Teaching

Questions

- Why must "our interest and concern . . . always be with the individual," even in a worldwide church? (See section 1.) When have you been blessed by someone who took a personal interest in you? What are some ways we can be more sensitive in looking after each individual?

- What can we learn and apply from the letter that President Hinckley shares in section 2? Ponder what you can do to strengthen those who are working to build their faith.

- Why does every new convert need friendship, responsibility, and nurturing with the word of God? (See section 3.) What are some ways we can befriend new converts? How can we support new converts in their Church responsibilities? How can we help new converts be "nourished by the good word of God"?

- Why is it sometimes difficult for members to return to Church activity? (See section 4.) How can we help people return? When have you experienced or witnessed the rejoicing that accompanies a return to Church activity?

- What do you learn from the account that President Hinckley shares in section 5? Consider how you can reach out to help someone who is not active in the Church "come home again."

Related Scriptures

Luke 15; John 10:1–16, 26–28; 13:34–35; Mosiah 18:8–10; Helaman 6:3; 3 Nephi 18:32; Moroni 6:4–6; D&C 38:24

Study Help

"Many find that the best time to study is in the morning after a night's rest. . . . Others prefer to study in the quiet hours after the work and worries of the day are over. . . . Perhaps what is more important than the hour of the day is that a regular time be set aside for study" (Howard W. Hunter, "Reading the Scriptures," *Ensign,* Nov. 1979, 64).

Notes

1. "Converts and Young Men," *Ensign,* May 1997, 47–48.
2. "Converts and Young Men," 48.
3. "Inspirational Thoughts," *Ensign,* Oct. 2003, 5.
4. "This Work Is Concerned with People," *Ensign,* May 1995, 52–53.
5. *Teachings of Gordon B. Hinckley* (1997), 537–38.
6. "There Must Be Messengers," *Ensign,* Oct. 1987, 5.
7. "Find the Lambs, Feed the Sheep," *Ensign,* May 1999, 108.
8. "Messages of Inspiration from President Hinckley," *Church News,* Apr. 5, 1997, 2; see also "Inspirational Thoughts," 3.
9. "Converts and Young Men," 47.
10. "Some Thoughts on Temples, Retention of Converts, and Missionary Service," *Ensign,* Nov. 1997, 51.
11. "Inspirational Thoughts," 4.
12. "Latter-day Counsel: Excerpts from Recent Addresses of President Gordon B. Hinckley," *Ensign,* July 1999, 73.
13. "Words of the Prophet: Reach Out," *New Era,* Feb. 2003, 7.
14. "Inspirational Thoughts," 3–4.
15. *Teachings of Gordon B. Hinckley,* 538.
16. "Inspirational Thoughts," *Ensign,* July 1998, 4.
17. "Find the Lambs, Feed the Sheep," 108.
18. "Converts and Young Men," 48.
19. "Find the Lambs, Feed the Sheep," 108.
20. "Everything to Gain—Nothing to Lose," *Ensign,* Nov. 1976, 95–96.
21. "And Peter Went Out and Wept Bitterly," *Ensign,* May 1979, 67.
22. "Everything to Gain—Nothing to Lose," 97.

The Colonia Juárez Chihuahua Mexico Temple

The Blessings of the Holy Temple

"The temple ordinances become the crowning blessings the Church has to offer."

From the Life of Gordon B. Hinckley

"I believe that no member of the Church has received the ultimate which this Church has to give until he or she has received his or her temple blessings in the house of the Lord," said President Gordon B. Hinckley in the October 1997 priesthood session of general conference. "Accordingly, we are doing all that we know how to do to expedite the construction of these sacred buildings and make the blessings received therein more generally available."[1] He named several temples that were in various stages of planning and construction, and then he made an announcement that would change the lives of people all over the world:

"There are many areas of the Church that are remote, where the membership is small and not likely to grow very much in the near future. Are those who live in these places to be denied forever the blessings of the temple ordinances? While visiting such an area a few months ago, we prayerfully pondered this question. The answer, we believe, came bright and clear.

"We will construct small temples in some of these areas. . . . They [will] be built to temple standards, which are much higher than meetinghouse standards. They [will] accommodate baptisms for the dead, the endowment service, sealings, and all other ordinances to be had in the Lord's house for both the living and the dead."[2]

The inspiration for this plan had begun more than 20 years earlier, when President Hinckley was serving as chairman of the Church's Temple Committee. Concerned that many Latter-day Saints did not have easy access to temple blessings, he wrote in his journal, "The Church could build [many smaller] temples for the cost of the Washington Temple [then under construction]. It would take the temples to the people instead of having the people travel great distances to get to them."[3]

In 1997 a revelation from the Lord brought this idea to life. President Hinckley shared something about that revelation when he offered the dedicatory prayer for the Colonia Juárez Chihuahua Mexico Temple. "It was here in Northern Mexico," he prayed, "that Thou didst reveal the idea and the plan of a smaller temple, complete in every necessary detail, but suited in size to the needs and circumstances of the Church membership in this area of Thy vineyard. That revelation came of a desire and a prayer to help Thy people of these colonies who have been true and loyal."[4]

Six months after announcing the plan to build smaller temples, President Hinckley made another significant announcement:

"We have traveled far out among the membership of the Church. I have been with many who have very little of this world's goods. But they have in their hearts a great burning faith concerning this latter-day work. They love the Church. They love the gospel. They love the Lord and want to do His will. They are paying their tithing, modest as it is. They make tremendous sacrifices to visit the temples. They travel for days at a time in cheap buses and on old boats. They save their money and do without to make it all possible.

"They need nearby temples—small, beautiful, serviceable temples. Accordingly, I take this opportunity to announce to the entire Church a program to construct some 30 smaller temples immediately. . . .

"This will be a tremendous undertaking. Nothing even approaching it has ever been tried before. . . . This will make a total of 47 new temples in addition to the 51 now in operation. I think we had better add 2 more to make it an even 100 by the end of this century, being 2,000 years 'since the coming of our Lord and Savior Jesus Christ in the flesh' (D&C 20:1). In this program we are moving on a scale the like of which we have never seen before."[5]

On October 1, 2000, President Hinckley dedicated the Boston Massachusetts Temple, the 100th temple in operation. Before the end of the year, he dedicated two temples in Brazil. And when he died on January 27, 2008, the Church had 124 temples in operation, with 13 more announced. Of the 124 operating temples, President Hinckley had participated in the planning and construction of most of them and had personally dedicated 85 of them.

Even as President Hinckley announced large numbers of new temples, and even as he marveled at their beauty, he reminded Latter-day Saints of the purpose of those sacred edifices: to bless individuals and families, one by one. Speaking of the San Diego California Temple, he said: "What a magnificently beautiful building that is. But with all the beauty of that building, that structure is only a means to an end and not an end in itself. That facility was erected and dedicated for the performance of the sacred ordinances which the Lord has revealed in this time."[6]

On another occasion he said: "No person has all of the gospel until he is able to receive [the ordinances of the temple]. And the responsibility rests with us to see that the facilities are available. I do not know how much longer I am good for, but I hope to end out my days building temples of the Lord, taking the temples to the people so that they can have the marvelous blessings that are to be obtained [there]."[7]

Teachings of Gordon B. Hinckley

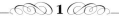 1

Temples are expressions of our testimony, and they represent the ultimate in our worship.

Each temple built by The Church of Jesus Christ of Latter-day Saints stands as an expression of the testimony of this people that God our Eternal Father lives, that He has a plan for the blessing of His sons and daughters of all generations, that His Beloved Son, Jesus the Christ, who was born in Bethlehem of Judea and crucified on the cross of Golgotha, is the Savior and Redeemer of the world, whose atoning sacrifice makes possible the fulfillment of that plan in the eternal life of each who accepts and lives the gospel.[8]

Everything that occurs in [the] temple is of an uplifting and ennobling kind. It speaks of life here and life beyond the grave. It speaks of the importance of the individual as a child of God. It speaks of the importance of the family as a creation of the Almighty. It speaks of the eternity of the marriage relationship. It speaks of going on to greater glory. It is a place of light, a place of peace, a place of love where we deal with the things of eternity.[9]

Every temple . . . has in effect stood as a monument to our belief in the immortality of the human soul, that this phase of mortal life through which we pass is part of a continuous upward climb, so to speak, and that as certain as there is life here, there will be life there. That is our firm belief. It comes about through the Atonement of the Savior, and the temple becomes, as I have indicated, the bridge from this life to the next. The temple is concerned with things of immortality.[10]

These unique and wonderful buildings, and the ordinances administered therein, represent the ultimate in our worship. These ordinances become the most profound expressions of our theology.[11]

Sacred matters deserve sacred consideration. . . . When you leave the doors of the House of the Lord, be true to a sacred trust to speak not of that which is holy and sanctified.

Said the Lord, "Remember that that which cometh from above is sacred, and must be spoken with care, and by constraint of the Spirit." (D&C 63:64.) And again, "Trifle not with sacred things." (D&C 6:12.)[12]

Through temple ordinances, we receive the crowning blessings of the gospel.

These temples, which now dot the earth, are necessary to the total fulfillment of the Savior's Atonement. Here, under the authority of the Holy Priesthood, will be administered those ordinances which lead not only to salvation, but also to eternal exaltation.[13]

Jesus Christ, the Son of God, gave His life on Calvary's cross as an atonement for the sins of mankind. His was a vicarious sacrifice for each of us. Through that sacrifice came the promise of the resurrection for all. This has come through the grace of God, without effort on the part of men. And beyond this, through the keys of the holy priesthood conferred upon the Twelve by the Lord when He walked among them, which keys were restored in this dispensation by those who held them anciently—through these have come great added blessings, including those unique and remarkable ordinances administered in the house of the Lord. Only in those ordinances is there realized the exercise of "the fulness of the priesthood." (D&C 124:28.)[14]

The temple ordinances [are] the crowning blessings the Church has to offer.[15]

The blessings of the temple for both men and women who are worthy to enter therein . . . include our washings and anointings that we may be clean before the Lord. They include the instruction service in which we are given an endowment of obligations and blessings that motivate us to behavior compatible with the principles of the gospel. They include the sealing ordinances by which that which is bound on earth is bound in heaven, providing for the continuity of the family.[16]

I was [once] called to the hospital bedside of a mother in the terminal stages of a serious illness. She passed away a short time later, leaving her husband and four children, including a little boy of six. There was sorrow, deep and poignant and tragic. But shining through their tears was a faith beautiful and certain that as surely as there was now a sorrowful separation, there would someday be a glad reunion, for that marriage had begun with a sealing for time and eternity in the house of the Lord, under the authority of the holy priesthood. . . .

Many have traveled [great distances] to receive the blessings of temple marriage. I have seen a group of Latter-day Saints from Japan who—before the construction of a temple in their homeland—had denied themselves food to make possible the long journey to the Laie Hawaii Temple. Before we had a temple in Johannesburg, we met those who had gone without necessities to afford the 7,000-mile (11,000-km) flight from South Africa to the temple in Surrey, England. There was a light in their eyes and smiles on their faces and testimonies from their lips that it was worth infinitely more than all it had cost.

And I remember hearing in New Zealand many years ago the testimony of a man from the far side of Australia who, having been previously sealed by civil authority and then joined the Church with his wife and children, had traveled all the way across that wide continent, then across the Tasman Sea to Auckland, and down to the temple in the beautiful valley of the Waikato. As I remember his words, he said, "We could not afford to come. Our worldly possessions consisted of an old car, our furniture, and our dishes. I said to my family, 'We cannot afford to go.' Then I looked into the faces of my beautiful wife and our beautiful children, and I said, 'We cannot afford not to go. If the Lord will give me strength, I can work and earn enough for another car and furniture and dishes, but if I should lose these my loved ones, I would be poor indeed in both life and in eternity.'"[17]

Small wonder, my brethren and sisters, that with the opening of . . . temples I have seen the tears of strong men who have embraced their wives at the altars in these sacred houses. I have seen the tears of fathers and mothers as they have embraced their children at these same altars. Through the power here exercised they have come to know that neither time nor death can destroy the bonds which bind them together.[18]

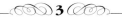

3

The temple is a sanctuary of service where we receive saving ordinances in behalf of those who have died without receiving the gospel.

There are uncounted millions who have walked the earth and who have never had the opportunity to hear the gospel. Shall they be denied such blessings as are offered in the temples of the Church?

Through living proxies who stand in behalf of the dead, the same ordinances are available to those who have passed from mortality. In the spirit world they then are free to accept or reject those earthly ordinances performed for them, including baptism, marriage, and the sealing of family relationships. There must be no compulsion in the work of the Lord, but there must be opportunity.[19]

This is a sanctuary of service. Most of the work done in this sacred house is performed vicariously in behalf of those who have passed beyond the veil of death. I know of no other work to compare with it. It more nearly approaches the vicarious sacrifice of the Son of God in behalf of all mankind than any other work of which I am aware. Thanks is not expected from those who in the world beyond become the beneficiaries of this consecrated service. It is a service of the living in behalf of the dead. It is a service which is of the very essence of selflessness.[20]

Boys and girls in large numbers have . . . been reminded that these temples are not only for their parents but also for them. When 12 years of age, they may enter the house of the Lord and stand as proxies in baptisms for those beyond the veil of death. What a great and unselfish service this is. What a wonderful thing for our youth to be involved in this totally selfless act in behalf of others who are powerless to help themselves.

Going hand in hand with . . . increased temple activity is an increase in our family history work. The computer in its various ramifications is accelerating the work, and people are taking advantage of the new techniques being offered to them. How can one escape the conclusion that the Lord is in all of this? As computer facilities improve, the number of temples grows to accommodate the accelerated family history work.[21]

We are responsible for the blessing, the eternal blessing, of all who have lived upon the earth, the uncounted, unnumbered generations of men and women who have lived upon the earth, all who today live upon the earth, and all who will yet live upon the earth. How great is our responsibility. We must stand a little taller and work a little harder to accomplish it.[22]

Those on the other side, who are not dead but who are alive as to the spirit, will rejoice and be made glad as they awaken and go forward on their way to "immortality and eternal life" (Moses 1:39).[23]

Great blessings await us as we keep ourselves worthy and go to the temple frequently.

I make . . . a challenge for each of you this day to put your lives in order, to be worthy to go to the house of the Lord and there to partake of the blessings that are peculiarly yours. . . . Great are the requirements, but greater still are the blessings.[24]

I urge our people everywhere, with all of the persuasiveness of which I am capable, to live worthy to hold a temple recommend, to secure one and regard it as a precious asset, and to make a greater effort to go to the house of the Lord and partake of the spirit and the blessings to be had therein.[25]

Whether you can go [to the temple] frequently or not, qualify for a temple recommend and keep a recommend in your pocket. It will be a reminder to you of what is expected of you as a Latter-day Saint.[26]

I am satisfied that every man or woman who goes to the temple in a spirit of sincerity and faith leaves the house of the Lord a better man or woman. There is need for constant improvement in all of our lives. There is need occasionally to leave the noise and the tumult of the world and step within the walls of a sacred house of God, there to feel His Spirit in an environment of holiness and peace.[27]

This sacred edifice becomes a school of instruction in the sweet and sacred things of God. Here we have outlined the plan of a loving Father in behalf of His sons and daughters of all generations. Here we have sketched before us the odyssey of man's eternal journey from premortal existence through this life to the life beyond. Great fundamental and basic truths are taught with clarity and simplicity well within the understanding of all who hear. . . .

The temple is also a place of personal inspiration and revelation. Legion are those who in times of stress, when difficult decisions must be made and perplexing problems must be handled, have come to the temple in a spirit of fasting and prayer to seek divine direction. Many have testified that while voices of revelation were not heard,

"Go to the house of the Lord and there feel of His Spirit and commune with Him and you will know a peace that you will find nowhere else."

impressions concerning a course to follow were experienced at that time or later which became answers to their prayers.

This temple is a fountain of eternal truth. "Whosoever drinketh of the water that I shall give him shall never thirst." (John 4:14.) Here are taught those truths which are divine in their substance and eternal in their implications.

For those who enter these walls, this house becomes a house of covenants. Here we promise, solemnly and sacredly, to live the gospel of Jesus Christ in its finest expression. We covenant with God our Eternal Father to live those principles which are the bedrock of all true religion.[28]

Is life filled with cares for you? Do you have problems and concerns and worries? Do you want for peace in your heart and an opportunity to commune with the Lord and meditate upon His way? Go to the house of the Lord and there feel of His Spirit and commune with Him and you will know a peace that you will find nowhere else.[29]

In times of darkness, try to get to the house of the Lord and there shut out the world. Receive His holy ordinances, and extend these to your forebears. At the conclusion of a session in the temple, sit quietly in the celestial room and ponder the blessings you have received in your own behalf or that you have extended to those who have gone beyond. Your heart will swell with gratitude, and thoughts of the eternal verities of the Lord's great plan of happiness will infuse your soul.[30]

In this noisy, bustling, competitive world, what a privilege it is to have a sacred house where we may experience the sanctifying influence of the Spirit of the Lord. The element of selfishness crowds in upon us constantly. We need to overcome it, and there is no better way than to go to the house of the Lord and there serve in a vicarious relationship in behalf of those who are beyond the veil of death. . . .

. . . I encourage you to take greater advantage of this blessed privilege. It will refine your natures. It will peel off the selfish shell in which most of us live. It will literally bring a sanctifying element into our lives and make us better men and better women.[31]

I know your lives are busy. I know that you have much to do. But I make you a promise that if you will go to the House of the Lord, you will be blessed; life will be better for you. Now, please, please, my beloved brethren and sisters, avail yourselves of the great opportunity to go to the Lord's house and thereby partake of all of the marvelous blessings that are yours to be received there.[32]

Suggestions for Study and Teaching

Questions
- President Hinckley said that temple ordinances are "the most profound expressions of our theology" (section 1) and "the crowning blessings the Church has to offer" (section 2). What are some blessings you have received through these ordinances?
- President Hinckley spoke of men and women shedding tears of joy in temples (see section 2). From your experience, why do temple ordinances stir such deep feelings?

- Of the work to redeem the dead, President Hinckley said, "What a wonderful thing for our youth to be involved in this totally selfless act" (section 3). What can parents and youth do to work together in this service?

- What can we do to make time to serve and worship in the temple? In what ways can our service in the temple influence our life outside the temple? (For some examples, see section 4.) How has going to the temple blessed you?

Related Scriptures

Exodus 25:8; 1 Kings 6:11–13; D&C 88:119–20; 109:12–13, 24–28; 110:1–10; 128:22–24

Study Help

"Share what you learn. As you do this, your thoughts will become clearer and your power of retention will increase" (*Teaching, No Greater Call* [1999], 17).

Notes

1. "Some Thoughts on Temples, Retention of Converts, and Missionary Service," *Ensign,* Nov. 1997, 49.

2. "Some Thoughts on Temples, Retention of Converts, and Missionary Service," 49.

3. In Sheri L. Dew, *Go Forward with Faith: The Biography of Gordon B. Hinckley* (1996), 325.

4. "This Is a Day Long Looked Forward To" (text of the dedicatory prayer for the Colonia Juárez Chihuahua Mexico Temple, Mar. 6, 1999), *Church News,* Mar. 13, 1999, 7.

5. "New Temples to Provide 'Crowning Blessings' of the Gospel," *Ensign,* May 1998, 87–88.

6. *Discourses of President Gordon B. Hinckley, Volume 1: 1995–1999* (2005), 311–12.

7. *Teachings of Gordon B. Hinckley* (1997), 641.

8. "This Peaceful House of God," *Ensign,* May 1993, 74.

9. *Teachings of Gordon B. Hinckley,* 623–24.

10. "Inspirational Thoughts," *Ensign,* Apr. 2002, 4.

11. "Of Missions, Temples, and Steward-ship," *Ensign,* Nov. 1995, 53.

12. "Keeping the Temple Holy," *Ensign,* May 1990, 52.

13. "Shining Star in a World Oppressed with Darkness" (text of the dedicatory prayer for the Manhattan New York Temple, June 13, 2004), *Church News,* June 19, 2004, 5.

14. "Rejoice in This Great Era of Temple Building," *Ensign,* Nov. 1985, 59.

15. "New Temples to Provide 'Crowning Blessings' of the Gospel," 88.

16. "Temples and Temple Work," *Ensign,* Feb. 1982, 3.

17. "The Marriage That Endures," *Ensign,* July 2003, 4–6.

18. "Rejoice in This Great Era of Temple Building," 60.

19. "Why These Temples?" *Ensign,* Aug. 1974, 40.

20. "The Salt Lake Temple," *Ensign,* Mar. 1993, 5.

21. "Welcome to Conference," *Ensign,* Nov. 1999, 4–5.

22. *Teachings of Gordon B. Hinckley,* 640.

23. *Discourses of President Gordon B. Hinckley, Volume 1,* 154.

24. *Discourses of President Gordon B. Hinckley, Volume 1,* 362.

25. "Of Missions, Temples, and Stewardship," 53.

26. "Inspirational Thoughts," 4.

27. "Of Missions, Temples, and Stewardship," 52.

28. "The Salt Lake Temple," 5–6.

29. "Excerpts from Recent Addresses of President Gordon B. Hinckley," *Ensign,* Apr. 1996, 72.

30. *One Bright Shining Hope: Messages for Women from Gordon B. Hinckley* (2006), 103.

31. "Closing Remarks," *Ensign* or *Liahona,* Nov. 2004, 104–5.

32. *Teachings of Gordon B. Hinckley,* 624.

The Atonement of Jesus Christ: Vast in Its Reach, Intimate in Its Effect

*"I bear witness [of] the Atonement of the Lord
Jesus Christ. Without it life is meaningless.
It is the keystone in the arch of our existence."*

From the Life of Gordon B. Hinckley

On January 1, 2000, President Gordon B. Hinckley led the First Presidency and the Quorum of the Twelve Apostles in publishing their unified testimony of the Savior. In this message, titled "The Living Christ," they declared: "We offer our testimony of the reality of His matchless life and the infinite virtue of His great atoning sacrifice. None other has had so profound an influence upon all who have lived and will yet live upon the earth."[1]

In a general conference address three months later, President Hinckley testified of the profound influence the Savior had on his own life. He spoke tenderly and personally, at times choked with emotion:

"Of all the things for which I feel grateful this morning, one stands out preeminently. That is a living testimony of Jesus Christ, the Son of the Almighty God, the Prince of Peace, the Holy One. . . .

"Jesus is my friend. None other has given me so much. 'Greater love hath no man than this, that a man lay down his life for his friends' (John 15:13). He gave His life for me. He opened the way to eternal life. Only a God could do this. I hope that I am deemed worthy of being a friend to Him.

"Everything depended on Him—His atoning sacrifice. . . .
That was the keystone in the arch of the great plan [of] the Father."

"He is my exemplar. His way of life, His absolutely selfless conduct, His outreach to those in need, His final sacrifice all stand as an example to me. I cannot measure up entirely, but I can try. . . .

"He is my healer. I stand in awe at His wondrous miracles. And yet I know they happened. I accept the truth of these things because I know that He is the Master of life and death. The miracles of His ministry bespeak compassion, love, and a sense of humanity wonderful to behold.

"He is my leader. I am honored to be one in the long cavalcade of those who love Him and who have followed Him during the two millennia that have passed since His birth. . . .

"He is my Savior and my Redeemer. Through giving His life in pain and unspeakable suffering, He has reached down to lift me and each of us and all the sons and daughters of God from the abyss of eternal darkness following death. He has provided something better—a sphere of light and understanding, growth and beauty where we may go forward on the road that leads to eternal life. My gratitude knows no bounds. My thanks to my Lord has no conclusion.

"He is my God and my King. From everlasting to everlasting, He will reign and rule as King of Kings and Lord of Lords. To His dominion there will be no end. To His glory there will be no night.

"None other can take His place. None other ever will. Unblemished and without fault of any kind, He is the Lamb of God, to whom I bow and through whom I approach my Father in Heaven. . . .

"Gratefully, and with love undiminished, I bear witness of these things in His Holy name."[2]

Teachings of Gordon B. Hinckley

 **1**

Our Heavenly Father's love is expressed in the gift of His Only Begotten Son.

My heart is subdued when I think of the great love of my Heavenly Father. How grateful I am to know that God loves us. The incomprehensible depth of that love found expression in the gift of His Only Begotten Son to come into the world to bring hope into our hearts, to bring kindness and courtesy into our relationships, and above all to save us from our sins and guide us on the way that leads to eternal life.[3]

The Savior's premortal ministry

The Father of us all, with love for us, His children, offered a . . . plan under which we would have freedom to choose the course of our lives. His Firstborn Son, our Elder Brother, was the key to that plan. Man would have his agency, and with that agency would go accountability. Man would walk the ways of the world and sin and stumble. But the Son of God would take upon Himself flesh and offer Himself a sacrifice to atone for the sins of all men. Through unspeakable suffering He would become the great Redeemer, the Savior of all mankind.[4]

The Savior's earthly ministry

In all of history there has been no majesty like His majesty. He, the mighty Jehovah, condescended to be born to mortal life in a stable of Bethlehem. He grew as a boy in Nazareth and "increased in wisdom and stature, and in favour with God and man" (Luke 2:52).

He was baptized by John in the waters of Jordan, "and, lo, the heavens were opened unto him, and he saw the Spirit of God descending like a dove, and lighting upon him:

"And lo a voice from heaven, saying, This is my beloved Son, in whom I am well pleased" (Matt. 3:16–17).

During the three years of His earthly ministry, He did what none other had ever done before; He taught as none other had previously taught.

Then came His time to be offered. There was the supper in the Upper Room, His last with the Twelve in mortality. As He washed their feet, He taught a lesson in humility and service they would never forget.[5]

Suffering in the Garden of Gethsemane

There followed the suffering of Gethsemane, "which suffering," He said, "caused myself, even God, the greatest of all, to tremble because of pain, and to bleed at every pore, and to suffer both body and spirit" (D&C 19:18).[6]

In the Garden of Gethsemane, He suffered so greatly that he sweat drops of blood as He pleaded with His Father. But this was all a part of His great atoning sacrifice.[7]

[I once sat] in the shadow of an old olive tree [in the Garden of Gethsemane] and read of that terrible wrestling of the Son of God as He faced the certain future, sweating drops of blood and praying to His Father to let the cup pass if it might—but saying, Nevertheless, Thy will be done, not mine. . . . I had an overwhelming feeling that He wasn't making His plea, He wasn't facing that ordeal in terms of the physical pain He was about to face, the terrible, brutal crucifixion on the cross. That was part of it, I am sure. But in large measure it was, I think, a sense on His part of His role in the eternal welfare of all of the sons and daughters of God, of all generations of time.

Everything depended on Him—His atoning sacrifice. That was the key. That was the keystone in the arch of the great plan which the Father had brought forth for the eternal life of His sons and daughters. Terrible as it was to face it, and burdensome as it was to realize it, He faced it, He accomplished it, and it was a marvelous and wonderful thing. It is beyond our comprehension, I believe. Nevertheless, we glimpse it in small part and must learn to appreciate it more and more and more.[8]

Arrest, crucifixion, and death

He was taken by rough and crude hands, and in the night, contrary to the law, was brought before Annas, and then Caiaphas, the wily and evil officer of the Sanhedrin. There followed early the next morning the second appearance before this scheming, vicious man. Then He was taken to Pilate, the Roman governor, to whom his wife said in warning, "Have thou nothing to do with that just man" (Matt. 27:19). The Roman, thinking to evade responsibility, sent Him to Herod, the corrupt, debauched, and evil tetrarch of Galilee. Christ was abused and beaten. His head was crowned with sharp and platted thorns; a mocking robe of purple was thrown upon His bleeding back. Again He was taken before Pilate, to whom the mob cried, "Crucify him, crucify him" (Luke 23:21).

With stumbling steps He walked the way to Golgotha, where His wounded body was nailed to the cross in the most inhumane and pain-ridden method of execution that sadistic minds could conjure.

Yet He cried out, "Father, forgive them; for they know not what they do" (Luke 23:34).[9]

There is no more poignant picture in all history than that of Jesus in Gethsemane and upon the cross, alone: the Redeemer of mankind, the Savior of the world, bringing to pass the Atonement.

I remember being with President Harold B. Lee . . . in the Garden of Gethsemane in Jerusalem. We could sense, if only in a very small degree, the terrible struggle that took place there, a struggle so intense, as Jesus wrestled alone in the spirit, that blood came from every pore (see Luke 22:44; D&C 19:18). We recalled the betrayal by one who had been called to a position of trust. We recalled that evil men laid brutal hands upon the Son of God. We recalled that lonely figure on the cross, crying out in anguish, "My God, my God, why hast thou forsaken me?" (Matt. 27:46). Yet, courageously, the Savior of the world moved forward to bring about the Atonement in our behalf.[10]

The hours passed as His life ebbed in pain. The earth shook; the veil of the temple was rent. From His parched lips came the words, "Father, into thy hands I commend my spirit: and having said thus, he gave up the ghost" (Luke 23:46).

It was over. His mortal life was finished. He had offered it as a ransom for all. Gone were the hopes of those who loved Him. Forgotten were the promises He had made. His body was hurriedly but tenderly placed in a borrowed tomb on the eve of the Jewish Sabbath.[11]

Resurrection

Early in the morning of Sunday, Mary Magdalene and other women came to the tomb. They wondered as they hurried how the stone might be rolled from the door of the sepulchre. Arriving, they

"He is not here: for he is risen, as he said" (Matthew 28:6).

saw an angel who spoke to them: "I know that ye seek Jesus, which was crucified.

"He is not here: for he is risen, as he said" (Matt. 28:5–6).

It had never before happened. The empty tomb was the answer to the question of the ages. Well did Paul say: "O death, where is thy sting? O grave, where is thy victory?" (1 Cor. 15:55).[12]

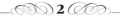

2

Through the Savior's redeeming sacrifice, all people will rise from the grave.

The miracle of that resurrection morning . . . is a miracle for all mankind. It is the miracle of the power of God, whose Beloved Son gave His life to atone for the sins of all, a sacrifice of love for every son and daughter of God. In so doing He broke the seals of death.[13]

There is nothing more universal than death, and nothing brighter with hope and faith than the assurance of immortality. The abject sorrow that comes with death, the bereavement that follows the passing of a loved one are mitigated only by the certainty of the Resurrection of the Son of God. . . .

Whenever the cold hand of death strikes, there shines through the gloom and the darkness of that hour the triumphant figure of the Lord Jesus Christ, He, the Son of God, who by His matchless and eternal power overcame death. He is the Redeemer of the world. He gave His life for each of us. He took it up again and became the firstfruits of them that slept. He, as King of Kings, stands triumphant above all other kings. He, as the Omnipotent One, stands above all rulers. He is our comfort, our only true comfort, when the dark shroud of earthly night closes about us as the spirit departs the human form.

Towering above all mankind stands Jesus the Christ.[14]

I remember speaking at a funeral service of a good man, a friend whose goodness caused me to reach a little higher. Through the years I had known his smiles, his kind words, the play of his brilliant intellect, the great breadth of his service to others. And then he who had been so bright and good suddenly died. I looked upon his lifeless form. There was neither recognition nor motion nor word of any kind. . . .

I looked up at his weeping widow and children. They knew, as I knew, that never again in mortality would they hear his voice. But a tender sweetness, indescribable in nature, brought peace and reassurance. It seemed to say, "Be still, and know that I am God" (Ps. 46:10).

It seemed further to say, "Don't worry. All of this is part of my plan. None can escape death. Even my Beloved Son died upon the cross. But through so doing He became the glorious firstfruits of the Resurrection. He took from death its sting and from the grave its victory."

I could hear in my mind the Lord speaking to the sorrowing Martha: "I am the resurrection, and the life: he that believeth in me, though he were dead, yet shall he live: And whosoever liveth and believeth in me shall never die" (John 11:25–26).[15]

Through the Savior's atoning sacrifice, we are offered the opportunity of exaltation and eternal life.

Thanks be to the Almighty. His glorified Son broke the bonds of death, the greatest of all victories. . . . He is our triumphant Lord. He is our Redeemer, who atoned for our sins. Through His redeeming sacrifice all men shall rise from the grave. He has opened the way whereby we may gain not only immortality but also eternal life.[16]

I sense in a measure the meaning of His Atonement. I cannot comprehend it all. It is so vast in its reach and yet so intimate in its effect that it defies comprehension.[17]

The magnitude of [the] Atonement is beyond our ability to completely understand. I know only that it happened, and that it was for me and for you. The suffering was so great, the agony so intense, that none of us can comprehend it when the Savior offered Himself as a ransom for the sins of all mankind.

It is through Him that we gain forgiveness. It is through Him that there comes the certain promise that all mankind will be granted the blessings of salvation, with resurrection from the dead. It is through Him and His great overarching sacrifice that we are offered the opportunity through obedience of exaltation and eternal life.[18]

Are we not all prodigal sons and daughters who need to repent and partake of the forgiving mercy of our Heavenly Father and then follow His example?

His Beloved Son, our Redeemer, reaches out to us in forgiveness and mercy, but in so doing he commands repentance. . . . Said the Lord—and I quote from a revelation given to the Prophet Joseph:

"Therefore I command you to repent—repent, lest I smite you by the rod of my mouth, and by my wrath, and by my anger, and your sufferings be sore—how sore you know not, how exquisite you know not, yea, how hard to bear you know not.

"For behold, I, God, have suffered these things for all, that they might not suffer if they would repent;

"But if they would not repent they must suffer even as I;

"Which suffering caused myself, even God, the greatest of all, to tremble because of pain, and to bleed at every pore, and to suffer both body and spirit. . . .

"Learn of me, and listen to my words; walk in the meekness of my Spirit, and you shall have peace in me." (D&C 19:15–18, 23.)[19]

When all is said and done, when all of history is examined, when the deepest depths of the human mind have been explored, nothing is so wonderful, so majestic, so tremendous as this act of grace when the Son of the Almighty, the Prince of His Father's royal household, He who had once spoken as Jehovah, He who had condescended to come to earth as a babe born in Bethlehem, gave His life in ignominy and pain so that all of the sons and daughters of God of all generations of time, every one of whom must die, might walk again and live eternally. He did for us what none of us could do for ourselves. . . .

Declared the prophet Isaiah:

"Surely he hath borne our griefs, and carried our sorrows: . . .

". . . He was wounded for our transgressions, he was bruised for our iniquities: the chastisement of our peace was upon him; and with his stripes we are healed" (Isa. 53:4–5).

This is the wondrous and true story of Christmas. The birth of Jesus in Bethlehem of Judea is preface. The three-year ministry of the Master is prologue. The magnificent substance of the story is His sacrifice, the totally selfless act of dying in pain on the cross of Calvary to atone for the sins of all of us.

The epilogue is the miracle of the Resurrection, bringing the assurance that "as in Adam all die, even so in Christ shall all be made alive" (1 Cor. 15:22).

There would be no Christmas if there had not been Easter. The babe Jesus of Bethlehem would be but another baby without the redeeming Christ of Gethsemane and Calvary, and the triumphant fact of the Resurrection.

I believe in the Lord Jesus Christ, the Son of the Eternal, Living God. None so great has ever walked the earth. None other has made a comparable sacrifice or granted a comparable blessing. He is the Savior and the Redeemer of the world. I believe in Him. I declare His divinity without equivocation or compromise. I love Him. I speak His name in reverence and wonder. I worship Him as I worship His Father, in spirit and in truth. I thank Him and kneel before His Beloved Son, who reached out long ago and said to each of us, "Come unto me, all ye that labour and are heavy laden, and I will give you rest" (Matt. 11:28).

. . . I wish for each of you a time, perhaps only an hour, spent in silent meditation and quiet reflection on the wonder and the majesty of this, the Son of God.[20]

I bear witness [of] the Atonement of the Lord Jesus Christ. Without it life is meaningless. It is the keystone in the arch of our existence. It affirms that we lived before we were born in mortality. Mortality is but a stepping-stone to a more glorious existence in the future. The sorrow of death is softened with the promise of the Resurrection.[21]

Jesus is the Christ, the foreordained Son of God who condescended to come to earth, who was born in a manger, in a conquered nation among a vassal people, the Son of God, the Only Begotten of the Father in the flesh, the Firstborn of the Father and the Author of our salvation. He is our Redeemer, our Savior, through whose Atonement eternal life is made possible for all who will walk in obedience to His teachings.[22]

Suggestions for Study and Teaching

Questions
- Why did Heavenly Father give us the "gift of His Only Begotten Son"? (See section 1.) What can you do to show gratitude for this gift? What are your thoughts and feelings as you read President Hinckley's summary of what the Savior has done for us?

- In section 2, compare the words President Hinckley uses to describe death with the words he uses to describe resurrection. What do you learn from the differences in these words? How does your testimony of the Savior's Resurrection influence your life?

- What do you learn from President Hinckley's testimony of the Atonement of Jesus Christ? (See section 3.) How has the Atonement blessed you personally? What are your feelings as you ponder the Savior's sacrifice for you? Plan a time to have "silent meditation and quiet reflection" about the Savior.

Related Scriptures

Isaiah 53; John 3:16; 11:25; 2 Nephi 9:6–13; Alma 7:11–13; 34:8–10; Helaman 14:13–19; D&C 18:10–12

Teaching Help

"As you prayerfully prepare to teach you may be led to emphasize certain principles. You may gain an understanding of how best to present certain ideas. You may discover examples, object lessons, and inspiring stories in the simple activities of life. You may feel impressed to invite a particular person to assist with the lesson. You may be reminded of a personal experience that you can share" (*Teaching, No Greater Call* [1999], 48).

Notes

1. "The Living Christ: The Testimony of the Apostles," *Ensign,* Apr. 2000, 2.
2. "My Testimony," *Ensign,* May 2000, 69, 71.
3. "The Wondrous and True Story of Christmas," *Ensign,* Dec. 2000, 2.
4. "We Look to Christ," *Ensign,* May 2002, 90.
5. "The Victory over Death," *Ensign,* Apr. 1997, 2.
6. "The Victory over Death," 2.
7. "The Things of Which I Know," *Ensign* or *Liahona,* May 2007, 83–84.
8. *Teachings of Gordon B. Hinckley* (1997), 29–30.
9. "The Victory over Death," 2, 4.
10. "Living with Our Convictions," *Ensign,* Sept. 2001, 2.
11. "The Victory over Death," 4.
12. "The Victory over Death," 4.
13. "The Victory over Death," 4.
14. "This Glorious Easter Morn," *Ensign,* May 1996, 67.
15. "The Wondrous and True Story of Christmas," 2, 4.
16. "He Is Not Here, but Is Risen," *Ensign,* May 1999, 72.
17. "The Wondrous and True Story of Christmas," 2.
18. "Forgiveness," *Ensign* or *Liahona,* Nov. 2005, 84.
19. "Of You It Is Required to Forgive," *Ensign,* June 1991, 5.
20. "The Wondrous and True Story of Christmas," 4–5.
21. "The Things of Which I Know," 84.
22. In Sheri L. Dew, *Go Forward with Faith: The Biography of Gordon B. Hinckley* (1996), 560.

Move Forward with Faith

*"If there is any one thing that you and I need, . . . [it is]
the kind of faith that moves us to get on our knees and
plead with the Lord for guidance, and then, having
a measure of divine confidence, get on our feet and
go to work to help bring the desired results to pass."*

From the Life of Gordon B. Hinckley

"When I left for a mission [as a young man]," recalled President
Gordon B. Hinckley, "my good father handed me a card on which
were written five words. They were the words of the Lord to the
ruler of the synagogue who had received news of his daughter's
death: 'Be not afraid, only believe.' (Mark 5:36.)"[1] As young Elder
Hinckley served in England, he faced many challenges in which
he needed to remember those five words. He later described one
such experience:

"One day three or four of the London papers carried reviews of
a reprint of an old book, snide and ugly in tone, indicating that the
book was a history of the Mormons. President Merrill [my mission
president] said to me, 'I want you to go down to the publisher and
protest this.' I looked at him and was about to say, 'Surely not me.'
But I meekly said, 'Yes, sir.'

"I do not hesitate to say that I was frightened. I went to my room
and felt something as I think Moses must have felt when the Lord
asked him to go and see Pharaoh. I offered a prayer. My stomach
was churning as I walked over to the Goodge Street station to get
the underground train to Fleet Street. I found the office of the president and presented my card to the receptionist. She took it and went
into the inner office and soon returned to say that the president was
too busy to see me. I replied that I had come five thousand miles

"Faith is, when all is said and done, our only genuine and lasting hope."

[8,000 kilometers] and that I would wait. During the next hour she made two or three trips to his office; then finally he invited me in. I shall never forget the picture when I entered. He was smoking a long cigar with a look that seemed to say, 'Don't bother me.'

"I held in my hand the reviews. I do not recall what I said after that. Another power seemed to be speaking through me. At first he was defensive and even belligerent. Then he began to soften. He concluded by promising to do something. Within an hour word went out to every book dealer in England to return the books to the publisher. At great expense he printed and tipped in the front of each volume a statement to the effect that the book was not to be considered as history, but only as fiction, and that no offense was intended against the respected Mormon people. Years later he granted another favor of substantial worth to the Church, and each year until the time of his death I received a Christmas card from him."[2]

In accepting the assignment to visit the publisher's office, Elder Hinckley practiced what would become a lifelong pattern: with faith, accept the challenge; plead with the Lord for help; then go to work.

Teachings of Gordon B. Hinckley

1

Faith in Heavenly Father and Jesus Christ can become the wellspring of purposeful living.

If there is any one thing that you and I need, to help us find success and fulfillment in this world, it is faith—that dynamic, powerful, marvelous element by which, as Paul declared, the very worlds were framed (see Hebrews 11:3). I refer not to some ethereal concept but to a practical, pragmatic, working faith—the kind of faith that moves us to get on our knees and plead with the Lord for guidance, and then, having a measure of divine confidence, get on our feet and go to work to help bring the desired results to pass. Such faith is an asset beyond compare. Such faith is, when all is said and done, our only genuine and lasting hope.

. . . Faith can become the very wellspring of purposeful living. There is no more compelling motivation to worthwhile endeavor than the knowledge that we are children of God, that God expects us to do something with our lives, and that He will give us help when help is sought. . . .

. . . When I discuss faith, I do not mean it in an abstract sense. I mean it as a living, vital force that comes with recognition of God as our Father and Jesus Christ as our Savior. . . .

. . . Faith in a Divine Being, in the Almighty, is *the* great moving power that can change our lives.[3]

Long ago I worked for one of our railroads whose tracks threaded the passes through [the] mountains. I frequently rode the trains. It was in the days when there were steam locomotives. Those great monsters of the rails were huge and fast and dangerous. I often wondered how the engineer dared the long journey through the night. Then I came to realize that it was not one long journey, but rather a constant continuation of a short journey. The engine had a powerful headlight that made bright the way for a distance of 400 or 500 yards. The engineer saw only that distance, and that was enough, because it was constantly before him all through the night into the dawn of the new day. . . .

And so it is with our eternal journey. We take one step at a time. In doing so we reach toward the unknown, but faith lights the way. If we will cultivate that faith, we shall never walk in darkness. . . .

The challenge which faces every member of this Church is to take the next step, to accept that responsibility to which he is called, even though he does not feel equal to it, and to do so in faith with the full expectation that the Lord will light the way before him.[4]

2

Faith is the basis of testimony and the strength of the Lord's work on the earth.

The only real wealth of the Church is in the faith of its people.[5]

It is a marvelous and wonderful thing that thousands are touched by the miracle of the Holy Spirit, that they believe and accept and become members [of the Church]. They are baptized. Their lives are forever touched for good. Miracles occur. A seed of faith comes into their hearts. It enlarges as they learn. And they accept principle upon principle, until they have every one of the marvelous blessings that come to those who walk with faith in this, The Church of Jesus Christ of Latter-day Saints.

. . . This precious and marvelous gift of faith, this gift from God our Eternal Father, is still the strength of this work and the quiet vibrancy of its message. Faith underlies it all. Faith is the substance of it all. Whether it be going into the mission field, living the Word of Wisdom, paying one's tithing, it is all the same. It is the faith within us that is evidenced in all we do.

. . . The strength of this cause and kingdom is not found in its temporal assets, impressive as they may be. It is found in the hearts of its people. That is why it is successful. That is why it is strong and growing. That is why it is able to accomplish the wonderful things that it does. It all comes of the gift of faith, bestowed by the Almighty upon His children who doubt not and fear not, but go forward. . . .

Faith is the basis of testimony. Faith underlies loyalty to the Church. Faith represents sacrifice, gladly given in moving forward the work of the Lord.[6]

The gospel is good news. It is a message of triumph. It is a cause to be embraced with enthusiasm. . . .

Let us not be afraid. Jesus is our leader, our strength, and our king.

This is an age of pessimism. Ours is a mission of faith. To my brethren and sisters everywhere, I call upon you to reaffirm your faith, to move this work forward across the world. . . .

"Brethren, shall we not go on in so great a cause? Go forward and not backward. Courage, brethren; and on, on to the victory!" (D&C 128:22). So wrote the Prophet Joseph in a psalm of faith.

How glorious is the past of this great cause. It is filled with heroism, courage, boldness, and faith. How wondrous is the present as we move forward to bless the lives of people wherever they will hearken to the message of the servants of the Lord. How magnificent will be the future as the Almighty rolls on His glorious work, touching for good all who will accept and live His gospel, and even reaching to the eternal blessing of His sons and daughters of all generations through the selfless work of those whose hearts are filled with love for the Redeemer of the world. . . .

I invite every one of you, wherever you may be as members of this church, to stand on your feet and with a song in your heart move forward, living the gospel, loving the Lord, and building the kingdom. Together we shall stay the course and keep the faith, the Almighty being our strength.[7]

3

With faith, we can rise above fear and any obstacle or challenge in our lives.

Who among us can say that he or she has not felt fear? I know of no one who has been entirely spared. Some, of course, experience fear to a greater degree than do others. Some are able to rise above it quickly, but others are trapped and pulled down by it and even driven to defeat. We suffer from the fear of ridicule, the fear of failure, the fear of loneliness, the fear of ignorance. Some fear the present, some the future. Some carry the burden of sin and would give almost anything to unshackle themselves from those burdens but fear to change their lives. Let us recognize that fear comes not of God, but rather that this gnawing, destructive element comes from the adversary of truth and righteousness. Fear is the antithesis of faith. It is corrosive in its effects, even deadly.[8]

Paul wrote to Timothy: "God hath not given us the spirit of fear; but of power, and of love, and of a sound mind.

"Be not thou therefore ashamed of the testimony of our Lord" (2 Tim. 1:7–8).

I wish that every member of this church would put those words where he might see them every morning as he begins his day. They would give us the courage to speak up, they would give us the faith to try, they would strengthen our conviction of the Lord Jesus Christ. I believe that more miracles would happen over the earth.[9]

I spoke one day to a friend who had escaped from his native land. With the fall of his nation, he was arrested and interned. His wife and children were able to get away, but for three years and

"Be not . . . ashamed of the testimony of our Lord" (2 Timothy 1:8).

more he was a prisoner without means of communication with those he loved. The food was wretched, the living conditions oppressive, with no prospects for improvement.

"What sustained you through all those dark days?" I asked.

He responded: "My faith; my faith in the Lord Jesus Christ. I put my burdens on him, and then they seemed so much the lighter."[10]

It all works out. Don't worry. I say that to myself every morning. It will all work out. If you do your best, it will all work out. Put your trust in God, and move forward with faith and confidence in the future. The Lord will not forsake us. He will not forsake us.[11]

Could not any of us say that if we had greater faith in God we could do better than we are now doing? There is no obstacle too great, no challenge too difficult, if we have faith. With faith we can rise above those negative elements in our lives that constantly pull us down. With effort we can develop the capacity to subdue those impulses that lead to degrading and evil actions. With faith we can school our appetites. We can reach out to those who are discouraged and defeated, and we can warm them by the strength and power of our own faith.[12]

 **4**

As we exercise our faith, the Lord will help it increase.

As you exercise your time and talents in service, your faith will grow and your doubts will wane.[13]

The Church will ask you to do many things. It will ask you to serve in various capacities. We do not have a professional ministry. You become the ministry of this Church, and whenever you are called upon to serve may I urge you to respond, and as you do so your faith will strengthen and increase. Faith is like the muscle of my arm. If I use it, if I nurture it, it grows strong; it will do many things. But if I put it in a sling and do nothing with it, it will grow weak and useless, and so will it be with you. If you accept every opportunity, if you accept every calling, the Lord will make it possible for you to perform it. The Church will not ask you to do anything which you cannot do with the help of the Lord.[14]

This is my prayer for all of us—"Lord, increase our faith" [see Luke 17:5]. Increase our faith to bridge the chasms of uncertainty and doubt. . . .

. . . Lord, increase our faith to rise above the feeble detractors of this Thy great and holy work. Strengthen our will. Help us to build and expand Thy kingdom according to Thy great mandate, that this gospel may be preached in all the world as a witness unto all nations. . . .

. . . Grant us faith to look beyond the problems of the moment to the miracles of the future. Give us faith to pay our tithes and offerings and put our trust in Thee, the Almighty, to open the windows of heaven as Thou hast promised. Give us faith to do what is right and let the consequence follow.

Grant us faith when storms of adversity beat us down and drive us to the ground. In seasons of sickness may our confidence wax strong in the powers of the priesthood. May we follow the counsel of James:

"Is any sick among you? let him call for the elders of the church; and let them pray over him, anointing him with oil in the name of the Lord:

"And the *prayer of faith* shall save the sick, and the Lord shall raise him up" (James 5:14–15; italics added). . . .

Lord, when we walk in the valley of the shadow of death, give us faith to smile through our tears, knowing that it is all part of the eternal plan of a loving Father, that as we cross the threshold from this life we enter another more glorious, and that through the atonement of the Son of God all shall rise from the grave and the faithful shall go on to exaltation.

Give us faith to pursue the work of redemption of the dead that Thine eternal purposes may be fulfilled in behalf of Thy sons and daughters of all generations.

Father, grant us faith to follow counsel in the little things that can mean so very much. . . .

Lord, increase our faith in one another, and in ourselves, and in our capacity to do good and great things. . . .

Father, increase our faith. Of all our needs, I think the greatest is an increase in faith. And so, dear Father, increase our faith in Thee, and in Thy Beloved Son, in Thy great eternal work, in ourselves as Thy children, and in our capacity to go and do according to Thy will, and Thy precepts, I humbly pray in the name of Jesus Christ, amen.[15]

Suggestions for Study and Teaching

Questions

- President Hinckley taught that faith in God is "the great moving power that can change our lives" (section 1). What experiences have helped you learn about the power of faith? How have you seen that when "we reach toward the unknown, . . . faith lights the way"?

- What can we learn from section 2 about the source of the Church's strength? How are faith and sacrifice related to each other? Consider how you can heed President Hinckley's call to "move this work forward across the world."

- Why do you think faith has the power to help us in times of trial? (See section 3.) When has faith helped you rise above fear? When has faith helped you rise above other obstacles?

- Review President Hinckley's prayer in section 4. What words in this prayer have special meaning for you? How can faith help us overcome uncertainty and doubt? How can faith help us look beyond problems to see miracles?

Related Scriptures

John 14:12–14; Romans 5:1–5; 2 Nephi 26:12–13; Moroni 7:33–38; D&C 27:16–18

Teaching Help

"When we study the scriptures regularly and diligently, earnestly seeking guidance from the Spirit, we will be receptive to enlightenment about how to prepare lessons. We will also be prepared to receive and follow promptings from the Spirit while we teach" (*Teaching, No Greater Call* [1999], 14).

Notes

1. In Conference Report, Oct. 1969, 114.
2. "If Ye Be Willing and Obedient," *Ensign,* July 1995, 5.
3. *Standing for Something: Ten Neglected Virtues That Will Heal Our Hearts and Homes* (2000), 109–10.
4. "We Walk by Faith," *Ensign,* May 2002, 72–73.
5. "The State of the Church," *Ensign,* May 1991, 54.
6. "The Miracle of Faith," *Ensign,* May 2001, 68–69.
7. "Stay the Course—Keep the Faith," *Ensign,* Nov. 1995, 71–72.
8. "God Hath Not Given Us the Spirit of Fear," *Ensign,* Oct. 1984, 2.
9. "Be Not Afraid, Only Believe," *Ensign,* Feb. 1996, 5.
10. "Be Not Faithless," *Ensign,* Apr. 1989, 4.
11. "Latter-Day Counsel: Excerpts from Addresses of President Gordon B. Hinckley," *Ensign,* Oct. 2000, 73.
12. *Standing for Something,* 109–10.
13. "He Is Risen, As He Said," *Ensign,* Apr. 1983, 7.
14. "Inspirational Thoughts," *Ensign,* June 1999, 2.
15. "Lord, Increase Our Faith," *Ensign,* Nov. 1987, 52–54.

List of Visuals

Index

of Gordon B. Hinckley, 6–9, 69,
201, 283–85, 333–35
helping the full-time missionaries
in, 287–89
is a priesthood responsibility, 290
in the latter days, 283–93
the Lord will bless our efforts in,
292–93
preparing children for, 289–90
reaching out to the world
through, 285–86

Mothers
responsibilities of, 168
sacred calling of, 99–101
See also Family; Parents

O

Obedience
blessings come through, 64,
182–83
is required of us in every aspect,
181
is the way to happiness, 72
means living the gospel, 177–87
strengthens the Church, 186–87

Optimism, 69–78

Ordinances
for the dead, 51, 314–15
of the temple are the crowning blessings of the Church,
312–14

P

Parents
are responsible for teaching
and caring for their children,
167–69
should bridle anger, 173–74
should create an atmosphere
of learning in their homes,
239–40
should not give up on rebellious
children, 173

should pray for their children,
109, 169, 173
should prepare children early for
missionary work, 289–90
single, 168–69

Peace
can be found in the temple,
316–18
praying for, 110
through self-reliance, 189–98
through virtuous living, 251–53

Perpetual Education Fund, 30–31,
191, 194

Pioneers
all members of the Church are,
89–91
brought their faith to reality,
83–84
of the early Church, 3, 58–61,
81–88
legacy of, 81–92
modern-day, 82, 89–91
of the Willie and Martin handcart
companies, 86–88

Plan of salvation, 52, 316

Pornography, 123, 218, 251–55

Pratt, Parley P., 229–31

Prayer
brings blessings and happiness,
107–9
family, in Gordon B. Hinckley's
home, 107
family, helps children grow in
faith, 169–70
family, leads to miracles, 110–13
power of, 107–15
seeking answers to, 113–15

President of the Church
called by the Lord, 260–61
the senior Apostle becomes the
next, 262–63